ACPL ITEM
DISCARD SO-AUH-053

DO NOT REMOVE
CARDS FROM POCKET

Negotiating Debt

The IMF Lending Process

Kendall W. Stiles

Westview Press

BOULDER • SAN FRANCISCO • OXFORD

This Westview softcover edition is printed on acid-free paper and bound in library-quality, coated covers that carry the highest rating of the National Association of State Textbook Administrators, in consultation with the Association of American Publishers and the Book Manufacturers' Institute.

Published in 1991 in the United States of America by Westview Press, Inc., 5500 Central Avenue, Boulder, Colorado 80301, and in the United Kingdom by Westview Press, 36 Lonsdale Road, Summertown, Oxford OX2 7EW

Library of Congress Cataloging-in-Publication Data
Stiles, Kendall W.
  Negotiating debt : the IMF lending process / Kendall W. Stiles.
    p. cm.
  Includes bibliographical references and index.
  ISBN 0-8133-8146-0
  1. International Monetary Fund. 2. Debts, External—Developing
countries—Case studies. 3. Loans, Foreign—Developing countries—
Case studies. I. Title.
HG3881.5.I58S85 1991
332.1'52—dc20   91-299
                                                                        CIP

Printed and bound in the United States of America

The paper used in this publication meets the requirements
of the American National Standard for Permanence of Paper
for Printed Library Materials Z39.48-1984.

10   9   8   7   6   5   4   3   2   1

Contents

Tables and Figures

Acknowledgments

A work of this type is, almost by definition, a collective effort. I deeply appreciate the time invested by many individuals on its behalf. In particular, I would like to thank my colleagues in academia who helped guide this work over the past five years: William Ascher, Michael Doyle, Ernst Haas, Valerie Assetto, Stephen Krasner, Ladd Hollist, Christopher Chase-Dunn, Miles Kahler, Michael Schechter, Robert Russell, and John T. Rourke. Of course, I alone bear responsibility for the book's flaws.

I would like to express appreciation for those individuals at the International Monetary Fund who gave of their time and thoughts in spite of considerable personal inconvenience. While many must remain nameless for reasons of professional courtesy and confidentiality, I can mention Frank Southard, Tom deVries, Margaret deVries, Azizali Mohammed, Sir Joseph Gold, Edward Bernstein, Jacques Polak, and William Dale. These individuals did far more than simply grant an interview. They offered substantive comments on early drafts and articles, offered advice on interviewing techniques and etiquette, and even pointed me toward other helpful colleagues at the Fund. Although some no doubt will disagree with my conclusions, I am certain that they and other IMF staff support the general effort of expanding public understanding of the institution. For that I am grateful.

Many individuals have walked me through the steps of completing and refining this manuscript. I would in particular like to thank Barbara Ellington, who has been my principal sponsor at Westview, and Miriam Gilbert, who offered encouragement at a pivotal point in the process. Don Butler and Jim Youll provided critical technical advice and service in the final phase of manuscript completion. They had answers the highly paid "experts" did not.

Finally, I would like to thank my wife, Rebecca, for her continuous support over these years. Her bemused comments about an endeavor that at times was all-consuming gave me perspective and balance. It is to her that I would like to dedicate this book.

Kendall W. Stiles

1

Introduction

The date is November 10 of the year 2000. A new U.S. President has just been elected on a promise of "no new taxes." With the federal budget deficit at $400 billion and the public debt at five trillion dollars, confidence in the U.S. economy is at an all-time low abroad. Slowly at first, then with increasing velocity, dollars are being exchanged for Japanese yen and Deutsch marks on international markets. A panic erupts when the value of the dollar finally breaks the psychologically important 100 yen mark. Within minutes reports arrive in Washington that the dollar will be worth only 85 yen by the end of the day, with more dismal prospects for the rest of the week. The President-elect calls the chairmen of the four major central banks in Europe and Japan as well as the Bank for International Settlements only to learn that they are all unwilling to coordinate an intervention to shore up the dollar's value. He is informed that his only hope is to immediately begin negotiations for a loan from the International Monetary Fund (IMF or "Fund"). Overnight, the United States slips into foreign financial dependency.

This scenario, though unlikely, is not at all far-fetched. In November of 1988, George Bush's electoral victory was met with a 100-point drop in the Dow-Jones Industrials Average and a roughly ten percent drop in the dollar's value relative to the yen. (*Time* 1988, 20) It is entirely possible that in the next fifteen years the United States will go to the IMF to negotiate a conditional transfer of hard currency, just as have Great Britain, Brazil, Mexico, Argentina and many other nations in the past. In such an event, what will be most valuable to American policymakers will be a knowledge of how the IMF develops and implements its lending policies at the national level and how a loan recipient might influence that process. Unfortunately, this knowledge is not readily available in the writings on the IMF to date.

In spite of its status as one of the most, if not the most powerful international organization in history, very few systematic studies has been made of the internal decision-making processes of the IMF. Many scholars have focused on the impact of the Fund's decisions on societies with which it has dealings. (Williamson 1983; Payer 1974; Killick 1984; IMF 1986; Dell 1982; Sidell 1988) Several scholars have written on decision-making in the executive board (Lister 1984; Kwitney 1983), categorized the types of decisions taken by the Fund (Strange 1973), and offered some tentative observations on overall decision-making processes (Strange 1973; Southard 1982; Eckhaus 1985; Assetto 1988). There has yet to be, however, a major study that asks the single question: Through what logic and process does the IMF carry out its lending policies at the level of the individual debtor nation? It is to this question that I will address myself in this volume.

I will focus specifically on one of the most controversial and significant aspects of IMF decision-making: the application of "conditionality" to "upper-tranche" loans. Put briefly, the IMF makes available hard currencies and Special Drawing Rights (SDRs–a "world currency" administered by the Fund) to its member countries on the basis of their contributions to the organization, or "quotas." These transfers are typically referred to as "loans" in the literature, but are officially termed "repurchases" in IMF documents because the borrowing nations provide their own domestic currency in exchange for hard currency. If a nation desires to use the Fund's hard currency temporarily, it may do so freely up to a prescribed limit. Once a nation requests large amounts of currency in proportion to its quota (25 percent or more), it is dealing in the "upper tranches" and the Fund has the obligation to require greater and greater policy reforms on the part of the country, such as trade liberalization and reduced government debt, as a condition of lending. These quasi-mandated policy reforms are referred to collectively as "IMF conditionality." Conditionality is naturally perceived as intrusive and threatening to nations that have no alternative to the Fund to deal with their international obligations. The questions that emerge are: Which conditions does the IMF impose on which cases? How strictly will it enforce them? How sensitive will the Fund staff be to the requests of the borrower? Do politics matter—or will the decisions be made purely on the basis of economic criteria?

My objective is to develop and test a model of IMF decision-making that will offer a better understanding of how the IMF applies its lending terms to individual countries. This decision-making model will emphasize the importance of bargaining and negotiation between the IMF and its borrowers on the one hand, and among the various organs within the Fund itself on the other. I do not expect the model to explain decision-making in other international organizations, but I do believe that the insights gained from my emphasis on unit-level dynamics may move scholars of North-South relations away from an emphasis on systemic-level analysis.

A word on what I am not doing and why. By emphasizing the implementation of conditionality, I will be neglecting the Fund's long-range "programmatic" decisions. (Strange 1973) The executive board, the board of governors, and certain major "creditors" (the major industrialized nations that have the largest quotas and may appoint their own executive directors unilaterally—see chapter two) are instrumental in setting long-range Fund policies such as limits on annual lending, quota levels, creation of new lending accounts, and membership. Other decisions which I am not addressing are those involved in the IMF's "soft" lending—non-conditional, longer-term loans made on the basis of "need" rather than "merit," such as the "compensatory financing facility" which assists primary product exporters in dealing with shortfalls resulting from fluctuations in global commodity prices. These types of decisions have been omitted from this study because: (1) an explanation of how conditionality is implemented is the most urgent political problem for many of the Fund's borrowers, (2) the application of conditionality to individual cases has been critical to attempts at resolving the debt crisis since 1982, and (3) much of the programmatic and non-conditional decision-making is heavily influenced by systemic forces that have already been studied elsewhere. (Kahler 1986, Lister 1984, Keohane & Nye 1977, Gilpin 1987)

The purpose of this study is specifically to illuminate the decision-making processes of those organs of the IMF involved in applying conditionality to country borrowing. The question of which method of analysis to employ is an important and complex one. Officially, the IMF staff are not available for external interviews. (See "By-Laws, Rules and Regulations" of the IMF, Section N) Therefore, the obvious methods of participant observation, staff interviews, and inspection of internal memoranda are essentially unavailable. I was fortunate enough to gain access to over thirty senior and mid-level IMF officials largely because of the kindness of Messrs. William Dale and Frank Southard, both former Deputy Managing Directors of the Fund, who facilitated my research with personal references. The substance of each interview was different, but each focused generally on the individual's role in the Fund and his or her experiences and observations regarding conditional lending. The findings of these interviews are presented primarily in chapter two. These interviews offer only general, though important, observations about Fund policy implementation. In order to determine more precisely how certain key factors influence Fund decision-making, I also conducted seven detailed country studies of IMF borrowers. Each of the seven countries has attempted to borrow from the Fund during the past fifteen years. They differ markedly in terms of levels of economic development, regime types, openness of economic systems, types of economic problems, and past experience with the Fund. The experiences of these countries illustrate the bargaining and negotiation dynamics in rich detail and indicate areas where theoretical refinement is needed. Because of the variety of these countries' characteristics and experiences, they will serve well as representatives of broader classes of Fund borrowers, thereby lending to the research results a significant degree of generalizability.

The "internal" dynamics of IMF decision-making, as revealed by the interviews and published sources, can be related to their "external" manifestations as shown in the case studies of actual conditionality, through a process of critical analysis using three competing models of IMF decision-making. Each of the models (especially the "political" and "functional" models) is familiar in the literature on the IMF and proposes a set of assumptions regarding how the IMF operates. By comparing the utility of each of the models in explaining and predicting IMF policy, it is possible to select the most promising one. All told, then, this study will provide the reader with an opportunity to assess different general models of IMF decision-making by analyzing historical lending experience, the possibility of focusing on a more promising model of IMF decision-making that will provide a starting point for future research, and, new information with which scholars can pursue similar or unrelated research questions.

Competing Models of IMF Decision-Making

There are in the writings on the International Monetary Fund, implicit in most and explicit in a few, three distinct "models" of how the IMF "really" works. I have labelled these models "functionalist," "political," and "bargaining and negotiation." What follows is a brief description of each approach's basic characteristics, assumptions, and theoretical origins in the literature. (Note: These models are necessarily simplified and presented as "ideal-types" for purposes of this study. In actuality, most scholars hold a more sophisticated conception than that found in any one model.)

Functionalist Model

The functionalist model (also termed the "technocratic" model in Assetto 1988, 8-10) of IMF decision-making is dominated by a conception of the Fund as the depository of economic rationality in the area of international finance. It is assumed that through calm, thorough analysis of a country's economy and the systematic application of economically sound principles, the IMF dispenses its impartial advice in the form of conditionality to all nations that seek its help. (Dell 1981) The staff are assumed to be politically neutral and technically expert. (Gold 1983; *Articles of Agreement* Art. XII, sec. 4,c) The senior staff are assumed to play relatively passive roles as analysts, liaisons, and overseers (Strange 1973, 267). Politically sensitive decisions are confined to the executive board, where diplomatic representatives of the various member states sort out their differences and arrive at policy decisions through consensus, based on "rational" staff recommendations (Southard 1979; Pion-Berlin 1985).

Historically, this view has dominated IMF documents and histories. Lord Keynes, speaking at one of the founding meetings of the IMF in 1944, voiced his view of the proper role of the IMF staff:

> We want to aim at a governing structure doing a technical job and developing a sense of corporate responsibility to all members, and not the need to guard the interests of particular countries (Strange 1973, 267).

Although it took several years for the IMF to emerge from American dominance after World War II (Tew 1969), in the late-1950s the institution achieved a high degree of autonomy and self-respect (Pion-Berlin 1985). The most active minds of the Fund, in particular, Director of Research Jacques Polak and Director of the Legal Department Sir Joseph Gold, with the encouragement of U.S. Executive Director Frank Southard, developed a basic and simple formula for calculating conditionality for specific types of loans (Polak 1957; IMF 1977; IMF 1987). For a clear explanation of the monetarist "paradigm," see David 1985). With this formula, it was possible for the IMF staff to propose concrete and straight-forward recommendations to virtually any nation seeking assistance (Rhomberg and Miller 1977). This intellectual coherence allowed the staff to dominate executive board deliberations (Strange 1973; Southard 1979; Kwitney 1983). Among the staff, the Exchange and Trade Relations Department (ETR), which compares each loan agreement to assure conformity of conditionality to the Polak model and other agreements, is seen as dominant (confidential interviews with Fund staff).

Interestingly enough, both sympathetic and critical observers of the Fund hold the assumptions of the functionalist model. Buira and Horowitz each criticize the Fund for straying in recent years from the functionalist ideal and allowing too much politics to enter staff operations (Buira 1983; Horowitz 1985–86). Kwitney criticizes the executive directors for taking too passive a role in the Fund and allowing the staff to control decision-making (Kwitney 1983). Julius Nyerere condemned the staff in 1980 for its inflexible and systematic application of conditionality by asking, "When did the IMF become an International Ministry of Finance?" (Sampson 1981, 379). Former Managing Director Jacques DeLarosière denied charges that the Fund was politically motivated or aimed to increase poverty in Third World by stating that the Fund does not "impose austerity" (DeLarosière 1984).

To summarize, the principal actors of the functionalist model are the staff, led by the Managing Director and the Exchange and Trade Relations Department. It is assumed that decisions are made almost exclusively on the basis of economic rationality and objective need of the borrower. It is very easy to predict the content of any given conditionality agreement by simply identifying the values for a few key variables and "plugging" them into the modern variations of the "Polak model" (Nowzad 1981; David 1985; Dell 1983). The only changes in Fund policy that might be expected according to this model would be an expansion of Fund authority into new areas of policy and an increasingly secure status of the staff over time relative to other Fund organs. The principal risks to the IMF, according to this model are political penetration, on the one hand, and intellectual sterility, on the other (DeLarosière 1984).

Political Model

Many, if not most, analysts of the IMF single out the political forces that are posited as surrounding and penetrating the institution as the most important factor in IMF decision-making (Payer 1974; Aronson 1977; deVries 1985; Helleiner 1983). These political forces express themselves most directly through the Executive Board (Lister 1984). The Executive Board is a body composed of twenty-two elected and appointed representatives of various nations and regions, called Executive Directors. Through a system of weighted voting, the nations with the largest quotas have the most voting power (Gold 1979). All conditional loans must be approved by the Executive Board according to the Articles of Agreement of the Fund. The staff are expected to serve a purely supportive role.

The Fund, rather than acting as the international economic physician, has more strategic objectives, according to the political model. Under the leadership of the Executive Board and the major creditors, the Fund aims to increase the liberalization of the international economic system and to directly sustain the economic viability of nations considered "strategic allies" of the major creditors (Payer 1974, Appendix II). Assetto points out that IMF (and World Bank) policy toward Eastern Europe from 1947 to 1978 is best explained in terms of East-West relations. She points out that both Yugoslavia and Romania were permitted membership in the Fund in part because their relationship with the Soviet Union was poor (1988, 187).

A change in Fund policy is conceivable, according to the model, if the attitudes of major Executive Board members changed, or if the membership itself shifted. Helleiner is quick to point out that the election of Ronald Reagan in the United States marked the beginning a more restrictive Fund approach to lending (1983, 13). Likewise, some have seen the rise in Saudi, Chinese, Eastern European, and Latin American voting power on the Board as a factor in an increasingly concessional IMF lending approach (deVries 1976, 1985). This discussion can be found in large-scale studies of "hegemonic decline" (Keohane 1984; Gilpin 1987, chapter 8; Kennedy 1987).

In the literature on the Fund, both critics and proponents of IMF policy often implicitly adopt the political model. Radical thinkers, such as Payer, argue that the Fund serves merely as an enforcer of the interests of the world's capitalists. By favoring liberalization, the IMF makes the world more hospitable to multinational corporations and developed country exports. (1974, Appendix II) By isolating radical regimes and requiring excessive austerity in return for limited funds, the IMF has facilitated the collapse of several democratically elected Third World governments (Paul 1983). Some radical thinkers, such as Aronson and Körner, adopt a more structuralist approach by allowing for the possibility that the executive board and the major creditors may only represent one of many forces influencing IMF policy (Aronson 1977; Körner 1986). Interestingly, this difference of emphasis reflects the broader debate between "instrumental" Marxists (Lenin and the "New Left Review" school), and "structural" Marxists (Trotsky and the "Monthly Review" school).

Conservative critics of the Fund argue simply that the "wrong" political elements have gained ascendancy in the institution and are promoting a "global welfare system" at the expense of the developed nations, consistent with the New International Economic Order agenda of the developing world (Smith 1984). Note that both of these schools agree that political forces are more important than economic rationality, and the only differences relate to which political forces are dominant.

To summarize, then, the principal actors in the political model are the dominant creditors who express their interests through the Executive Board. The Board is the dominant organ of the institution and the staff serve to implement and justify its goals. These goals are, essentially, preservation of a liberal international system and support to strategically important allies of the major creditors. Although these political objectives have been subverted in favor of Third World development according to some, the essential logic of political dominance persists.

Bargaining Model

Both the functionalist and political models are based on what Ascher refers to as "first principles," meaning that they rely on an essentially unidirectional line of causality with very little dynamic interaction (Ascher 1985). The bargaining model differs from the other two in that it emphasizes dynamic processes and multiple levels of analysis.

The alternative that I present draws on the concepts of bargaining and negotiation. According to this view, no single entity controls Fund policy, but each sub-unit—political divisions, technical experts, or managerial staff—shares influence depending on the circumstances. This model stresses the dynamic processes involved in IMF policy-making rather than the static dimensions emphasized in the functionalist and political models. Although not a purely pluralist view, the model does allow for organizational sub-goals (Haas 1964; Cox 1969; Gordenker 1967; Sewell 1975; Luard 1977). Policy-making, according to this model, is best understood as a disaggregated process, consisting of a variety of realms of decision-making, both substantive and sequential. Policy outcomes emerge, not from the imposition of either technical or political power, but through pragmatic and fluid give-and-take, where the ultimate goal of all actors is the perpetuation of the relationship itself. Depending on the circumstances, the actors involved, and the specific tactics employed, the resulting policies are determined.

The bargaining model is more than a mere amendment of the preceding approaches. The bargaining model assumes a much less simple lending process than the earlier models. This model portrays the IMF as a constellation of often competing entities with their own interests and goals, none of which can be achieved without the support or compliance of other actors. What is most important from this perspective is the fact that lending negotiations take place over a rather long period of time and through several very different negotiating formats. Although it may be possible to expect that either political or technical values might prevail at any given stage of the negotiating process, it is not possible to predict the final outcome without taking into account a multi-layered model of interests, resources and bargaining skills. Depending on the case, a nation's particular resources and skills might outweigh whatever strength other actors might wield.

By way of illustration, the first step any nation takes in requesting Fund assistance is either initiated by the Fund staff or by the member country. If there is general agreement between Fund staff and country officials, then negotiations may proceed fairly smoothly along technical lines. If, however, the Fund mission is pressing for more rapid adjustment than the country is willing to undertake, then a variety of political tactics will likely come into effect, with the member country pleading for "leniency" on the grounds that its political and social system would not tolerate the adjustments, and the Fund enlisting the help of major economic powers to urge the member state to carry out its reforms. At other stages of the negotiation process various actors will have the opportunity to assert their own position, such as during face to face talks, when the IMF mission in the field it operates with the full legal and political support of the Fund. For example, the personal values of the mission chief may significantly alter the outcome of negotiations. Finally, after the negotiations are completed and the managing director has approved the package, the board has the opportunity to express its views and approve or reject the plan. Although in general the board approves plans, these reviews provide the opportunity for political representatives to influence future Fund policy (The above is based on confidential interviews with IMF officials and other sources, such as Assetto 1988, 12–16, and Gold 1983).

The key players in the decision-making "game" are the managing director, the staff (broken down into their various institutional units) the missions themselves, and the executive directors. The key process is competition and negotiation. Because no single unit or actor can achieve its individual or group objectives without the cooperation of many other elements, the key question is what negotiations and trade-offs will be achieved. For example, the influence that comes from the voting power of the U.S. Executive Director may be negated by the persuasiveness and charm of the Brazilian representative. The economic vulnerability of a prospective debtor in fact can be an asset if it can demonstrate a willingness to default on its private loans. The logically sound recommendations of the Exchange and Trade Relations Department to cut off a nation in arrears may be overruled by a managing director interested in preserving the Fund's reputation for fairness. What is perhaps most important in the bargaining model is not the answers but the questions. Are there any actors that have more "bargaining chips" than others? Are there alliances between actors that endure? How are interests communicated? At what point in the negotiating process is one actor dominant over another? In the political and functionalist models, these questions can be answered easily and consistently because they rely on an essentially static process. In the bargaining model the answers to these questions vary from situation to situation and from case to case.

The bargaining model draws heavily from traditional organizational behavior literature. Graham Allison's "Model II" and "Model III" go beyond the simple "Rational Actor" model of organizational decision-making by taking into account institutional forces. "Organization process" and "bureaucratic politics" are the terms used to describe how decision-making in large-scale organizations is better understood if one takes into account such institutional forces as parochialism (the tendency for small agencies within an institution to promote their own welfare over the institution's), the personal ambitions of certain agency heads, and poor communication among institutional actors (Allison 1971, chapter 7; see also Davis 1972). Lindblom, Braybrooke, March, and Simon have articulated well-known theories of institutional decision-making that refute the classic rational actor model on the grounds that rationality is simply not possible given the constraints of time, money, and other resources that exist even in large organizations. March and Simon argue that the most rational decision-making one can expect is a close approximation thereof, or "satisficing," while Lindblom argues that most decisions are simply slight variations on past procedure and do not involve any substantial creative thought and analysis (Lindblom & Braybrooke 1970; March & Simon 1958). The bargaining model incorporates these findings with its emphasis on institutional idiosyncrasies and dynamics. One could even consider this part of the school of "new institutionalism" (March & Olsen 1984).

In the area of international organization literature, several classic texts place a great deal of emphasis on institutional autonomy and decision-making processes. In his important analysis of the International Labor Organization (1964) Ernst Haas devoted a great deal of attention to the role of the ILO head in shaping policy and organization agenda, illustrating this point through a vivid contrast in the leadership styles of successive directors general. John Sewell's treatment of UNESCO (1975) likewise focused on the processes through which the institution developed its character and related to its "clients" and "patrons."

More recent authors have identified a need for a more process-oriented model of international organization decision-making. William Ascher comments:

> I suggest a process-oriented, multi-actor, 'exchange' model that analyzes what each significant actor wants, how that actor sees the opportunities for achieving these objectives, and the ensuing open or tacit arrangements that arise among actors. (1985, 15)

His findings on World Bank lending policy support the claim that a process-oriented model can be useful (Ascher 1983).

Frank Southard, in his candid portrayal of Fund policy-making, illustrates some of the dynamic aspects of the process. On the one hand, he points out, the appointed executive directors representing the major contributors will often recommend Fund policies that are self-interested, but they will only do so upon recommendation of the staff and with a sound research memorandum before them. On the other hand, the Fund staff are aware of the desires and goals of what they call the "major shareholders" and will rarely submit recommendations they know will be vetoed (Southard 1979).

In a recent work that analyzes the experiences of Eastern European nations in both the IMF and the International Bank for Reconstruction and Development (IBRD or World Bank), Assetto concludes that the Bretton Woods institutions are clearly neither dominated by political or technocratic forces, and that instead it is best to understand IMF policy-making in terms of country-specific factors that revolve around bargaining and limited coercion:

> The nature of the relationship between the IMF and IBRD and their Soviet Bloc members in the near future, therefore, will most likely be a result of a combination of factors including the status of the Cold War and the Bank and Fund's assessments of priorities in their environment. Past successes and failures of the Bank and Fund in their relations with Soviet Bloc members will also surely influence future policy. . . . (1988, 193)

Many legal scholars of the Fund have also emphasized the "division of powers" of the various IMF organs. Their research on the legal parameters of the institution tends to focus attention on the limits of IMF power as well as the limits of the various organs themselves. Gold, for example, stresses the balance between the executive board and the managing director, as well as the balance between national interests and Fund interests:

> A member's letter of intent is not a contractual relationship, but neither is it a unilateral declaration that creates obligations for the member to pursue its announced policies. . . . A member's failure to observe any of its declared purposes. . . does not automatically amount to an improper use of Fund resources. . . . (1979a, 20)

To summarize, then, the bargaining model differs from its political and functionalist alternatives in that it is dynamic rather than static, multidimensional rather than one-dimensional, inductive rather than deductive, and historical rather than universal. While it does not necessarily provide all of the answers, at least it raises the right questions.

Empirical Validity of Competing Models

Essential Empirical Features of Models

Thus far, I have described the essence of three very different models of IMF decision-making. They clearly differ in terms of their assumptions, logic, and implications. However, to be truly instructive, this analysis must go beyond the mere description of models. Rather, it is essential that the validity and utility of these models be tested against the actual behavior of the Fund. The models each describe a set of processes at work within the institution. These hypothetical processes can be compared to those observed directly by members of the institution and other analysts. More importantly, these models propose hypothetical outcomes of these processes in the form of specific application of IMF conditionality to individual nations. These hypothetical outcomes should be compared to the actual experiences of nations that have dealt with the Fund. In order to make these connections, it will be necessary to identify the key variables that distinguish each model. Some of this was done earlier in the chapter but will be made more explicit here.

First, with regard to the functionalist model, the central task is to determine whether the economic conditions of a country truly are the single best predictor of conditionality. Do all nations that are in the same economic boat and requesting the same level of assistance receive the same terms for their loans? Does a nation whose economic conditions and requests remain the same receive the same terms for successive loans over time? These are the key variables and questions to be asked in assessing the validity of the functionalist model.

The functionalist approach implies that the Fund has developed a fairly coherent and consistent logic with regard to the implementation of conditionality. The Exchange and Trade Relations Department is expected to guard against excessive variations in the terms that different countries receive. A recent director of ETR, David Finch, defended Fund application of conditionality against Third World criticism that it is applied arbitrarily and irresponsibly by saying, "[T]he nature of the problem facing the member dictates many of the policy responses that are [criticized]." (Finch 1983, 76) The "Polak Model" for balance of payments adjustments would seem to be the epitome of a consistent logic within the IMF. This model calls on governments of nations experiencing balance of payments shortfalls to rely on internal economic forces to adjust. These include, for example, expansion of production and sale of exports and contraction of demand for imports, liberalization of trade, elimination of exchange controls, reduction of public sector borrowing through reduced expenditures and increased revenues (which typically targets industrial subsidies, social spending, and price controls), and upward adjustment of domestic interest rates. All of this is based on an essentially monetarist economic approach that emphasizes the flow of money itself over the flow of goods and services (Finch 1983; Guitán 1981; Mikesell 1983; Johnson 1979). The functionalist model would predict relatively consistent treatment across time and across countries.

The functionalist model, with regard to the internal dynamics of policy implementation, assumes that the technical staff, dominated by ETR and the managing director, will carry out policy unilaterally. The executive board will be expected to play a very passive role.[1] Likewise, one would expect the borrowing nation to be relatively quiescent relative to Fund programs, since these terms would contain the best of economic wisdom and could not be improved upon by negotiation. The only input the recipient would have, according to the functionalist model, would be in the form of the initial request. Once the request is made, the decision would be out of the borrower's hands.

In summary, then, the most significant variable in the functionalist model is simply the economic condition of the borrower in terms of balance of payments disequilibrium. One could determine with a significant degree of confidence that the functionalist model was adequate to explain IMF decision-making if: (1) Fund conditionality is highly responsive to the economic conditions of the borrower, (2) the staff is the dominant actor within the Fund, (3) the Managing Director and ETR are dominant among the staff, and (4) the member country plays a passive role.

The political model is based on the assumption that economic policy is merely a tool in the hands of political actors. The most important way of determining whether the political model is the most appropriate analytical tool is to focus on the political characteristics of the recipient nations on the one hand, and the political characteristics of the executive board on the other. Because the major creditors of the IMF—the United States, France, Germany, and Japan—are each capitalist nations, one would expect that all Western capitalists would receive the best treatment from the Fund. Conversely, one would expect the IMF to deal quite sternly with anti-Western socialist states—perhaps even going so far as to exclude them from the institution or attempting to undermine their governments with "punitive" conditionality.

Going beyond the mere "East-West" dichotomy, a distinction that was still meaningful during the period of this study, one could expect to see any borrowers' programs which limit foreign access (whether restrictions on foreign investment, trade barriers, export subsidies, nationalizations, or exchange controls) struck down, since these would go against the interests of the major creditors of the institution. As put by Payer:

> This brings us to the final component of the typical IMF stabilization program: greater hospitality to foreign investment. This item is in a sense redundant, since we have seen that the entire complex of stabilization policies is designed to ensure that the country can manage its foreign exchange policies with the minimum recourse to restrictions on payments, which would damage primarily foreign investors and suppliers of that country's imports. (1974, 38)

It will be important, then, to determine whether nations which have severe restrictions on foreign economic access but which have relatively healthy economies would be required to carry out more comprehensive adjustments than a nation which has an open, if very unhealthy, economy. If it is, then one could say that politics had likely taken precedence over economics.

With regard to internal dynamics, the political model would lead us to expect a strong, dynamic executive board and a relatively passive—although complicitous—staff. One would expect the U.S. Executive Director to be the dominant figure in the institution, wielding at the very least a veto power over all decisions. One might even expect to find that the professionals on the staff resent the intrusion of "political" factors into what they see as a purely "technical" matter.

In sum, then, the political model emphasizes the variables of (1) political affiliation of the borrowers and creditors, and (2) openness of the borrower's economic systems. One would expect that: (1) Nations which are members of the Western bloc—broadly speaking—would receive more lenient treatment than non-aligned or anti-Western states, (2) nations with closed economies will be expected to make greater adjustments than nations with open economies, (3) the executive board will dominate the institution, and (4) the major creditors will dominate the executive board.

The bargaining model identifies a whole new set of variables as especially significant. First of all, what are the objectives of each of the participants in the process? Before one can begin to predict the outcome, one must understand what each actor seeks. In most cases, the objectives of any given actor can be summarized in terms of power and influence, but these are often only the means to much more urgent ends. The borrowing country, for example, may at any given point in time seek and/or as much money as possible with as lenient conditionality as possible, to make symbolic gestures of accommodation in order to appease foreign financial markets, to make symbolic gestures of intransigence to appease domestic nationalistic political forces, to resolve structural economic difficulties through short-term solutions. The process and outcome of negotiations will obviously vary greatly depending on the objectives of the borrower. The same applies to each of the participants. For example, an up-and-coming mid-level official will likely argue on behalf of his recently negotiated agreement with more vigor than a soon-to-retire senior official.

Second, it is important to identify the specific attributes of each actor relative to its negotiating partners at various points in time. One should consider the following as important to an actor's bargaining skill: economic expertise, authority to make binding decisions, persuasiveness, flexibility, institutional support, experience, and familiarity with the process. The key question will be which actor has more "assets" at a given point during the negotiation process. The managing director negotiating an agreement with a mid-level finance ministry official will likely be more effective than a mid-level mission member negotiating with the minister of finance. A stubborn, senior official of a newly-formed military government may have more success than an insecure, junior official of an unstable democracy.

Third, it is important to have an idea of the "tactics" and strategy each participant uses. According to the bargaining model, a confrontational strategy, employed either by the Fund or the borrower, could be expected to yield very different results than a conciliatory one. Obstructionism on the part of the borrower, a common strategy, may yield very different results from the "pre-emptive" reform strategy that is used more rarely. Each of these strategies are understandable only in the historical context, however. According to the bargaining model, one cannot simply look at a statistical description of the country to determine whether a nation had adopted a particular strategy relative to IMF negotiations. One must study the "play-by-play" of the "game."

In the final analysis, it will not always be easy to predict the outcome of IMF negotiations. There is no simple algorithm to determine the level of public sector borrowing, nor can one simply look at the alliance configuration of the borrowers to determine who gets a "good deal." Rather, each program will tend to be unique to the nation at hand and may vary from year to year depending on which individuals occupy which seat in the Fund or in the borrowing nation's government, which administration is in office, and whether they are learning anything as they go along.

To summarize, the bargaining model requires one to focus on: (1) the objectives of each of the Fund negotiation participants, (2) the negotiating assets held by each participant, (3) the strategy and tactics of each participant in using their assets to achieve their aims. With regard to predictions, the most the bargaining model can say is that those actors with the best strategy for using their assets will tend to achieve their aims when matched with actors that have fewer assets and less coherent strategies.

The reader may find Table 1.1 a useful summary of the preceding descriptions of the models.

The Case Studies

Before discussing the remainder of the work, I believe a clarification is appropriate. As mentioned earlier, these models are meant to be "ideal-types," rather than sophisticated elaborations of complex theory. They are meant to provide the extremes in explanations of IMF behavior. The question of whether the actual experience of a particular country fits only partially the assumptions of one or another model will be dealt with on a case-by-case basis. It is hoped that the detail for each case will be sufficient to clearly establish the logic of its experience. However, by comparing the experiences of several nations, it should be possible to identify a single model which best explains all of the cases. The key objective is to identify a model which requires minimal qualification to "fit" the reality of several cases.

I have selected seven different countries, each of which dealt with the Fund in a major way at some point over a fifteen year period from 1973 to 1988. They are: Jamaica, Zaire, Sudan, India, Turkey, Argentina, and Great Britain. These nations differ dramatically in terms of their levels of economic development, openness of the economy, regime type, alliance patterns, and economic expertise available in the nation. In addition, each nation employed a very different negotiating strategy with the Fund, sometimes changing tactics from year to year. Some nations were denied funding, while others received more than they expected. By taking these cases as a group, one may identify all of the variables mentioned above, which will allow us to more clearly assess the utility of the models in explaining Fund behavior.

I will supplement these case studies with a more detailed description and discussion of IMF structure and organization, as seen primarily through the eyes of its members and staff. This will provide a beginning of a "test" of the three models' assumptions regarding process.

One final word before embarking on a presentation of the findings. Although I have at times used the word "test" in the previous section, the reader should understand that this term is used primarily for convenience. I am not attempting a definitive, quantitative determination of the truthfulness of my hypotheses. What I will be doing is far more interpretive, rather than scientific. I do expect to conclude that the

TABLE 1.1 Competing Models of IMF Decision-Making

	FUNCTIONALIST MODEL	POLITICAL MODEL	BARGAINING MODEL
DOMINANT ACTORS	Staff, Managing Director	Executive Board	Managing Director, Staff sub-units, Executive Board
GOALS OF DOMINANT ACTORS	Economic adjustment Institutional enhancement	Political Dominance, Enrichment through access to debtors' economies	Goals vary accross time and from actor to actor
MEANS OF DOMINANCE	Intellectual dominance	Voting power, Lending capacity	Adroit tactics and careful strategy
PROSPECTS FOR CHANGE	Institutional enhancement leads to expanded Fund role	Changes in power/wealth distribution can alter voting majorities	Personalities, circumstances bring about new forces and bargaining resources
RATIONALE FOR PROGRAMS	Economic disequilibria	Stability/vitality of global economic structures of capitalism	Rationale varies depending on dominant bargainer
PROGRAM CONSISTENCY	Contingent on borrower's willingness/ability to carry out adjustment program	Consistent with dominant global political alignment and borrower's alliance pattern	Learning, changes in assets affect successive bargains
PREDICTABILITY OF PROGRAMS	High, given dominant economic rationale	High, assuming stable alliance patterns during period under study	Low, given information requirements for accurate prediction of bargaining

P R O C E S S

O U T C O M E S

Source: Author.

bargaining model is more useful—but not necessarily universal. If the bargaining and negotiation model is found to be relevant to institutions other than the IMF, it will only be through the work of others.

Notes

1. *Articles of Agreement* Article XII, Section 4, Part b: "The Managing Director shall be chief of the operating staff of the Fund and shall conduct, under the direction of the Executive Board, the ordinary business of the Fund. Subject to the general control of the Executive Board, he shall be responsible for the organization, appointment, and dismissal of the staff of the Fund."

Bibliography

Allison, Graham. 1971. *Essence of Decision: Explaining the Cuban Missile Crisis.* Boston, MA: Little, Brown. Argy, Victor. 1977. "Monetary Variables and the Balance of Payments," in IMF, *The Monetary Approach to the Balance of Payments.* Washington, D.C.: International Monetary Fund: 185–204.

Aronson, Jonathan. 1977. *Money and Power: Banks and the World Monetary System.* Beverly Hills: Sage Library of Social Research.

Ascher, William. 1985. "Preface to Exploring the Fund and the Bank." Paper Presented to the Annual Meetings of the International Studies Association, Washington, D.C., April.

————. 1983. "New Development Approaches and the Adaptability of International Agencies: The Case of the World Bank." *International Organization* 37 (Summer): 415–439.

Assetto, Valerie. 1988. *The Soviet Bloc in the IMF and the IBRD.* Boulder, CO: Westview.

Balassa, Bela. 1983. "The Adjustment Experience of Developing Economies After 1973." in J. Williamson, ed. *IMF Conditionality.* Washington, D.C.: Institute for International Economics: 145–174.

Buira, Ariel. 1983. "IMF Financial Programs and Conditionality." *Journal of Development Economics* 12: 111–136.

Cline, William R. 1983. "Economic Stabilization in Developing Countries: Theory and Stylized Facts." in Williamson, ed. *IMF Conditionality.* Washington, D.C.: Institute for International Economics: 175–208.

David, Wilfred L. 1985. *The IMF Policy Paradigm: The Macroeconomics of Stabilization, Structural Adjustment, and Economic Development.* New York: Praeger Publishers.

Davis, David H. 1972. *How the Bureaucracy Makes Foreign Policy: An Exchange Analysis.* Lexington, MA: D.C. Heath.

DeLarosière, Jacques. 1984. "Does the Fund Impose Austerity?" Washington, D.C.: International Monetary Fund.

Dell, Sidney. 1983. "Stabilization: The Political Economy of Overkill." in Williamson, ed. *IMF Conditionality.* Washington, D.C.: Institute for International Economics: 17–46.

_____. *On Being Grandmotherly: The Evolution of IMF Conditionality.* Essays in International Finance #86 Princeton, N.J.: Princeton University Press.

De Vries, Margaret G. 1976. *The International Monetary Fund, 1965-1971: The System Under Stress.* Washington, D.C.: International Monetary Fund.

_____. 1985. *International Monetary Fund, 1972-1978: Cooperation on Trial.* Washington, D.C.: International Monetary Fund.

Eckhaus, R.S. 1985. "How the IMF Decides on its Conditionality." Paper Presented to the Annual Meeting of the International Studies Association, Washington, D.C., April.

_____. 1986. "How the IMF Lives with its Conditionality." *Policy Sciences* 19: 237-52.

Finch, C. David. 1983. "Adjustment Policies and Conditionality." in Williamson, ed. *IMF Conditionality.* Washington, D.C.: Institute for International Economics: 75-86.

Gilpin, Robert. 1987. *The Political Economy of International Relations.* Princeton, N.J.: Princeton University Press.

Gold, Joseph. 1983. "Political Considerations Are Prohibited By Articles of Agreement When the Fund Considers Requests for Use of Resources." *IMF Survey* 12 (May 11): 146-148.

_____. 1979a. *Legal and Institutional Aspects of the International Monetary System: Selected Essays.* Washington, D.C.: International Monetary Fund.

_____. 1979b. *Conditionality.* IMF Pamphlet Series #31 Washington, D.C.: International Monetary Fund.

Guitán, Manuel. 1981. "Fund Conditionality and the International Adjustment Process." *Finance and Development* (June): 16-19.

Haas, Ernst. 1964. *Beyond the Nation-State: Functionalism and International Oorganization.* Stanford, CA: Stanford University Press.

Helleiner, G.K. 1983. *The IMF and Africa in the 1980s.* Essays in International Finance #152 Princeton, N.J.: Princeton University Press.

Horowitz, Irving L. 1985-86. "The 'Rashomon' Effect: Ideological Proclivities and Political Dilemmas of the International Monetary Fund." *Journal of Interamerican Studies and World Affairs* 27 (Winter): 37-55.

International Monetary Fund. 1986. "Fund-Supported Programs, Fiscal Policy, and Income Distribution: A Fiscal Affairs Department Study." *Occasional Papers* 46 Washington, D.C.: International Monetary Fund.

_____. 1984. *By-Laws, Rules and Regulations.* 41st Issue. Washington, D.C.: International Monetary Fund.

_____. 1977. *The Monetary Approach to the Balance of Payments.* Washington, D.C.: International Monetary Fund.

Johnson, Harry C. 1979. "The Monetary Approach to the Balance of Payments: A Nontechnical Guide." in Adams, John, ed., *The Contemporary International Economy: A Reader.* New York: St Martin's Press: 192-209.

Kahler, Miles, ed. 1986. *The Politics of International Debt.* Ithaca, NY: Cornell University Press.

Kennedy, Paul. 1987. *The Rise and Decline of the Great Powers: Economic Change and Military Conflict from 1500 to 2000.* New York: Random House.

Keohane, Robert. 1984. *After Hegemony: Cooperation and Discord in the World Political Economy*. Princeton, N.J.: Princeton University Press.

————— & Joseph Nye. 1977. *Power and Interdependence: World Politics in Transition*. Boston: Little, Brown Publishers.

Killick, Tony, ed. 1982. *Adjustment and Financing in the Developing World: The Role of the International Monetary Fund*. Washington, D.C.: International Monetary Fund.

—————. ed. 1984. *The IMF and Stabilisation: Developing Country Experiences*. London: Gower.

Kindleberger, Charles P. 1973. *International Economics*. 5th edition. Homewood, Ill: Richard D. Irwin.

Körner, Peter, Mass, Gero, Siebold, Thomas, and Tetzlaff, Rainer. 1986. *The IMF and the Debt Crisis*. translated by Paul Knight. London: Zed Books.

Kuhn, Thomas. 1962. *The Structure of Scientific Revolutions*. Chicago: University of Chicago Press.

Kwitney, Jonathan. 1983. "The 'Yes' Men Atop the IMF." *Wall Street Journal* May 12: 37.

Lister, Frederick. 1984. *Decision-Making Strategies for International Organizations: The IMF Model*. Monograph Series in World Affairs, Denver, CO: University of Denver Press.

Luard, Evan. 1977. *International Agencies: The Emerging Framework of Interdependence*. London: MacMillan.

March, James G. and Johan Olsen. 1984. "The New Institutionalism: Organizational Factors in Political Life." *American Political Science Review* 78 (September): 734–749.

March, James G. and Herbert Simon. 1958. *Organizations*. New York: John Wiley & Sons.

Mikesell, Raymond F. 1983. "Appraising Fund Conditionality: Too Loose, Too Tight, or Just Right?" in Williamson, ed. *IMF Conditionality* Washington, D.C.: Institute for International Economics: 47–62.

Nowzad, Bahram. 1981. *The IMF and Its Critics*. Essays in International Finance #146 Princeton, NJ: Princeton University Press.

Paul, Alix-Herard. 1983. "The 'Destabilization' Program of the IMF in Jamaica." *Inter-American Economic Affairs* 37 (Autumn): 45–61.

Payer, Cheryl. 1974. *The Debt Trap: The International Monetary Fund and the Third World*. New York: Monthly Review Press.

Pion-Berlin, David. 1985. "The Role of Ideas: The International Monetary Fund and Third World Policy Choices." Paper Presented at the Annual Meeting of the American Political Science Association, New Orleans, September.

Polak, J.J. 1957. "Monetary Analysis of Income Formation and Payments Problems." *IMF Staff Papers* 6: 1–40.

————— and Victor Argy. 1977. "Credit Policy and the Balance of Payments." in IMF. *The Monetary Approach to the Balance of Payments*. Washington, D.C.: International Monetary Fund: 205–225.

Rhomberg, Rudolf R. and H. Robert Miller. 1977. "Introductory Survey." in IMF. *The Monetary Approach to the Balance of Payments*. Washington, D.C.: Institute for International Economics: 1–14.

Sampson, Anthony. 1981. *The Money Lenders: The People and Politics of the World Banking Crisis.* New York: Penguin Press.

Sewell, James P. 1975. *UNESCO and World Politics.* Princeton, NJ: Princeton University Press.

Sidell, Scott. 1988. *The IMF and Third-World Political Instability: Is There a Connection?* New York: St. Martin's Press.

Smith, Fred L., Jr. 1984. "The Politics of IMF Lending." *Cato Journal* 4 (Spring/Summer): 211–241.

Southard, Frank. 1979. *The Evolution of the International Monetary Fund.* Essays in International Finance #135 Princeton, NJ: Princeton University Press.

Strange, Susan. 1973. "IMF: Monetary Managers." in Cox, Robert and Jacobson, H., eds., *The Anatomy of Influence: Decision-Making in International Organizations.* New Haven, CN: Yale University Press: 263–297.

Tew, Brian. 1969. "The International Monetary Fund." typescript.

Time 1988. November 28: 20.

Williamson, John. 1983. "On Judging the Success of IMF Policy Advice." in Williamson, ed. *IMF Conditionality.* Washington, D.C.: Institute for International Economics: 175–208.

Williamson, John, ed. 1983. *IMF Conditionality.* Washington, D.C.: Institute for International Economics.

2

Internal IMF Policy
Structures and Process

Before proceeding to a description of the case-studies discussed in chapter one, it is important to describe in more detail the internal dynamics, both routine and unusual, that characterize the IMF's way of doing business. This chapter offers such a picture.

Structure of the IMF

Although independent, the International Monetary Fund is officially a United Nations specialized agency. It opened for business in 1946. Based on the view that most countries' monetary problems are the result of flawed domestic policies, the IMF focuses primarily on monitoring and regulating members' economic and financial programs. The IMF was also endowed with financial resources with which to assist countries experiencing balance-of-payments difficulties. In 1958 the Fund began applying conditions for receipt of especially large loans: the "stand-by arrangement" came into full force (Horsefield 1969). This has since become the principal vehicle of Fund lending. Member countries may receive Fund assistance if they agree to alter their domestic economic and financial policies as suggested by the Fund staff.

The organization of the IMF has remained fairly stable over the years, especially in comparison with its sister institution, the World Bank. The reader is invited to consult figure 2.1. The Fund has expanded steadily in both membership and staff over its lifetime, with a spurt of roughly 35 new members from 1960 to 1964 (deVries 1985). The People's Republic of China, Yugoslavia, and Viet Nam are among the few socialist members of the Fund which as yet does not include the Soviet Union. This may soon change as Czechoslovakia, Bulgaria and others seek accession and East Germany enjoys the fruits of unification with the Federal Republic. Finance ministers, central bank presidents and/or other officials of these members constitute the governing body of the institution: the Board of Governors. They meet once each autumn to set overall lending ceilings and broad policies. A few also meet as an "Interim Committee" twice yearly to offer general advice regarding broad matters of international financial management as guidance for the Executive Board.

Everyday operation of the Fund is supervised by twenty-two executive directors. The five largest contributors to the fund appoint one director each, while other countries combine their voting power to "elect" an Executive Director (since these appointments are very rarely contested, it is misleading to call them elections*). At three fixed weekly meetings, and on a continuous basis as residents at the Fund headquarters, the executive directors monitor and direct Fund activities, under the chairmanship of the managing director who is elected for a five-year renewable term by the Board of Governors. Country-specific policies are often discussed at this level, as well as the overall policies of the Fund. A range of issues, from staffing to conditionality, are also considered and ruled upon. Each Executive Director wields a certain number of votes, largely in proportion to the "quota" or contribution of his constituency. (Lister 1984, chapter 3) On this basis, the United States' Executive Director, working with board members from France, Germany, Japan and Britain, has the ability to determine Fund policy, or at least veto many types of decisions. In addition to the weighted voting system, categories of decisions require different majorities for resolution, in much the same way as extraordinary majorities are required for amendments of most constitutions. The political model assumes numerous important and controversial votes in the executive board. We will see that in fact the behavior of the board is not strictly tied to voting majorities.

The structure of the staff is rather simple in that roughly one-fourth of the Fund's staff of 1,600 deals directly with its membership via a number of "area" departments and another one-fourth deals with overall Fund concerns via several "functional" departments. The remainder of the staff fill a variety of support functions for the other half of the staff and outside clients. Some of these functions are critical, such as the research activities of the Statistics department. Of particular importance to us in this study are the activities of area departments and functional departments.

There are five area departments, each with a quasi-continental jurisdiction: European, Asian, African, Middle Eastern and Western Hemisphere. Within each area department are the typical country desks and

---

*Because much of the material in this chapter is taken from confidential interviews with thirty of the IMF's senior staff, I will use an asterisk (*) as a substitute for a full citation.

FIGURE 2.1 Simplified IMF Organizational Structure

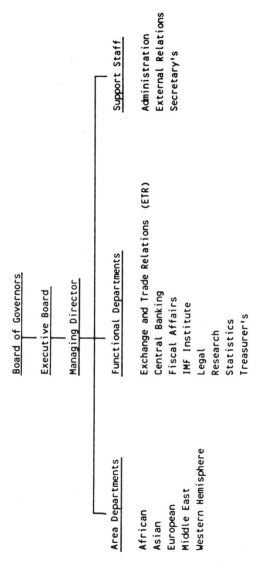

Board of Governors

Executive Board

Managing Director

Area Departments

African
Asian
European
Middle East
Western Hemisphere

Functional Departments

Exchange and Trade Relations (ETR)
Central Banking
Fiscal Affairs
IMF Institute
Legal
Research
Statistics
Treasurer's

Support Staff

Administration
External Relations
Secretary's

Source: IMF.

regional divisions that would be found in any foreign ministry. The functional departments provide specialized advice to Fund staff and member countries and are organized according to specialty: Legal, Central Banking, Fiscal Affairs (FAD), Exchange and Trade Relations (ETR), Research and Treasurer's Departments. ETR is perhaps the most influential department in the IMF because it monitors all stand-bys to assure that overall Fund policies are enforced. ETR has the authority to block any new lending packages that could be considered extraordinary even after the Fund mission and the borrowing country have formally reached agreement. An internal IMF document states that ETR:

> reviews individual programs in the light of current Fund policies and practices on conditionality and helps to ensure that such policies are applied uniformly with respect to member countries.

The energetic pursuit of this mission has earned ETR the reputation of IMF watchdog and whistle-blower.*

The division of labor between the area and functional departments, while originally intended to foster specialization and avoid unneccesary duplication of effort, has also resulted in a natural tension within the staff. Much of the decision-making in the IMF revolves around this dichotomy and its associated differences in goal, philosophy, and perspective.*

IMF Lending Process

Although the IMF is said to "lend" money, the transactions that take place differ markedly from the traditional "loan." Rather than simply providing money, the Fund exchanges hard currency for a member country's soft currency—thereby reducing its fungible assets. These transactions are formally called "repurchases" (Gold 1979b). Through a wide variety of transactions, the Fund makes available the temporary use of hard currency. This hard currency comes either from the Fund's regular resources (derived from quotas and interest payments) or indirectly from ad-hoc contributions by major creditor states through the "General Arrangements to Borrow" or GAB. In general terms, the larger the transaction, the larger the proportion of GAB resources. In this study, we focus on the "stand-by arrangement." Such a transaction involves the temporary (usually 12 to 36 months) use of Fund-provided resources in exchange both for domestic currency of the member as well as interest. In addition to these financial transactions, the member state is invited to carry out, or at least maintain, adjustment policies. The specific policies (conditions) are agreed upon through negotiations between the Fund and member country officials. There are five phases through which the conditions of the arrangement are decided upon: (1) initiation, (2) internal preparation, (3) negotiations in the field, (4) internal review of letter of intent, and (5) disbursement and monitoring.

Initiation

A request for Fund assistance can come either at the initiation of the member country or upon the advice of IMF staff. Especially at times of a crisis of unforeseen and sudden shortfalls in export earnings (a drop in commodity price, for example), a member might approach officials of the Fund regarding the possibility of negotiating a stand-by, or some other form of Fund assistance. More typically, the Fund staff, in the course of its annual visit to the member country, will identify emerging problems and situations, at which point "the member country may request Fund assistance in designing a suitable program, or the Fund staff may itself suggest the advantages of a comprehensive adjustment supported by the use of the Fund's resources," as a Fund official diplomatically described it. (Crockett 1982, 11)

Internal Preparations

Upon learning of a desire for assistance, the Fund's area department staff sets about drawing up a "briefing paper," or program proposal. This represents the Fund's concept of the program the recipient ought to undertake in order to qualify for the stand-by. The briefing paper is usually drawn up in consultation with officials from ETR and is forwarded to the managing director for final approval. The executive board is not involved at this phase, although the borrowing member's executive director would probably inquire privately concerning the progress of the loan. Once approved, a team is assembled to fly to the country in order to negotiate a final "letter of intent." Such a team, called a "mission," typically consists of 5–8 members: the director of the division with jurisdiction over the country at the helm, accompanied by "economists" (junior Fund staff) from the same division, ETR and perhaps another functional department, depending on the particular problems of the country. It is also common that a World Bank staff member familiar with the country will accompany the mission. This is especially important where a World Bank structural adjustment loan—similar to a stand-by arrangement—is already in place* (Crockett 1982).

Negotiations

The mission arrives in the member country and usually stays two to three weeks. During this time, mission members will hold confidential discussions with senior (though usually sub-ministerial level) officials from the member country's finance ministry, central bank and other agencies. The objective is to arrive at agreement between the Fund officials and the prospective loan recipient concerning the terms of the stand-by: How much of a devaluation is necessary? How much restriction ought there be on domestic credit expansion? Ought wages and prices be frozen? The visit may be painless or difficult depending on "the difficulty of obtaining the necessary information, the complexity of the program, and the constraints faced by member authorities in marshaling a consensus for needed adjustment measures." (Crockett 1982, 13) Of course, the degree of flexibility of the mission itself is an important factor, and the length of the "leash" varies from mission to mission.

In the vast majority of cases, a letter of intent is drafted and signed by the member country and provisionally approved by the mission pending final approval by the Managing Director. This letter of intent represents the program of adjustment that the member-state will attempt to put into practice.

Internal Review of the Letter of Intent

Before the request for assistance is passed on to the executive board for approval, the letter of intent must be accepted by the Managing Director, who obtains the comments and advice of senior staff in the process. It is then sent on to the Executive Board, along with analytical papers prepared by the mission and other Fund staff, for final discussion and approval. While the board has full authority to reject or amend any stand-by arrangement, it is sensitive to the amount of work already completed on the project, as well as the political costs involved in a rejection, and almost always assents. Members of the board nonetheless often express concerns over particular features of a stand-by and recommend that such features not be included in future cases (while retaining them in the package under review).* Later I will discuss some of the other ways the board attempts to influence the content of stand-bys.

Disbursement and Review

Once the stand-by is officially approved by the executive board, funds are made available to the member country. Disbursements are usually staggered such that a large portion (up to half of the agreed-upon amount) is available immediately and the rest is available at roughly six month intervals over the twelve to thirty-six month period of the stand-by. In order to insure compliance with the terms of the letter of intent, studies are carried out periodically and government financial data are compared with lending conditions. Should it be determined that the recipient has strayed too far from the conditions of the loan, disbursement is cut off. (See country cases and Sutton 1984, 14) This action does not require executive board approval. At this point, new negotiations are typically undertaken and may result in a new letter of intent, following the procedures discussed earlier.

In recent times, many recipients of IMF lending have suffered from structurally maladjusted economies, such that short-term lending and minor policy alteration as undertaken in the stand-by have proven insufficient to remedy the problem. In such cases, the country must often enter into a series of successive stand-bys (Compare IMF 1988, 182 to IMF 1984, 175). These often involve drawing on the recently created "extended fund" drawing which disburses funds over a three-year period in larger amounts and on different conditions. In either case, the termination of one stand-by is sometimes a prelude to new negotiations and the inauguration of a new stand-by. In a few cases, countries are in continuous negotiation with the IMF, as successive plans are implemented or implementation fails (See Zaire, Argentina, and Jamaica cases).

Staff Perspectives on Fund Decision-Making

There is a broad consensus among Fund staff that bargaining is the dominant decision-making dynamic*, in spite of the official IMF position that it operates along strictly functional lines.[1]

Interactions Between Missions and Member Countries

Regardless of the way in which the stand-by negotiations are initiated, a Fund "mission" will be organized to conduct these talks with the member country in question. Although usually formed along the lines described earlier, important differences emerg eamong missions, both in personnel and style. The mission chief, while usually the division chief responsible for the country in question, may be a much more senior individual. Even department heads themselves have led teams into especially difficult or politically sensitive negotiations (the cases of David Finch, ETR head, in Jamaica and L.A. Whittome, head of the European dept., in Britain will be reviewed later in the work). (deVries 1985)

The mission stays in a country for several weeks, dealing with senior officials from the member's finance ministry, central bank and others involved in economic and financial policy-making. The object of these discussions is arrival at a consensus between mission and country officials regarding the content of the letter of intent to be addressed to the Fund managing director. The mission will have in their briefcases the letter of intent drafted in Washington, while the country officials will have in their minds, usually, a rough idea of what type of concessions they are willing and not willing to make in order to obtain the maximum funds from the IMF. Thus the stage is set for a process that, amazingly enough, the Fund only recently acknowledged to be a "negotiation."*

What is at stake for each participant? For the Fund staff, the credibility of the institution, both in terms of its fairness and its consistency of treatment of member countries is a high priority. Not only are mission members concerned about promoting the interests of the Fund, their own career will be enhanced if "their" nation is successful.* For the country officials, the financial credibility of the regime, the prosperity of its citizens, and possibly their own jobs and the survival of the government are on the line. Both groups of participants, by virtue of their past relationships as individuals in earlier meetings and discussion, have a personal desire for cordiality and civility.* And, presumably, it is fair to think that both groups have the desire to solve the genuine problems of the country in question and put in place "good" policy.

What types of resources are available to each of the actors to achieve these goals? First, let us consider the IMF mission's assets. More than anything, what gives the IMF team influence in these discussions is its formal and legal *authority*. The mission's official status places it in a unique position vis-à-vis the member country. To begin with, the mission's recommendations carry extra weight because they represent a close approximation of the "will of the Fund," something an independent consultant's advice would not. Even if the mission is off-target in its assessment of the "will of the Fund," its opinion cannot be seriously questioned by outsiders to the Fund* (this process, known as the "OZ method," has been adopted by some country officials, who argue that a Fund proposal will not be acceptable to a secluded and sometimes hypothetical senior official with final decision-making capacity. See the case of Great Britain). More importantly, the mission holds the keys to the coffers of the Fund, and failure to conclude an agreement may result in failure to secure the sought-after loan. Finally, as Fund "insiders," the mission can play a crucial role of advocate on behalf of the member country after its return to headquarters in Washington.* While not all countries seek leniency, in terms of policy recommendations and conditions that would be neither difficult nor destabilizing, this is certainly one of the objects of most countries when dealing with the Fund.* If the country officials can persuade the Fund mission that its case is unique and warrants special treatment, the size of the arrangement and the policy conditions may be more tolerable to the debtor.

An experienced and alert team of member country officials can often minimize the significance of these mission assets, however. For example, during the tenure of Jacques DeLarosière as Managing Director (1978–1987), country officials tended in an increasing number of cases to minimize the salience of the mission in the field.* Many such officials have attempted, often successfully, to deal directly with the managing director, rather than the mission. This has been especially true for the small number of extremely indebted states. This has had a negative impact on mission morale. Such a situation was extremely rare under Managing Director Pierre-Paul Schweitzer, and some staff remember his tenure with fondness. For example, in 1967, during intense stand-by negotiations with Britain, Schweitzer was invited by U.K. officials to conduct direct negotiations with the British government. Schweitzer is said to have declined, rather indignantly, and to have reminded the visiting officials that the Fund's mission chief was empowered to negotiate on behalf of the Fund and was, additionally, eminently qualified to do so. One can understand the staff's affectionate recollection of such incidents.*

Not only do Fund mission members hold a certain official status, they also carry with them a great deal of expertise. Fund staff are recruited from the highest levels of academia, as either graduates or faculty members of internationally prominent universities and economics departments. A few have combined excellent academic qualifications with extensive experience (note the case of William Hood, Director of Research: professor of Economics at the University of Toronto for twenty years, followed by twelve years in Canada's Central Bank and Ministry of Finance).* In almost all cases, members of Fund missions have far more professional expertise than their counterparts in member countries in the field. This is especially the case where small Third World nations are involved. This also helps to explain why African governments tend to defer to the mission on matters of financial and economic policy and more willingly abide by the original provisions of the briefing paper. On the other hand, those few developed countries that have borrowed from the Fund in a major way (Britain and Italy in the 1970s) have been able to marshal their expertise and effectively debate the objective worth of Fund recommendations. (deVries 1985, chaps. 23, 24)

What resources are available to the member country in the face of such overwhelming power? First and foremost, member country officials have formal authority to adopt and *implement* economic policies for the most part, or at least a significant role in proposing such policies. A recently-elected government with a substantial parliamentary majority and loyal bureaucracy will be able to more effectively carry out an adjustment package of its choosing in comparison to a weak coalition government surrounded by a corrupt and self-serving governing apparatus. This may not be an advantage for first-time loan recipients, but in successive negotiations, compliance with earlier conditions often makes it easier to conclude a new program. It appears that in a few cases, compliance is later "rewarded" with less onerous terms (See cases of Turkey and Sudan as well as Assetto's treatment of Yugoslavia and Romania in 1988).*

Ironically, it may also be to the member country's advantage to lack authority to implement policies. The recent fall of several governments that tried to implement IMF conditionality (Sudan's Nimeiry, to cite a recent case) has made the IMF somewhat more aware of the political constraints of member governments in implementing economic reform* (IMF 1986). Thus, the argument that a particular policy recommendation is "politically unfeasible" carries weight with the mission. A result of this constraint is the tendency for Fund programs to offer only incremental reform and to show tolerance for non-compliance, both of which are illustrated in Tables 2.1 and 2.2. All of this has come to the attention of most debtor countries, to the point that some have, through their manipulation of the media and the masses, contrived "discontent and instability." For example, Argentina and Brazil, in the midst of the upheaval of democratization in the past few years, seem to have simply "allowed" riots to take place when negotiations with the IMF became deadlocked (See the cases of Argentina and Zaire).

Governments also have control over the production and transfer of the economic and statistical data which the IMF mission will analyze. In some cases, countries have used this simple resource in order to affect the outcome of negotiations. For example, Mobutu's Zairian government delayed adjustment by impeding the accumulation of data regarding the overall quantity of external debt owed by his country. Simply to measure the total amount of Zairian debt required two years' effort by a team of foreign officials and financiers who took control of key ministries in Kinshasa (Callaghy 1984). Already, it should be clear that participants in stand-by negotiations at the level of direct mission-member talks use their resources to exact concessions. The government yields its "political will" (in the sense of political authority) in order to gain a more lenient set of conditions. Mission staff yields their attachment to the briefing paper in order to achieve consensus and preserve cordiality.* There is in fact little coercion, in spite of press statements to the contrary (See all case studies).*

Interactions Among Fund Staff

The structure of the IMF itself has a significant impact upon staff attitudes and values, in spite of its high degree of professional training. As in most "bureaucratic" organizations, the staff develops organizational

TABLE 2.1 IMF Conditionality Compared to Country Performance in Africa, 1979-1983

Parameter	Number of cases for which IMF tar-gets equals +/-10% previous year's performance	Number of cases for which IMF tar-gets equals 10% to 20% previous year's performance	Total number of cases
Consumer Price Index	9	5	23
Savings/GDP Ratio	6	4	18
Investment/GDP Ratio	6	8	18
Government Revenue/GDP	15	7	25
Government Expenditure/GDP	16	4	25
External Debt/GDP	9	1	17
Growth of Money Supply	11	8	29

Source: Zulu & Nsouli 1985.

TABLE 2.2 Compliance with IMF Conditionality and Later
Borrowing by African Countries, 1981-1983

Country	Degree of Compliance with IMF Conditionality in 1980-1981	Successive Lending by IMF, 1981-1983
Gambia	Partial	SBA*: 1981-1982
Kenya	Non-compliance	SBA: 1981-1982 SBA: 1982-1983
Madagascar	Non-compliance	SBA: 1981-1982
Malawi	Partial	SBA: 1981-1982 EFF*: 1982-1983
Morocco	Partial	SBA: 1981-1982 SBA: 1982-1983
Senegal	Partial	SBA: 1981-1982 SBA: 1982-1983
Zaire	Non-compliance	SBA: 1982-1983
Zambia	Non-compliance	SBA: 1982-1983

*SBA=Stand-by Arrangement
*EFF=Extended Fund Facility

Source: Zulu & Nsouli 1985.

"sub-goals" that may or may not be compatible with overall organization goals. These revolve around issues of department and individual dominance over policy-making, job security and career enhancement.

The staff of the IMF determine, at headquarters, much of the content of most stand-by arrangements. This input takes place at three levels: (1) background information and analysis of the country's situation, (2) preparation of the briefing paper, and (3) review of the letter of intent agreed upon by the country and the Fund mission. Important actors in the process include not only the mission, but senior staff, department heads, and the managing director. The executive board injects itself only indirectly into these phases* (Kwitney 1983).

General data gathering and analysis is scattered throughout the Fund. While one would expect the area departments to dominate country-specific expertise, this is not always the case. Both ETR and the Research Department carry out extensive cross-national and country-specific analysis at the request of the Executive Board, at staff initiative (the Research department in this way resembles an academic department) and in connection with preparation of the semi-annual *World Economic Outlook* or WEO. [2]

In initial phase of a particular stand-by, a mission is assembled and begins drafting a "briefing paper." When discussing the content of the briefing paper, Fund staff openly air personal feelings and candidly comment on political questions such as regime stability, welfare effects, and administrative competence.* The staff almost always agree on the ultimate objectives of such programs: an open, growing, free-market economy void of maladjustments in the international sector. Debates revolve around issues of "timing" and the "pace" of adjustment, rather than whether adjustment is needed at all* (Edwards 1987). Much of the discussion at the briefing paper stage is based on weak empirical data (projections, estimates), since one of the mission's principal tasks is the gathering of statistics. In this situation, it is typically the mission chief, with his or her authority, seniority, and experience, who dominates the outcome.*

The IMF is structured in such a way that ETR is a natural "balancer" against the area departments. ETR, with a widely accepted role of custodian of the virtues of "consistency" and "fairness," typically opposes the proposals of the area department staff, which it suspects are based on "favoritism" and "special concessions."* The area departments, on the other hand, due to their more intimate acquaintance with overall conditions within the country, oppose ETR's "arbitrary" application of "inflexible rules" in favor of a "custom made" program to suit the particular needs and constraints of the country in question. Some senior officials of the Fund surmise that the institutional balance was created by design in order to promote more balanced policy.* Although Edward Bernstein, founding father of the Fund, denied this intent, he acknowledged the result (1985).

With the growth in the number of stand-bys since 1970, ETR has emerged as the most significant IMF department.* Its influence has grown in proportion. Even more important, it has succeeded in attracting the best of the IMF's mid-level staff, thus giving it additional intellectual resources in an agency where intellect is highly respected. There is therefore a tendency on the part of other departments to defer to ETR.* This is especially so in the case of the African department, to which relatively less talented staff have been migrating (a fact grudgingly acknowledged by senior staff).*

Managing Director DeLarosière, tended to intervene directly in the internal staff deliberations, thereby lessening ETR's influence.* For example, he decided that debt negotiations with the large, debtor nations of Latin America will be handled on a "case by case" basis (Rowan 1986). This phrase means that political idiosyncracies will be explicitly taken into account and the stand-bys moulded to the situation of each country.* In other words, ETR's rule of uniform treatment is waived, and ETR's dominance with respect to these cases is consequently reduced. It also appears that, in the context of expanding aid to African nations by the World Bank in the late 'seventies, DeLarosière, very experienced in African development lending himself and sympathetic to the extreme need of that continent, allowed a dramatic and unwise (South 1985) expansion of Fund lending to Africa from 1979 to 1983. Total sums approved in stand-by and extended fund arrangements increased from SDR 455.2 million in 1979 to SDR 4.7 billion in 1981. (Zulu 1985, 4) Fund staff point out that even at the time, conditions in Africa did not warrant the Fund's style of short-term lending at nearly market rates of interest.* Thus, Africa appeared to be receiving "special treatment" over the objections of ETR and other conservative voices.*

In general, it has been difficult for the staff to wield the level of influence over Fund policy characteristic of the Schweitzer regime because of the style of management employed by DeLarosière. He limited the total number of meetings and tended to dominate those he held.* While Schweitzer delegated a great deal, DeLarosière has been described as a "micro-manager."* This has naturally led to a certain amount of tension and frustration on the part of once-influential senior staff. In spite of this morale overall is strong.*

The final phase of intra-staff involvement, the review of the letter of intent after the mission's return, takes place only at the highest levels. The mission prepares a background paper to accompany the signed agreement for review by the executive board. In writing this report, the staff will defend the provisions of the letter of intent, anticipating possible executive board objections.* The Legal Department may also be consulted at this point to comment of whether the provisions of the agreement violate any of the Fund Articles or other international law (Gold 1985). Finally, the managing director has the authority to approve the final version of all letters of intent prior to submission to the board. As mentioned earlier, the board rarely rejects the provisions of any given letter of intent. This is due in part to the careful groundwork and informal communication performed during the previous stages.

In summary, the Fund staff arrive at decisions and proposals through a complex process involving much more than simple institutional rules. While hierarchy makes some difference in staff influence, much of the interaction within the staff involves give-and-take and balance between contending groups and divisions. Resources available to the various participants differ. While ETR, by virtue of its institutional role, wields significant influence, it can be overridden by the Managing Director and by persuasive area department recommendations. The Research Department, while not always capable of influencing specific programs, can influence the framework of discussions by providing the backdrop of the WEO. Knowledge, rank, persuasiveness and institutional role all determine the relative influence of staff in policy-making, but it is difficult to predict a specific policy based on a knowledge of staff chracteristics.

The implications of the staff's decision-making process described thus far are rather counter-intuitive. It was the broad consensus of those interviewed that the treatment of member states was a function of how their cases were handled within the institution. Specifically, the more the managing director became directly involved in country negotiations, the the greater the leverage of the member country. This flows from the relative withdrawal of the Fund staff—especially ETR—from the final decision-making. The managing director has considerable latitude in his application of Fund principles and, as in the cases of Great Britain, Argentina, Mexico, and other major debtor, he has been able to bring the rest of the staff to agree with his interpretation of the problems and appropriate solutions.* (O'Donnell 1985, 29–30) Thus far, the political sensitivity of a case of the level of indebtedness are key factors in the managing director's decision to become heavily involved in the negotiation process. By extension, one can infer that nations of little political salience and low indebtedness (in global terms), will be treated in a more routine fashion and will find it more difficult to extract concessions from IMF negotiators.*We will see this dynamic evidenced in each of the cases under study in this work. Finally, the professional and personal relationship between Fund staff and member country officials is seen as playing a significant role according those interviewed. As member states work with Fund rules and procedures, they develop a greater sophistication and learn to use rules to their advantage. Further, as individuals develop relationships over time in IMF negotiations, a certain sensitivity for difficulties and obstacles beyond the individual's control emerges. This sometimes motivates particularly area department staff to become strong advocates for the countries they negotiate with. In the case of Turkey, for example, we can see that as a new-comer to IMF negotiations, Turgot Ozal had a difficult time convincing Fund officials of the seriousness of his intentions to carry out an adjustment program. Over time, his actions and character became better understood and appreciated and the staff were more eager to speak on his behalf in Fund councils.*

Executive Board Discussions

Official IMF documents emphasize the salience of executive board deliberations. In actual practice, however, its role is restrained.*

There are currently twenty-two executive directors. Six of these were "appointed" by one of six major economies, and China "elected" its own. The other members of the board were elected by groups of varying sizes, depending on the amount of votes controlled by each nation (See *Articles of Agreement* and any *Annual Report*). A variety of coalitions have been formed over the years to expedite this process. For example, it is customary for the Scandinavian countries to vote together and elect an individual from a different country every two years. Most Sub-Saharan African countries pool their votes together and elect one senior official. Some unusal combinations have arisen, such as Canada's membership in the Caribbean bloc, and some executive directors have acquired unofficial tenure, such as Alexandre Kafka from Brazil. In some cases, it seems that the mixture of group members has a moderating influence on position-taking by board members, a factor which might help to explain the lack of board voting to be discussed later.* (Southard 1979, 4)

Approval of a letter of intent requires a simple majority of the votes on the Executive Board. However, many types of measures (thirty-nine in all) require extraordinary majorities. (Gold 1977, 57–61) These special majorities were provided primarily to allow the large economies to protect their interests in the future, and amount to giving the five largest a collective veto. (Gold 1977, 39)

In spite of a very complex system of voting majorities and vote-calculation, in actual practice very few formal votes are ever taken by the executive board (Lister 1984).* Rather than voting, it is traditional that executive board decisions are arrived at by the managing director— who serves as chair of the board—rendering the "sense of the meeting." In other words, he simply restates what he believes to be the consensus of the board and enters it into the record. As described in the *By-Laws, Rules and Regulations,* "The Chairman shall ordinarily ascertain the sense of the meeting in lieu of a formal vote. Any executive director may require a formal to be taken." (Section C-10)

As put by Joseph Gold, "It is extraordinarily difficult to explain why the Fund has been so determined to avoid voting." (1972, 201) Richard Ekhaus offers a plausible explanation. In a 1986 article, he proposes that the principal reason poorer nations avoid voting is to ensure that they are not on the record as opposing policies approved by developed nations. They recognize that although they may object to specific provisions of a particular letter of intent, they fear retribution on the day that they themselves might seek assistance. Conversely, the wealthy nations, aware of the sensitivities involved in creditor–debtor relationships, are loath to impose their will be demanding a vote where an agreement is not to their liking. "[It] permits the Group of Ten to hide their power rather than revealing it over and over again through voting." (1986, 247) Furthermore, "[t]he process of making decisions through a sense of the meeting by the Managing Director permits the Executive Directors to avoid direct confrontations." (1986, 247)

Executive board members interviewed for this project generally concurred with Ekhaus' conclusions. A member of the U.S. Executive Director's staff pointed out that the managing director is always aware of Group of Ten positions of each item and what outcome a vote would have.* Other former board members indicated that the Fund Secretary keeps a "running tally" through most board discussions. This information is used by the managing director to guide his thinking. The result is that the "sense of the meeting" drawn by the managing director is in fact a shadow of what actual votes would have produced.*

In the case of India, we will see in some detail what happens when the board consensus breaks down. In this situation, the result was a request by the United States to lodge a "protest" abstention when a large loan to India was up for approval. (Gwin 1983, 529) When the United States failed to move the G-10 countries through lobbying, it simply retreated and added its abstention to the minutes of the meeting.*

It is difficult to know precisely which positions each board member takes on specific issues. Given the lack of votes and the confidentiality of meeting minutes, this information is only available through observation and interview. Even more challenging is the difficulty of identifying the nature of the many informal conversations between board members during the week. Since all board members are permanent residents at the Fund, and routinely dine at IMF facilities, opportunities for interaction are numerous. It is well known that G-10 members interact frequently and plan positions and strategy before meetings.* Gold opined that such collegiality "encourages those who possess [financial power] to act with restraint and to refrain from the exercise of greater voting power." (1972, 201)

Regarding executive directors' conflicts, suffice it to say that during the 1980s, the United States executive director was generally loyal to the Reagan administration's ideology and pressed for greater liberalization measures in IMF conditionality.* Likewise, Third World directors routinely called for relaxation of elements of letters of intent that appeared to seriously undermine social welfare.*

Added to the personal and national interests and behavior patterns of executive directors is a broad loyalty across directors to the IMF and its principles. (Kwitney 1983) It can be safely assumed that each executive director has an interest in preserving the Fund's financial strength and integrity. Both creditors and debtors, knowning the risks and dangers of a weakened institution, support the Fund.* This attachment to the institution is sometimes extended to a committment to IMF principles of liberal adjustment and economic openness. Especially since the decline of communism in the late-1980s, Chinese, Brazilian, and British directors find themselves speaking the same language and sharing the same basic economic assumptions. (Kwitney 1983)

Board members employ economic arguments when advocating or disparaging a policy provision.* While some Third World directors have complained of a lack of imformation (Buira 1983) the staff papers typically form the basis for what can be quite sophisticated discussions about the merits of this or that credit ceiling or currency devaluation. (Strange 1973, 284–87) There is often a rotation of personnel between the board and Fund senior staff, a tendency which reinforces the board's basic commonality of purpose and intellectual sophistication.

Furthermore, the executive directors are supported financially by the IMF, rather than by their home governments. This has prompted critics of the board to emphasize directors' quiescence to IMF policy in order to preserve their six-figure salary and extensive first-class air travel privileges. (Kwitney 1983) It should be mentioned that this dual loyalty—to home government and to the Fund—was precisely what IMF founder Lord Keynes had hoped to achieve when advocating the creation of an executive body in residence, according to Edward Bernstein (1985).

When there exists a consensus of dissaproval of a stand-by on the board, the typical method of executing authority consists of attaching a memorandum to the letter of intent in question, noting the objectionable feature. This message, while not removing the clause from the letter in question, is conveyed to the Fund staff so that future agreement will not contain this type of provision. For example, in 1987 a particular country was required to host six annual review visits by IMF missions rather than the customary four. After the board expressed its objection to what it saw as a rather demeaning and onerous practice, future letters of intent with this country provided only for four visits.*

In summary, then, the Executive Board works as a collegial body in which directors share many purposes. Customs have developed over the years which reinforce these commonalities of interest and deemphasize national cleavages. However, it is clear that discussions on the executive board are candid and meaningful, even if actions sometimes give the appearance of a "rubber stamp" supervisory body. The board clearly influences the general direction of Fund behavior in the long run. Staff members interviewed reinforced this perception by stating that many policy options are simply removed from letters of intent *à priori* because of concern over board objections. Staff members further described a subtle change of direction after the emergence of three conservative regimes in Britain, Germany and the United States around 1980 as evidence for the above. In fact, it may be, as argued by Lister (1984), that the decision-making procedures of the IMF Executive Board have achieved a status of "model" for other, more polemical and divisive international institutions.

Conclusion

By way of conclusion, it is appropriate to consider critically whether the bargaining model provides a better description of the patterns of organizational decision-making in the IMF than the functionalist and political models.

The functionalist model predicts, as mentioned in the previous chapter, that the staff will dominate internal decision-making in the Fund at the expense of the Board and will base its decision on purely economic criteria. In addition, it is assumed the IMF's monetarist model will be applied rather rigidly in determining the conditionality of a package. Finally, within the staff, ETR and the managing director will tend to dominate by virtue of their institutional roles and significant resources, both intellectual and in personnel terms.

Many of these predictions are in fact supported by the preceding material. In particular, it is clear that the managing director is the single most influential actor in the Fund, in that he controls much of the staff's composition and operation at both the initial and concluding phases in stand-by negotiations, he has the ability to directly involve himself in country negotiations, and he significantly influences board response to stand-by requrests. The managing director has, over time, emerged as the dominant player, over and above the Executive Board.

The role of ETR is somewhat more ambiguous, in that the rise of the managing director has at times undermined ETR's influence. While it is clear that ETR has the capacity to dominate intra-staff discussions, in actual fact the managing director has superceded ETR's authority by adopting case-by-case lending criteria. Overall, ETR is still first among equals within the Fund.

The role of economic rationality seems even more uncertain. Although staff discussions are couched in strict economic terms, it seems that final decisions are the result, not of the search for economic "truth," but of compromise and accomodation. We have seen already several specific cases in which non-economic factors (personality, learning, department rivalry) have been significant in country decisions as well as other IMF policies (WEO, briefing papers).*

In general, behavior in the executive board is poorly explained by the functionalist model, although the outcomes are sometimes consistent with the model's predictions. The implicit bargains between the powerful and the weak are superficially justified in economic terms but seem to have their roots in political pragmatism. The custom of non-voting, it was shown, seems to make sense primarily from a political point of view. Based on the comments made by various directors within and outside of board meetings, there does not seem to be as clear a consensus on Fund policy as the history of concensus votes would imply. Politics seems to matter in the Executive Board, but it has been largely concealed by an unusual set of customs and practices.

Finally, while the actual outcomes of IMF policy-implementation have not been reviewed in detail, there would appear to be strong evidence that economic factors do not explain all of the content of IMF conditionality. As mentioned, the managing director and the staff both take into account non-economic factors relating to a nation's adjustment program. Likewise, the executive board seems to take many non-economic factors into account in its review. Most importantly, while negotiating loans with the Fund, the member country itself often stresses the salience of many non-economic factors. Member countries will often use their political resources (regime stability, ideological tendencies) to increase their leverage with Fund missions. Assetto has termed this "reverse influence." (1988, 40–42) Countries have been known to use creative tactics to alter the negotiating dynamic to their advantage. While much more will be said further on this subject, suffice it to say that the functionalist model cannot account for these phenomena.

Overall, the functionalist model predicts much of the IMF's behavior, but does not allow for the dynamic and political aspects of the process. The political model, however, explains much of what the other model does not. For example, where the functionalist model does not explain executive board behavior, the political model, using such concepts as balance of power and parliamentary politics, does rather well. Because executive directors represent nation-states, each of which turn can be described as power maximizers, it is natural that they express the positions of their governments. Likewise, the political model anticipates the role of voting majorities as implied in interviewee comments above. The salience of political factors in debt negotiations is consistent with the political model. Such things as alliance patterns, regime type, and political stability are central to political decision-making.

However, as is the case for the functionalist model, the political model leaves many questions unanswered. First and foremost, the apparant passivity of the executive board is inconsistent with the dominance accorded it in the political model. The political model assumes a dominance and even a pro-active board—not one which approves nearly all stand-bys without amendment. Instances described further of G-10 acquiecense to objectionable agreements is directly contraditory to the political model. Executive board loyalty to IMF goals and staff recommendations is also inconsistent with political decision-making.

In some ways, the political model seems the yin to the functionalist model's yang. Assetto refers to this phenomenon in terms of coexisting arenas of decision-making. (1988, 27–30) An alternative explanation can be the existence of an over-arching model which explain all decision-making according to a single logic: the bargaining model.

Much of IMF behavior can be understood in terms of bargaining and negotiation. If, instead of employing the rather rigid conceptions of the other two models, one conceives IMF decision-making in terms of competing actors simultaneously seeking conflicting and complementary objectives, the coalitions and rivalries become understandable. The bargaining model predicts a shifting locus of power, as has been noted in the material presented above. Not only can one observe long-term conflicts and competition between major IMF actors, but at each decision-making juncture there are new rivalries and alliances. In the case of Turkey, as was mentioned, the government's growing experience was a key factor in its increasing influence vis-à-vis Fund staff. In the case of the major debtors, the managing director was able to exert more influence over ETR by injecting himself in the negotiations themselves. In the case of the WEO, area departments competed with each other and ETR and the Research Department.

The bargaining model also provides for the use of a variety of resources—political, technical, institutional—and therefore anticipates the possibility of a wide variety of outcomes, depending on the actors and the resources they choose to employ. This helps to explain such now-familiar phenomena as use of the "OZ method", executive board non-voting, ETR dominance in ordinary loan cases, and the long-term ascendence of the managing director over the board.

The bargaining model fails to explain the high degree of intellectual convergence on the monetarist model across all levels of the Fund, except to say that this has proved to enhance the influence and survivability of each actor in its own way. One might add that the monetarist model emerged dominant because of the power of those who promoted it in the past. Finally, one might speak in terms of "organizational culture" and "hegemonic ideology" (Horowitz 1985–86; Pion-Berlin 1985; Payer 1974), depending on one's approval or disapproval of the monetarist model. The dominance of the monetarist model might also soon be undermined by the general convergence of IMF and World Bank policy, as evidenced by current Managing Director Michel Camdessus' concern about poverty alleviation (*Finance and Development* 1988).

At this point, it is also possible to conclude that, although it might represent a residual and less elegant approach, the bargaining model provides concepts and tools that are especially useful in describing day-by-day Fund policy-making. This utility, however, may be attributable in large part to the questions asked, rather than the actual explanatory value of the model. What is of even greater interest is its ability to explain policy outcomes and the processes of bargaining and negotiation with Fund members. This question will be answered as we embark on the several case-studies that make up the larger portion of the work. It is to this task that we now turn.

Notes

1. As a methodological note, a word about the backgrounds of the IMF interviewees. Those interviewed represent each of the IMF's area departments, as well as almost all the functional agencies such as ETR and Fiscal Affairs. The interviewees included two former deputy managing directors, thirteen current or former department heads, and eighteen former or current division chiefs. Of the eight interviewees associated with the executive board, five are current or former executive directors and four are current and former alternate executive directors. The average tenure of the thirty interviewees was eighteen years at the Fund, although several senior officials were brought in from high-level positions in private finance and public service.

2. Because The WEO is the most comprehensive survey of the financial and economic conditions of the countries of the world, and is used by central bankers and academicians the world over, the method of its production deserves some note. The WEO is created from data and growth projections provided by each country specialist in the various area departments, which are then compiled and adjusted with each other by the Research department. According to the official responsible for compiling the WEO, some desks have a reputation for submitting slightly distorted figures for their assigned countries, especially at the level of estimation of future growth and stabilization.* It is the desk officer's hope that optimistic (even overly optimistic) projections will reflect well on himself. When the Research Department identifies such overly optimistic projections and requests their revision downward, the request is typically resisted. The implication is that, in some cases, the economic projections are more the result of bureaucratic self-interest than rigorous economic analysis.*

Bibliography

Assetto, Valerie. 1988. *The Soviet Bloc in the IMF and the IBRD.* Boulder, CO: Westview Press.

Bernstein, Edward. 1985. Interview with the Author. Brookings Institution, Washington, D.C. July 15.

Buira, Ariel. 1983. "IMF Financial Programs and Conditionality." *Journal of Development Economics* 12 (1983): 111–36.

Callaghy, Thomas. 1984. "The Ritual Dance of the Debt Game." *Africa Report* (September–October): 22–26.

Crockett, Andrew. 1982. "Issues in the Use of Fund Resources." *Finance & Development* 19 (June): 10–15.

Davis, David. 1972. *How the Bureaucracy Makes Foreign Policy: An Exchange Analysis.* Lexington, MA: D.C. Heath.

deVries, Margaret. 1985. *International Monetary Fund, 1972–1978: Cooperation on Trial.* Washington, D.C.: International Monetary Fund.

Ekchaus, Richard. 1986. "How the IMF Lives with its Conditionality." *Policy Sciences* 19 (October): 237–52.

Edwards, Sebastian. 1987. "Sequencing Economic Liberalization in Developing Countries." *Finance & Development* March: 26–30.

Finance & Development. 1988. December Special Issue.

Gold, Sir Joseph. 1985. Interview with the Author, IMF Headquarters, Washington, D.C., June 15.

———. 1979a. *Legal and Institutional Aspects of the International Monetary System: Selected Essays.* Washington, D.C.: International Monetary Fund.

———. 1979b. *Conditionality.* IMF Pamphlet Series #31 Washington, D.C.: International Monetary Fund.

———. 1977. *Voting Majorities in the Fund: Effects of Second Amendment of the Articles.* IMF Pamphlet Series #20 Washington, D.C.: International Monetary Fund.

———. 1972. *Voting and Decisions in the International Monetary Fund.* Washington, D.C.: International Monetary Fund.

Goode, Richard. 1985. *Economic Assistance to Developing Countries Through the IMF.* Washington, D.C.: Brookings Institution.

Guitán, Manuel. 1981. *Conditionality: Access to Fund Resources.* Washington, D.C.: International Monetary Fund.

Gwin, Catherine. 1983. "Financing India's Structural Adjustment." in Williamson, John. ed. *IMF Conditionality.* Washington, D.C.: Institute for International Economics.

Horowitz, Irving. 1985-86. "The 'Rashomon' Effect: Ideological Proclivities and Political Dilemmas of the International Monetary Fund." *Journal of Interamerican Studies and World Affairs* 27 (Winter): 37–55.

Horsefield, J.K. 1979. *The International Monetary Fund, 1945-1965: Twenty Years of International Monetary Cooperation.* Washington, D.C.: International Monetary Fund.

International Monetary Fund. 1988. *Annual Report–1988.* Washington, D.C.: International Monetary Fund.

———. 1986. "Fund-Supported Programs, Fiscal Policy, and Income Distribution: A Fiscal Affairs Department Study." Occasional Papers #46 Washington, D.C.: International Monetary Fund.

_____. 1984. *By-Laws, Rules and Regulations.* 41st Issue, Washington, D.C.: International Monetary Fund.

_____. 1978. *Articles of Agreement of the International Monetary Fund.* Washington, D.C.: International Monetary Fund.

Kwitney, Jonathan. 1983. "The 'Yes' Men Atop the IMF." *Wall Street Journal* May 12: 37.

Lister, Frederick. 1984. *Decision-Making Strategies for International Organizations: The IMF Model.* Monograph Series in World Affairs, Denver, CO: University of Denver Press.

O'Donnell, Guillermo. 1985. "External Debt: Why Don't Our Governments do the Obvious?" *CEPAL Review* 27 (December): 27–33.

Payer, Cheryl. 1974. *The Debt Trap: The International Monetary Fund and the Third World.* New York: Monthly Review Press.

Pion-Berlin, David. "The Role of Ideas: The International Monetary Fund and Third World Policy Choices." Paper Presented to the Annual Meetings of the American Political Science Association, New Orleans, September.

Rowan, Hobart. 1986. "Mexico Called Special Case." *Washington Post* October 4: C1–2.

South. 1985. July: 30–40.

Southard, Frank. 1979. *The Evolution of the International Monetary Fund Essays in International Finance.* Essays in International Finance #135 Princeton, NJ: Princeton University Press.

Strange, Susan. 1973. "IMF: Monetary Managers." in Cox, Robert and Jacobson, Harold, eds. *The Anatomy of Influence: Decision-Making in International Organizations.* New Haven, CT: Yale University Press: 263–297.

Sutton, Mary. 1984. "Introduction." in Killick, Tony, ed. *The IMF and Stabilization: Developing Country Experiences.* London: Overseas Development Institute: 1-18.

Zulu, Justin B. and Nsouli, Saleh. 1985. *Adjustment Programs in Africa: The Recent Experience.* Occasional Paper #34 Washington, D.C.: International Monetary Fund.

3

The Case of Jamaica: 1976–1981

This analysis of Jamaica's experiences with the IMF from 1976 to 1981 will follow a standardized format, as will succeding case studies. First, I will offer a few comments regarding economic conditions in Jamaica prior to IMF involvement. Second, I will summarize the major events connected with Jamaica's borrowing from the Fund. In the most important section of the study, I will analyze the roles of various major and minor actors in the negotiation process as well as the outcomes of their behavior. Finally, I will discuss how Jamaica's experiences reflect on the three models discussed earlier.

Background

Jamaica was a success story from independence in 1962 through the mid-1970s. Its economy expanded at an annual rate of roughly six percent each year, led by consistent growth in the service and industrial sectors. Inflation was kept in check at roughly four percent. Jamaica's political system was also one of the most democratic in the Western Hemisphere, with a long tradition of competitive elections and peaceful transfer of power. Agricultural export earnings fluctuated widely, however, and it was due to this movement, combined with growing populism among the electorate, that precipitated what has become a long and often strained relationship between Jamaica and the IMF.

Jamaica's growth in the 1960s is consistent with concept of "dependent development" described by Evans (1979) and characterized by a dynamic externally-oriented sector and profitable foreign direct investments. The engine of growth in such an economy is external to the society itself. In order to assure continued growth, concessions are made by the state to facilitate foreign investment and exports to developed nations. The result is what de Janvry calls a "disarticulated economy"—one with few social and economic horizontal linkages (de Janvry 1981; Bernal 1984, 56–57).

More specifically, three-fourths of Jamaica's agricultural output was exported, and the majority of the domestic food supply was imported. (Bernal 1984, 57) Foreign control of Jamaica's major businesses was high—especially in Bauxite, banking, manufacturing, and export agriculture. In particular, U.S. investments amounted to $645 million in 1977, of which $390 million was in bauxite. (Whichard 1977, 32–55) Alongside the dynamic, externally-oriented economy, was a shrinking local economy in Jamaica. Unemployment grew from thirteen percent in 1960 to 23 percent in 1972 and disparities in income between rich and poor increased by roughly thirty percent. (Bernal 1984, 58)

A radical interpretation of the situation in Jamaica in the early 1970s led Michael Manley, leader of the People's National Party (PNP), to espouse Fabian socialism in his successful 1972 campaign. He called for an expansion of the role of the state in the economy, nationalization of foreign-controlled banks and bauxite mines, redistribution of wealth and of land, and development of a non-aligned foreign policy which leaned toward nearby Cuba.

Once in office, Manley introduced several new programs, although his administration did not break as dramatically from his predecessor's as many expected (Stone 1980). The most significant new programs were: (1) a rapprochement with Cuba, (2) cooperative sugar production, (3) establishment of a state trading firm for importing food, drugs and other essential commodities, and (4) a levy on bauxite production combined with state investment in bauxite firms along the lines of Salvador Allende's 'phased nationalization' of Chilean copper.

These new programs which precipitated a crisis in foreign exchange and political good-will from the United States and which brought the Manley government to the IMF in 1976. As explained by a rather frank report from the IMF, "prior to 1972, current account deficits had been financed mainly by inflows of private foreign investment, but in the years between 1972 and 1976 extensive foreign official borrowing, especially from foreign commercial banks, became the major source of finance." (Kincaid 1980, 378) This was due to the fact that American bauxite firms began to disinvest in Jamaica at the same time earnings from other exports was declining and the oil crisis pushed the price of imports to record levels.

Following the examples of OPEC countries and Chile, the Manley government began exacting a production levy on bauxite producers, thereby increasing tax revenue on bauxite from J$25 million to J$200 million in one year (Paul, 1983 46), or an increase to J$12 per ton from J$2 per ton. (Maingot 1979, 278) Revere Jamaica Alumina, Ltd. shut down and Reynolds Metal Co. filed a suit against the government. Nonetheless, in the next four years, the government carried out its plan and acquired majority ownership in all bauxite firms (while leaving the day-to-day management up to the original staff), many public utilities, the largest commercial bank, the merchant marine, three-fourths of total sugar output, and half of the total hotel capacity. In addition, the PNP government established the State Trading Corporation, and was the catalyst in organizing the ten-member International Bauxite Association. (Bernal 1984, 62; Paul 1983, 47) According to Girvan and Bernal (both former Manley administration officials) the bauxite firms began to reduce production. "The bauxite companies cut back production by 25 percent in 1975 and a further 11 percent in 1976, reducing revenue in the latter year by $54 million compared with the 1974 level. Inflows of foreign private capital declined from $254 million in 1973-74 to $54 million in 1975-76; in 1976 a net outflow was recorded." (Girvan & Bernal 1982, 38–9) And from the IMF, "in the bauxite sector export volume dropped by about a third, owing, in part, to the combined impact of global recession and a production levy imposed in 1974." (Kincaid 1980, 378)

Along with the crisis of investment in bauxite, sugar and banana exports fell by 23 and 39 percent, respectively, in the period 1971 to 1976. Prices for oil imports nearly tripled in 1974, from $65 million to $178 million, or eleven percent of the total import bill to 21 percent. (Bernal 1984, 60; Paul claims it quadrupled. 1983, 46) Overall, Jamaica's GDP fell by roughly twelve percent from 1974 to 1976. Foreign public debt increased four-fold in 1972–1976, from about $200 million to $820 million. Private banks cut off credit in 1976 and the government began using up its reserves to cover the import bill, with foreign reserves dwindled from $120 million in 1972 to a deficit of $230 million by the end of 1976. (Kincaid 1980, 378)

In a new national election in 1976, Manley won a resounding victory over the JLP, led by Edward Seaga, winning nearly 80 percent of the seats in the legislature. The victory was interperted as a personal victory for Manley and a mandate for democratic socialism. (Stone 1980, 159–167)

Jamaica and the IMF: A Summary

Manley was held back from negotiating with the IMF in 1976 by an especially militant PNP (Stone 1980, 175), even though Jamaica had already borrowed $65 million in "non-conditional" loans during the previous year. The need for foreign exchange and credit was too great by mid-1977, however, and the Manley administration persuaded the PNP to support negotiations toward a stand-by arrangement. The IMF agreed to provide $75 million over one year on condition of fiscal restraint and wage ceilings. The IMF permitted the creation of a two-tiered exchange rate in order to bring about at least a partial devaluation of the Jamaican dollar. This agreement lasted until roughly December, when the government fell out of compliance with IMF conditions.

Negotiations toward a long-term (three-year) loan had already begun in late-1977, and culminated in the drafting of an Extended Facility Arrangement in August 1978. The IMF made available $260 million contigent on very strict terms (by the IMF's own admission). These involved an austerity package that covered a very wide array of parameters, such as wages, public deficit, exchange reserves, and devaluation. The IMF modified these requirements in 1979 in Jamaica's favor as this country fell slightly out of compliance. The program was cancelled, however, when Jamaica again breached the terms after the second oil crisis of 1979.

New negotiations got underway in early 1980, but without a settlement. By this time, the radical wing of the PNP had regained control of the party apparatus and forced Manley to adopt an intransigent negotiating approach. Negotiations broke down, as did Jamaica's access to foreign credit, throughout 1980. The economic crisis was ultimately resolved with the election of conservative Edward Seaga in 1980 and the restoration of warm ties to the United States. In 1981 an Extended Fund Facility Arrangement (EFF) worth nearly $700 million was granted to Jamaica, although it was not fully disbursed due to non-compliance in 1983–1984.

Analysis of Jamaica's IMF Experience

Information on the Jamaica case is often contradictory. There are many discrepencies in both the objective information and their interpretation across analysts. Some point to Jamaica as the classic case of capitalist exploitation via the IMF. (Bernal 1984, 53–82; Girvan & Bernal 1982, 34–48, Paul 1983, 45–61, Maingot 1979, 245–301) Others point to it as a case of socialism misapplied and mismanaged. (Kincaid 1980, 378–382; O'Flaherty 1979, 126–142; Forbes 1985; Stone 1980—although Stone's assessment is mixed and a bit contradictory) For this reason, many of the observations I make about the Jamaican experience will be tentative. Nonetheless, the case of Jamaica reveals certain inadequacies of each of the three models of IMF decision-making.

Primary Actors

The primary actors in the case of Jamaica were the Manley administration (including senior officials and Manley himself) and the IMF (especially ETR Director, David Finch). Each of these individuals and groups played a direct role in determining (or attempting to determine (the conditionality of each of the loans negotiated between the IMF and

Jamaica. Specifically, it was the Manley administration which, upon advice from the general PNP membership, initiated the various negotiations with the IMF. Further it was the IMF staff which directly communicated with the Manley government and drafted the various letters of intent.

The Manley Administration. In late-1976, after new credits from overseas had been cut off following the earnings crisis described above, the foreign exchange markets were closed in an effort to prevent capital flight. It was at this point of emergency that the Manley regime initiated formal negotiations with the IMF.

Shortly after the election, Manley had pledged never to work with the IMF. (Stone 1980, 175) Thereafter, the principal goal of the government was to keep the economic tightening to a minimum. Specifically, it wanted to protect the poor from the effects on food prices of a major devaluation which the IMF urged as a solution to Jamaica's 20 percent inflation rate. Also, it did not want the bauxite firms to reap a windfall from the devaluation. Therefore, he proposed a dual exchange rate— one for oil and food imports and another for other products. The rate on food and oil would be kept constant while the other would be devalued. In addition, Manley proposed the expansion of price subsidies for basic commodities. (O'Flaherty 1979, 139)

This represented a fairly significant attempt on the part of the government to control the conditionality of the upcoming loan. These proposals were all the more unusual in that their implementation would have violated Article 14 of the Fund Articles, which calls for the elimination of multiple exchange rates. What is even more impressive, as will be seen, is that the IMF ultimately conceded to this bold proposal.

Once the $75 million, two-year stand-by was approved by the Executive Board in August 1977, it was up to the Manley administration to implement it. Among the more significant policy changes required were a reduction of government spending in order to halve the budget deficit, a "severe incomes policy," and a ceiling on net assets in the central bank of J$355 million in order to reduce import consumption and lower the balance of payments deficit to 4.2 percent of GDP. (Kincaid 1980, 378)

In December 1978, one of the targets of the stand-by had been breached: the assets of the Bank of Jamaica exceeded the limit agreed upon in the stand-by. As explained by Girvan, et al.:

(On December 15th 1977) the net domestic assets of the Bank of Jamaica failed to be under the required ceiling of J$355 million by the ridiculously small amount of $9 million, or 2.6 percent. This was because certain foreign loans on which the Jamaicans had counted failed to materialize, at least in time. But the Fund seized immediately on Jamaica's deliquency as grounds for suspending the agreement, refusing payment of $15 million due on the second tranche of the stand-by facility. . . (Girvan et al. 1980, 51)

According to IMF accounts, the Manley regime's expansion of domestic credit also resulted in a significant departure from the fiscal deficit targets. (Kincaid 1980, 379)

It is important to recognize that the Manley administration more than likely had the political support needed to achieve the targets of the original stand-by, but failed to do so due to miscalculation. As will be discussed later, the general attitude of the electorate at this point was grudgingly sympathetic to the need for IMF intervention. Public unrest over reduction of certain benefits, such as a freeze on wage increases, was minimal. (Stone 1980, 176) It appears, based on the tone of Girvan's comments (above), who had been involved in the policy-making process, that the administration may have misjudged the IMF's inflexibility. If this is true, then it would be safe to assume that the IMF learned from this experience to distrust the Manley regime and be less forthcoming with concessional terms in the future. This will be seen to have been the case. By allowing the economic situation to fall out of compliance with Fund expectations, Manley had restricted his negotiating room.

Partly in order to obtain a large amount of funds and a rescheduling of foreign debt, and partly because of internal political pressures to be discussed later, Manley decided in late-1977 to seek an Extended Fund Facility Arrangement. (Kincaid 1980, 378–380, Paul 1983, 52) Negotiations began in February 1978 and were concluded in May. Manley apologized to radical PNP cadres by explaining he had "no choice but to go to the IMF." (*Weekly Gleaner* 1978, 7)

The three-year EFF was clearly more strict than the previous loan. Although it did provide far more resources ($260 million, or 270 percent of quota), it also required, according to Manley:

(1) An immediate 15 per cent devaluation, as of May 1978, and anadditional 15 percent devaluation in monthly installment over the first twelve months of the program, May 1978 to May 1979; (2) Unification of the exchange rate; (3) Additional taxes on consumer goods to raise tax revenues by over 20 percent; (4) Incentives given to the private sector by lifting price controls and guaranteeing 20 per cent rate of profit; (5) a 15 per cent ceiling on wage increases. (Paul 1983, 52)

Implementation of the 1978 agreement was far more difficult than the previous stand-by. Not only did the policy changes have a more direct negative effect on the poor of Jamaica, which put political pressure on Manley to postpone implementation, but exacerbated unanticipated shocks from the second oil crisis and wide-spread flooding. The result was an inability to achieve fiscal and balance of payments equilibria.

The net effect of all of this was a return to the negotiating table for the Manley government. Anticipating failure to meet the short-term targets for June 1979, the government approached the Fund regarding a waiver of certain conditions on the EFF program to keep the flow of Fund money coming. According to the IMF, the government was not only concerned about a cut-off of funds, but also growing political unrest at home. It was hoped that some loosening would stimulate growth over the short term. Perhaps because the unintended shocks to Jamaica accounted for much of the economic failure in 1979, the IMF consented to suspending additional devaluations of the currency. (Kincaid 1980, 380)

In early 1980, Jamaica failed yet another test of the IMF program. Wages were allowed to increase too far resulting in a public deficit of 15.1 percent of GDP, nearly 70 percent above the target of 8.9 percent agreed upon. The external deficit also widened beyond what was allowed. New negotiations were contemplated as early as September and were initiated in December. However, according to Manley:

> negotiations with the Fund broke down on the question of J$50 million of expenditure which the Fund wished removed from the Recurrent Budget in addition to all the other savings which had already been made. This would have created an impossible situation involving the laying-off of 10,000-11,000 workers or dismantling a large range of social programmes. (Paul 1983, 53)

Clearly, the Manley administration seems to have had less and less influence over conditionality over time. Unable to change the IMF's terms in 1980, Manley eventually adopted a more confrontational approach, to the delight of the radical wing of the PNP. By this point, Manley's general support among the Jamaican electorate was too weak to earn him reelection.

The IMF Staff. In general, the IMF displayed inconsistencies in its dealings with Manley. These cast doubt on the functionalist model.

The Jamaican negotiations were initiated by the Manley regime in 1977. Much of the content of the first stand-by was proposed by the Jamaican administration itself. In particular, the government urged creation of a dual exchange rate, contrary to Fund norms. The IMF's acceptance of this concession was likely conditioned upon Manley's willingness to comply with other, more strict, conditionality.* (O'Flaherty 1979, 139) One can easily imagine advocacy for the Jamaican program by Western Hemisphere Department staff, as described in chapter two. The growing role of ETR, however, may help to explain the overall trend toward more inflexibility on the Fund's part.

Specifically, ETR seems to have had greater influence over the "tightness" of conditionality after the government failed to comply with the first set of conditionality. The appointment of the Director of ETR to lead the IMF mission to Jamaica may serve to highlight this dynamic. This said, it is important to acknowledge that the IMF's continued support of Jamaica, even with stricter lending terms, is evidence that the regime maintained acceptable payment of interest and other obligations (Note Peru's ineligibility to receive funds after 1987).

The second loan was far more stringent in terms of policy changes; even the Fund staff conceded this in their press release:

> [The program involves] a major effort to reduce consumption as a proportion of [GDP], thus making resources available to stimulate production and investment in the private sector, and direct the productive efforts to exports and imports substitution by price incentives. (Kincaid 1980, 380)

In other words, the IMF and the government's goal was to impose austerity on the general public, while attempting to make investment in import-substitution sectors more inviting. IMF staff members of the day characterized the program as "shock treatment." (*NACLA Report* 1981, 27) This approach reflects the demand-management style of IMF lending based on rigid monetarism. Likewise, it is possible to understand this outcome in functionalist terms.

After the various difficulties experienced in 1979, the Fund decided to grant significant concessions to the Manley regime in the form of a waiving of the devaluation requirement. Considering devaluation has become an extremely common characteristic of IMF programs (perhaps even a prerequisite—see Buira 1983), this concession was significant. A further concession was granted on the deficit reduction targets. It should be noted that at the same time this concession was made, however, the IMF increased the restriction on wage increases. (Kincaid 1980, 380)

Up to this point, the IMF and the Manley regime seem to be engaged in a fairly constructive, if volatile, relationship. The Fund continued to provide funding while the Manley regime made good-faith efforts to adopt IMF conditionality. However, by late-1979, changes occurred in both actors which led to a polarization in the relationship. On the Jamaican side, the emergence of the radical wing of the PNP and the selection of D.K. Duncan as party Secretary-General dramatically increased the administration's resistance to austerity on ideological grounds.

On the IMF side, the appointment of David Finch, head of the Jamaican mission, as Director of ETR, seems to have significantly constricted the

Fund's negotiating flexibility. David Finch's dual role placed him in an awkward situation. On the one hand, as head of the IMF's mission to Jamaica he felt a natural tendency to act as advocate for the Manley regime in the halls of the Fund. Due to personal relationships and familiarity with local circumstances, the mission head typically plays this role. However, as head of ETR, he was obliged to critically evaluate all conditional lending packages in order to insure fairness and conformity to Fund customs and standards. In typical IMF decision-making, there exists and tension between these two roles, which typically results in a balancing of influence and a moderation of the outcome. In Jamaica's case, ETR's influence became more dominant, as indicated by the Fund's increasing intransigence. While difficult to demonstrate causality defin-itively, the coincidence of the developments is consistent with previous findings.

In November 1979, David Finch and Walter Robichek offered their interpretation of Manley's intentions in a confidential memo to the managing director:

> the Government is not seriously committed to its economic program, judging from perceived inconsistencies between its foreign policy and domestic political stances on the one hand and the dictates of the program on the other. (Bernal 1984, 72)

Negotiations lasted three months to no avail. As put by the IMF itself, "the loss of policy momentum resulted in such departures from the program's targets that the original objectives were clearly unattainable. Moreover, weakening social and political cohesion further complicated development of economic policy." (Kincaid 1980, 381)

The IMF, in an unusual political gesture, accepted, prior to the October election, a visit from Seaga at the Fund headquarters. Needless to say, after these discussions, presumably on the subject of a future extended fund arrangement, the JLP could credibly claim that it would be able to "mobilize the foreign exchange needed during the next three years." (Bernal 1984, 73) Without referring explicitly to the IMF, the JLP made it clear that they would work for warmer relations with foreign credits in general.

Key IMF officials made the decision in late-1979 that the Manley administration could no longer carry out the array of reforms required to maintain compliance with any conditional loan from the Fund. It is clear that it so doing, IMF officials took into account not only economic conditions, but also political will and legislative forces in Jamaica's government, as well as broader foreign policy priorities of the Manley administration. The consideration of such non-economic factors is inconsistent with the assumptions of the functionalist model, but not with the other approaches under consideration.

Secondary Actors

Three other groups of actors that had significant influence over the negotiation process and outcomes are the radical wing of the PNP under the informal leadership of D.K. Duncan, foreign creditors under the leadership of the United States, and Jamaica's opposition party, the JLP.

Radical PNP. D.K. Duncan was elected to the post of PNP General Secretary in 1976 and headed the Ministry of Mobilization in the newly elected Manley administration. As such, his influence was significant. Duncan felt that the "major obstacle in the path of our development is the domination of our economy by the imperialist system by which foreign interests have exploited our people and natural resources." (Bernal 1984, 61) It was primarily his idea to adopt a "non-IMF" path to economic and financial stability, and with the 1976 mandate and Manley's support, he set about drafting a plan.

It is important to note that Duncan's philosophy—as well as that of many other radicals in the PNP—was developed well before the nation initiated direct talks with the Fund. His antipathy did not result from disenchantment, but from ideology. Michael Manley, a moderate in the PNP, was sympathetic to Duncan's viewpoint, although he often objected to his methods. In spite of this, Duncan was assigned the task of leading an economic planning team which drafted proposals for dealing with Jamiaca's imbalances.

> The left advisors were given a mandate to prepare an anti-imperialist economic plan as an alternative to the IMF austerity route. In the process, there was a build-up of mass mobilization in meetings and teach-ins all over the country and in extensive left rhetoric on the government-owned mass media (television and radio). (Stone, 1980 175)

After several months of deliberations, no concensus emerged among the radicals of the PNP regarding a coherent economic adjustment program. The PNP vetoed an early IMF agreement in December 1976 on the grounds that it required too many austerity provisions. (Paul 1983, 49) The radicals could not prevent Manley from concluding an agreement with the Fund in early 1977.

In 1977 and 1978, the radical left wing of the party fell from grace. D.K. Duncan was removed from office as the PNP General Secretary and the Minister of Mobilization (propaganda) along with many of his immediate staff. His portfolios were taken over by Manley. (Maingot 1979, 281) The population at large favored warmer relations with the IMF and the US, rather than the autarky the left proposed. For example, in May 1977, 66 percent favored, while only 14 percent opposed, United States aid to Jamaica, and in September 1977, 60 percent "actively desired to migrate to the U.S.A." (Stone 1980, 176) While Manley expressed sympathy for those on the PNP left favoring a non-IMF path, he pointed out that Jamaica had no choice but to go to the IMF. (Maingot 1979, 281)

The debate within Jamaica was a struggle between the extremes of the PNP. As mentioned earlier, Duncan was removed from his cabinet post in 1977. He nonetheless retained power in the party apparatus. He also retained influence over economic policy as a member of the Planning Ministry. He often clashed with Jamaican Central Bank and Finance Ministry proponents of adjustment. He took an active role in foreign policy, leading the Jamaican delegation at the Non Aligned Conference in Havana in 1979. (*NACLA Report* 1981, 27) In general terms, the PNP membership became more radicalized in the late-1970s and by 1980 had formed an almost united front against IMF conditionality. Even Hugh Small, Finance Minister and Duncan rival, campaigned against IMF terms in 1980 because they "cut across those things that were fundamental to our philosophy and beliefs and their implementation interrupted the programs of the PNP." (Bernal 1984, 71) Ultimately, it was the PNP that definitively cut off talks with the IMF in 1980. (Bernal 1984, 71; Girvan & Bernal 1982; 44–45) By a two-to-one vote, the National Executive Committee "approved abandoning the IMF regimen in principle . . . [and] to do so immediately, rather than after the expiration of a new agreement. . . . " (Forbes 1985, 27)

The PNP hoped to make economic policy and the role of the IMF the major campaign issues in 1979. However, the public had already rejected a "non-IMF" path to adjustment. PNP support had dwindled to merely 37 percent and the JLP easily won election in October.

The policies of the Manley administration are largely explained by the varying degrees of influence of the radical wing of the PNP. Not only are the general positions, but also more detailed tactical maneuvers were often motivated by a need to satisfy the demands of PNP radicals. This vacillation had a direct effect on the content of the various IMF packages, as was seen earlier. These multi-level dynamics are consistent with a bargaining model of decision-making generally.

Foreign Creditors. The role of foreign creditors was also indirect, much like the radicals of the PNP. At various junctures, foreign creditos discontinued loans, while at other times they organized major reschedulings. The private creditors were more quick to declare Jamaica ineligible for new credits, but were not as rigid in the types of policy reforms required to restore lending.

In mid-1976, due to significant arrears, Jamaica could no longer obtain foreign loans, even on a short-term basis. Bankers urged the Manley administration to go to the Fund in late-1976 in order to put in place a rational adjustment strategy. (Stone 1980, 176) Bankers did not seem concerned about the distinctly socialist turn the Manley administration had taken. According to one banker, "half the world is socialist after all—Castro's visits [to Jamaica] have no bearing on our attitude. We're indifferent to the government's ideology as long as we show a profit in the long run." (O'Flaherty 1979, 140)

In 1978 the IMF coordinated a major rescheduling of Jamaica's foreign debt in connection with the three-year EFF:

> 87.5 percent of the amortization due foreign commercial banks by the public sector was arranged. . . Balance of payments support, excluding Fund resources, mobilized on behalf of Jamaica was $156.5 million. . . . (Kincaid 1980, 380)

While it involved only North American banks and took until December 1978 to finalize, this rescheduling was essential to Jamaica's economic survival. This process of IMF-coordinated rescheduling was rather uncommon in Fund experience in 1978, having been performed only rarely up to that point. This intervention on Jamaica's behalf was repeated in 1979 when $65 million in fresh funding was generated.

The support of private banks for Jamaica expanded after the accession of Seaga in 1980. In March 1981, roughly one fourth of Jamaica's outstanding private debt was rescheduled by a consortium of private banks. (*Wall Street Journal* 1981, 37) Seventy-one million dollars in fresh private loans was provided in July by a group of American and Canadian banks. Although private banks did expand their lending after Seaga's election, the increase was small compared to the growth in public lending.

Views of Jamaican politics in Washington during the 1976–1980 period were not always sympathetic. The Carter administration was tolerant of Manley's ideology, to the point of extending a $9.5 million loan in 1977. (O'Flaherty 1979, 139) Conservative politicians, however, were suspicious. As put by Senator Orrin Hatch, "Jamaica has become captive of Cuba through the type of leadership it now has. . . . I am saying it is an extension of Cuba, and I am saying that they are doing the same things as Cuba." (O'Flaherty 1979, 138)

After Carter's departure, conservatives in the Reagan administration orchestrated a $200 million, three-year loan to Jamaica, of which roughly $75 million was specifically targeted for balance of payments support. (Forbes 1985, 36) Other official lending included $10.1 million from Japan, $4.5 million from Canada, $37 million from the IBRD and a package from the IDA. Total new credit from private and public sources exceeded one billion dollars in 1981.

It is unclear whether the United States may have withheld possible funding from Jamaica prior to 1981. Because Manley was gone before Reagan came into office, there was never a direct confrontation in early-1980. Because Carter was generally tolerant and even understanding of Manley's anti-imperialist rhetoric, it is unlikely that his administration deliberately blocked support. Furthermore, public statements by private bank officials indicate an indifference to ideology. The small role banks and the United States seem to have played in the pace and direction of IMF-Jamaican negotiations is further underscored by the day-to-day momentum described earlier. Only at the outset, when private lenders cut off new loans to Jamaica on account of arrears—precipitating IMF intervention at Manley's request—did Western actors seem to stimulate IMF action. In general terms, the explanatory power of the political model seems limited in the case of Jamaica.

The JLP Opposition. The JLP, as an opposition party, did not have significant influence over the Manley regime except at election time. After a successful campaign in 1976, Manley did not have to worry about JLP activities. His majority in parliament was secure.

The JLP proposed a conservative, externally-oriented economic program in 1976. The problem with past experiences in export-led growth, according to the JLP, was mismanagement, rather than anything inherent in the development model. (Bernal 1984, 73) In addition to the rather vague promises of economic normalcy aimed at the capitalists, the JLP mounted a major propaganda campaign painting a frightening picture of Jamaica's future under yet another four years of Manley. Playing on the general fear of Communism, the JLP predicted nationalization on a massive scale, hinting that no private property was safe.

> What is intended is a Socialist model of eventual embracing State ownership of the means of production and exchange. . . . [The intent is for] the State to control everything. The State to decide everything. (Bernal 1984, 73)

By 1980, the radicalized PNP was very much a minority party in Jamaica. The JLP received 59 percent of the vote in 1979, and its support cut across classes and economic sectors. (Forbes 1985, 33)

Upon achieving the presidency, Seaga concluded new agreements with the IMF, although his long-term relationship with the institution has proved quite difficult. In general terms, the role of the JLP, while indirect, was significant, in that it constrained Manley's policy-making to a degree and presented the IMF with an alternative to dealing with the PNP.

Outcomes

A comparison of the content of various conditionality packages between the Fund and Jamaica from 1976 to 1981 reveals several patterns. First, the amount of resources made available to Jamaica increases dramatically from agreement to agreement. Small, initial loans in 1976 totalled roughly $65 million. In 1977 $75 million was provided to help alleviate a debt that had swollen to $800 million for the nation as a whole. In 1978, however, the IMF lent roughly $260 million and in 1982 increased the figure to $650 million. The scale of lending can be explained in part by the fact that each loan was drawn from a different lending window: the 1976 loans came from concessional windows (oil facility and compensatory financing facility), the later stand-by arrangements were limited by Jamaica's quota, while the Extended Fund Facility was able to provide significant sums over longer periods of time.

A second pattern is the increase in the demands made on the Jamaican government by the IMF over time, until 1981. The creation of a dual exchange rate in 1977 was reversed in 1978. A series of devaluations (15 to 50 percent) was required at this point. (Kincaid 1980, 379) The goal to control the increase in wages in the 1977 accords was modified in 1978 to a goal of actually reducing wages over the short term. In 1977 little was done to specifically reduce the role of parastatals in Jamaica, whereas in 1978 the program called for a strong encouragement of private investment—much of which would compete directly with the state-owned firms. In describing the increasing demands of the EFF, it would be appropriate to say that although many of the policy objectives remained in place, the policy instruments were elaborated more precisely (thus reducing the government's latitude) and directly threatened political and social values of the government.

A possible explanation for these two patterns is that they are interrelated. IMF conditions, as has been noted, tend to become more severe as the quantity lent increases. The fact that Jamaica was borrowing 270 percent of quota in 1978 versus 120 percent in 1977 could, in and of itself, explain the increased stringency of conditionality. The weakness of this simple explanation is revealed when the IMF offered more concessional terms of lending in 1979, following the failure of the Manley regime to abide by the terms of the 1978 agreement. Clearly something else was at work. One might ask whether the agreements themselves were not taken seriously at the level of implementation.

At the level of implementation, the IMF showed varying degrees of flexibility. When 1977 terms were breeched, the Fund ceased disbursement and tightened terms for the next loan. When the 1978 agreements were violated, a new, much larger loan was approved with more concessional terms. Finally, in 1980 agreement was not possible in spite of the IMF's willingness to negotiate new terms after Jamaica violated the 1979 agreement. These shifts in policy are not entirely consistent with a functionalist or technocratic model, since conditions in Jamaica had not changed significantly over the three year period in question.

The factors of Manley's political will, on the one hand, and the changes in IMF staffing and procedures, on the other, might account for some of the variation in policy. More will be said in this regard in the conclusion.

Conclusion

What lessons can be learned from this case? The deeper the problems in a nation's economy and the greater the dependence on foreign capital, the more difficult the government's task of influencing Fund conditionality. First, the depth of economic distress reduces the perios of time available for negotiation. Jamaica's time constraint was largely determined by foreign creditors and IMF terms of successive agreements. To prolong the negotiation process risked curtailment of credit. Second, the deeper the economic distress, the lower the level of public confidence in the governing regime and the greater the chance of anti-regime mobilization— especially in a relatively mature democracy such as Jamaica. This tends to limit the flexibility of the government in office and places greater time constraints on policy. Third, lack of resources combined with lack of size removes the one policy option (or threat) that has proven so vital to such countries as Mexico, Brazil, and (as will be seen) Argentina, namely the potential to disrupt global financial structures and processes in a fundamental way through non-payment of arrears. For a small, heavily indebted and dependent economy, there is little in the way of bargaining chips available.

What can be said of Manley's bargaining style? First, it is interesting to note that a strident ideological stand is not entirely counterproductive. It is clear that the IMF is willing to bend in order to conclude and agreement. Manley, however, found himself constrained by the ideological position of his advisors. Although capable of concluding an agreement, the Manley administration, in 1978–1979, was not able to overcome PNP radical opposition to implementation of conditionality. The debate was not so much over long-term, strategic objectives, but over tactics and specific short-term policies. One might see, in hindsight, that Jamaica was not in a position in 1978 to embark on a major social investment program which included rejection of foreign assistance and investment without addressing its chronic balance of payments deficit. The IMF's short-term orientation tended to make IMF staff especially impatient with this tenuous policy combination.

We have seen that the strength of the government itself, both at the cabinet level and among rank-and-file party members, increases government's ability to determine the outcome of negotiations. During periods of high party unity (1977–1978, 1980), the Fund made significant concessions.

The Fund demonstrated a capacity for innovation in the Jamaican case, which is not consistent with the functionalist model. For example, the Fund introduced a dual exchange rate in contravention of IMF Articles, it undertook a significant rescheduling of international private debt, and it dealt seriously with an anti-Western, non-aligned nation. In fact, the IMF seems to have worked with Jamaica up to the point where the Manley administration adopted a vocally confrontational and instransigent approach.

The record on the IMF and Jamaica leads to a much more mixed conclusion than is found in most of the existing literature. The IMF does not seem to have been dominated by Western interests as many radicals have claimed. It provided significant and increasing support at varying degrees of conditionality throughout the Manley period. In fact, it appears from the account that it was ultimately the PNP that severed ties definitively, rather than IMF staff. The roles of the executive board and managing director seem to have been marginal, as they are not discussed in either the published or interview-based material in this case study. This would be consistent with the general pattern for small debtors observed in chapter two.

Does the functionalist model clarify the dynamics of this situation? To the extent that IMF conditionality was tailored to the particular economic circumstances of Jamaica, yes. However, the model explains neither the inconsistencies nor the innovation displayed by IMF policy. In particular, it does not explain the conclusion of a concessionary EFF in 1978 and the relative willingness of the staff to work through a variety of very novel demands by a member country. Additionally, the functionalist model does not anticipate the new approaches employed by staff. There is evidence of far more learning and experimentation in the IMF's behavior than predicted by the functionalist model to make this explanation adequate.

Likewise the political model does not explain the 1978–1980 period, since according to this conception, one would have anticipated continual and even increasing "toughness" on the IMF's part, proportional to Manley's growing political intransigence toward the West. The strongest evidence of political processes at work in the Jamaican case relate to the dramatic expansion of public credit to Jamaica after 1980 and Seaga's election. Seaga held private talks with IMF officials before the election and assured them of his willingess to comply with conditionality in the future. Interestingly enough, all of this pro-Western rhetoric did not help Seaga retain the IMF's support when his administration began to violate IMF conditionality in the mid-1980s. His eventual ouster by a mellowed and wiser Manley in the late-1980s brought the cycle full-circle.

The bargaining model seems to offer promising tools with which to understand the Jamaican case. One can see Manley as a negotiator with very few resources at his disposal to trade. Jamaica was desperate and has no leverage in international financial markets. The IMF, for Jamaica, was a lender of last resort, and therefore had significant latitude in the talks in the mid-1970s. The Manley administration lacked not only economic resources, but it had few political strengths, given the division within the PNP over IMF conditionality. Finally, Manley had turned away from an important political resource—the West. Contrary to another weak nation, Zaire, Jamaica had nothing strategic to offer the West, and in fact had alienated much of the international business community with its attempts at nationalizing Alcoa and other foreign businesses. Jamaica was very weak in all respects, and it is impressive that the nation obtained as much help as it did.

During the period 1978–1980, Manley was able to assert control over the party and managed to improve the country's econmic condition marginally. As a consequence, he was able to more effectively persuade the IMF of his ability to implement conditionality. Also, he was able to bide his time without collapsing into economic chaos. The combination of new bargaining tools resulted in a much more conciliatory agreement. Note that the general economic environment was also in Jamiaca's favor, since the late-1970s was the apex of Third World influence in international economic diplomacy.

All told, one can understand better, though not fully, the IMF–Jamaica dynamic with concepts of bargaining and negotiation.

Bibliography

Bernal, Richard. 1984. "The IMF and Class Struggle in Jamaica, 1977-1980." *Latin American Perspectives* 11 (Summer): 53–82.

Buira, Ariel. 1983. "IMF Financial Programs and Conditionality." *Journal of Development Economics* 12: 111–136.

NACLA Report of the Americas 15 (Jan–Feb): 27.

De Janvry, Alain. 1981. *The Agrarian Question and Reformism in Latin America.* Baltimore, MD: Johns hopkins University Press.

Girvan, Norman and Bernal, Richard. 1982. "The IMF and the Foreclosure of Development Options: The Case of Jamaica." *Monthly Review* 33 (February): 34–48.

―――― and Hughes, Wesley. 1980. "The IMF and the Third World: The Case of Jamaica." *Development Dialogue* (Spring): 45-56.

Forbes, John D. 1985. *Jamaica: Managing Political and Economic Change.* Washington, D.C.: American Enterprise Institute.

Kincaid, Russel. 1980. "Fund's Assistance to Jamaica Has Sought to Check and Restore Economic Growth." *IMF Survey* December 15: 378–382.

Maingot, Anthony P. 1979. "The Difficult Path to Socialism in the English-Speaking Caribbean." in Fagan, Richard. ed. *Capitalism and the State in U.S.-Latin American Relations.* Stanford: Stanford University Press: 254–301.

O'Flaherty, J. Daniel. 1979. "Finding Jamaica's Way." in Franko, Lawrence and Seiber, Marilyn. eds. *Developing Country Debt.* New York: Pergamon Press: 126–142.

Paul, Alix-Herard. 1983. "The 'Destabilization' Program of the IMF in Jamaica." *Inter-American Economic Affairs* 37 (Autumn): 45–61.

Stone, Carl. 1980. *Democracy and Clientelism in Jamaica.* New Brunswick, NJ: Transaction Books.

Wall Street Journal. 1981. March 31, 1981: 37.

Weekly Gleaner. 1978. May 22: 7.

Whichard, Obie G. 1977. "U.S. Direct Investment Abroad in 1976." *Survey of Current Business* 57 (August): 32–55.

World Bank. 1982. *World Development Report 1982.* Washington, D.C.: World Bank.

4

The Case of Zaire: 1976–1981

Background

Zaire, formerly the Belgian Congo, has been officially independant since 1960. Since that time the country has seen the imposition of a unique form of clientelism at the local and international levels. While the country has been described as "dependent" (Gould 1980, 7) in the traditional sense, Zairian officials have developed over the years a unique relationship with foreign investors and creditors, maximizing their bargaining power in order to create a mutually-dependent relationship (Callaghy 1984a, 63–73; Callaghy 1984b, 22–26). Although struggling since 1975 in a seemingly never-ending series of crises on both the economic and political fronts, Mobutu Sese Seko, Zaire's long-time leader, has nonetheless preserved his regime without going bankrupt, thus beating the odds. Before embarking on an analysis of Mobutu's experience in the last half of the 1970s, it would be useful to acquaint the reader with the essential background to Zaire's IMF loans.

Mobutu Sese Seko, a former army officer, emerged in 1965 as Zaire's chief of state, elevated by a coup that received CIA support. The "Second Republic," as the new administration was dubbed, began immediately consolidating its power. With independence, Belgian civil servants left the country in large numbers, their posts filled by eager lower-level Zairian nationals. In many cases, mere clerks leaped to power by virtue of seniority. (Young & Turner 1985, 115) While very few Zairians were successful in business and trade, senior bureaucrats began making use of their privileged access to import licenses to engage in foreign trade. Mobutu was careful to placate the demands of this "politico-commercial" class since it was on their support that he depended. Mobutu undertook a massive reorganization of the civil service in order to concentrate power in the capital city and in his own hands, instituting a sort of "caesarism." (Kabwit 1979, 385)

The relationship of mutual dependence between the upper political bourgeoisie and Mobutu affected Zairian development throughout the

FIGURE 4.1 Zaire's General Price Index, 1960-1967

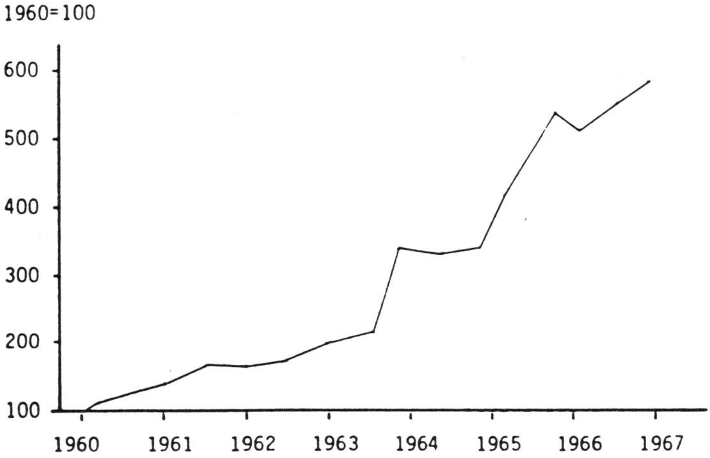

1960=100

Source: Young & Turner 1985, 279.

period under consideration. Excluded from the political process were the workers, the peasants and the "petty bourgeoisie" of school teachers and clerks. The new bureaucratic bourgeosie, or "intellectuals," as they were also called, maintained their status not through productivity or competence, but by virtue of the privileges of office. Corruption, as detailed in an exhaustive study by David Gould, became an integral part of the political and social system, rather than a mere aberration. (1980, 7)

The internal dependence of the bureaucratic bourgeosie on Mobutu and the state was mirrored by dependence of the Zairian state on a variety of foreign creditors and sponsors (Callaghy 1984c). This was especially the case after the initial period of consolidation, from 1965 to 1969. Some economic problems had emerged by the end of the decade, including a very high inflation rate and an overvalued official exchange rate for the Congo franc. As evidenced by Figure 4.1, prices swelled in a dramatic way in the years after the inauguration of the Second Republic.

In the context of an IMF program, Mobutu undertook a series of stabilization measures in 1968 included a three hundred percent devaluation, creation of a new currency, the zaire (1 zaire=1,000 Congo francs), elimination of import licenses, heavy taxation on imports and a relaxation of many foreign investment restrictions. The effect was immediate. Inflation fell to 2.5 percent in 1968, the Gross National Product went from a negative figure in 1967 to eight percent growth in 1968. Inflation remained between five and ten percent until 1973. (Young & Turner 1985, 278–280, 324) As described by Callaghy, "the financial condition of the Zairian state in the late 1960s and early 1970s was excellent. . . ." (1984a, 65) Foreign creditors were impressed with the skill and strength displayed by Mobutu and the financial agencies in Zaire in dealing successfully with a precarious economic situation, and Zaire's credit rating rose.

The IMF liberalization programs carried with them reforms of Zairian investment laws. Foreign corporations (particularly from Belgium and Italy) dramatically increased their holdings in Zairian mining and cash-crop production. The criticism of this investment by Zairian politicians was so intense that it forced Mobutu to pledge never to return to the Fund. The criticism came specifically from those high-ranking Zairian officials involved in managing state-owned corporations who directly benefitted from the existing system. The intensity of the nationalistic sentiment that emerged in 1973 was such that Mobutu further seized upon it to embark on an economic restructuring program known as "Zairianization." (Callaghy 1984c, 22)

Zairianization

Zairianization mimicked the policies of Salvador Allende in Chile and of Julius Nyerere in Tanzania at the time. It consisted of a sudden and large-scale transfer of ownership from foreign nationals and firms to local investors and public officials, all in the name of self-determination and economic independence. In effect, many foreign-owned firms were nationalized, while others were purchased by Zairian investors with substantial public backing over Western objections. The scope of the transfer was immense: all enterprises in the agricultural, commercial and transportation sectors were nationalized, with the exception of those firms established since the new 1969 investment code was in force. This involved over one hundred firms and establishments, effectively excluding those Mediterranean businessmen mentioned above. (American University 1979, 188–89) Although politicians were legally prohibited from controlling new parastatal firms, in fact they were the principal beneficiaries of the new policy. In the city of Lubumbashi, a major industrial pole in the Shaba mining region, thirty five percent of the nationalized firms were transferred to politicians, while only thirty-four were transferred to businessmen. Frequently such politicians-turned-industrialists were entirely unfit for the task and hired former foreign owners and executives to take over management. (Young & Turner 1985, 341–43)

Very soon the disruption of ownership brought about upheaval in the day-to-day traffic of goods at the local level. Short-term financing was stopped short pending finalization of ownership, while transfers took place so quickly and at different centers, giving rise to several multiple ownerships. It took months to work out such problems. Meanwhile, prices at the retail level rose dramatically, resulting in 30.4 percent inflation for 1974. The administration of Mobutu reacted to the troubles with arbitrary price controls. (Young & Turner 1985, 344)

In 1975 Mobutu further radicalized both domestic and foreign policy after formal state visits to China, Cuba, and North Korea. Mobutu undertook a new phase, termed "radicalization." Throughout the period, foreign borrowing continued apace, while the Bank of Zaire expanded credit and prices rose. More importantly, world copper prices fell precipitously back to pre-1970 levels after the peak of 1974, from $1.40 per pound to $0.53 per pound in 1975 (Young & Turner 1985, 308; Callaghy 1984a, 65).

Foreign reaction erupted in 1975 as Belgians cut off export insurance to Zairians selling to Belgium and international bankers became aware of arrears in repayment of interest. (Young & Turner 1985, 357) The American Ambassador Deane Hinton was expelled on charges of fomenting a CIA-sponsored coup, while the real reason lay in the fact the he had lectured Mobutu concerning the need for reform once too often. (Kabwit 1979, 395, 405) External debt had grown from $714.9 million in 1972 to over $3 billion in 1975 (see Table 4.1), or nearly half Zaire's total gross national product for the year. The GDP itself fell six percent in 1975. (American University 1979, 190) Reserves of hard foreign currency were entirely depleted in 1975, falling from a high of 110.5 million zaires in 1973 to a deficit of 46 million zaires by the beginning of 1976. (American University 1979, 191,194–5) In other words, the total Zairian debt had reached over 200 percent of total exports, and seemed to be rising out of control. (Cuhna & Donnelly 1983, 18) Budget deficits also skyrocketed with expenditures exceeding estimates by up to fifty percent due to failed military campaigns in Angola, shortfalls in revenues, and cost overruns in many public works projects. The 1974 deficit was 190 million zaires. (American University 1979, 188) In short, Zaire's finances were in a shambles.

Zaire's IMF Borrowing

The Mobutu administration began talks with the IMF in 1976 after an initial program of "retrocession" was initiated. The Mobutu administration returned "40 percent equity in foreign-owned radicalized or zairianized enterprises" to their original owners. (Young & Turner 1985, 357) At the recommendation of IMF officials, Mobutu created a special committee to deal with stabilization and he embarked on a rescheduling of Zaire's foreign private debt with Citibank officials. (Aronson 1977, 169)

TABLE 4.1 Zaire External Public Debt, 1972-1977 ($US million)

	1972	1973	1974	1975	1976	1977
Total Foreign Debt (including commitments)	715	1751	2877	3008	3305	3543
Private	238	763	1247	1268	1349	1376
Public - Bilateral	161	439	722	827	956	1121
Public - Multilateral	85	101	136	285	349	367
Total Foreign Debt (disbursed only)	544	862	1295	1655	2169	2639
Private	197	426	651	819	1031	1146
Public - Bilateral	124	134	251	404	589	801
Public - Multilateral	30	50	60	79	117	180

Source: Young & Turner 1985, **386.**

In March 1976, the IMF approved a $47 million one-year stand-by with the stated goals of achieving "limitations of the expansion of domestic demand, stimulation of domestic production, and furtherance of exports." (American University 1979, 191) Following the IMF agreement, both private creditors (The London Club) and public lenders (The Paris Club) orchestrated significant reschedulings of Zaire's interest payments. In addition, $250 million in fresh money was provided by the London Club in early 1977.[1]

During 1977, several economic reversals forced Zaire to return to the Fund for additional support. These included falling prices for copper which contributed to a 4.7 percent decline in Zaire's GNP and a higher fiscal deficit. (American University 1979, 191) In addition, the Mobutu regime broke several key provisions of the 1976 agreement by protecting subsidized state-owned firms during the recession. A critical IMF report in February attributed the fiscal deficit in part to excessive payments to the military. (Young 1983, 120–1) Callaghy contends that Mobutu had "no intention of living up to the agreement." (1984b, 23)

In spite of Zaire's poor performance, the Fund extended a further $52 million over eighteen months in 1977. The objectives of the new program were more immediate and urgent: preservation of Zaire's ability to trade and attraction of foreign investment. (*IMF Survey* 1977, 137) The IMF specifically sought a 50 percent reduction of the fiscal deficit and a tightening of domestic credit, neither of which were realized in any degree. (Young & Turner 1985, 382) Given Zaire's lack of success and clear unwillingness to repay its arrears, the IMF declared the country ineligible for further assistance in late-1977. A further explanation for the IMF's action was the chaotic state of Zaire's accounting mechanisms and their inability to calculate the total volume of Zaire's foreign private and public debt. (Young & Turner 1985, 383)

In a coordinated effort to clearly evaluate Zaire's economic state and create a modicum of financial order, the IMF and the Paris Club organized a team of senior financial experts to replace local officials in key economic posts in Kinshasa. (*Wall Street Journal* 1978b, 19) The team, led by Deutsche Bank official Erwin Blumenthal, was told to gain control over Zaire's high level of capital flight and provide support for those local officials committed to implementing conditionality. (Callaghy 1984a, 67) To contain capital flight, Blumenthal withdrew access to foreign capital for many senior Zairian officials. Such unpopular actions, combined with the natural aversion to direct foreign control, led local officials to withhold their cooperation from the Blumenthal team. Within one year, after writing a scathing report attacking local corruption and incompetence, Blumenthal withdrew the team. (Gould 1980, 95; Young 1983, 124; Callaghy 1984a, 68)

In 1979, the IMF extended yet another short-term loan to Zaire in the form of a $155 million stand-by arrangement. In justifying the program the IMF singled out poor management of the national budget as a major factor in Zaire's crisis—a direct indictment of Mobutu's government. (*IMF Survey* 1979, 265) The Fund also committed itself to a series of loans over a period of several years. Zaire benefitted from rising copper prices and carried out monetary and fiscal reforms to address inflation and budget deficits. (Turner & Young 1985, 323–24) Zaire's performance improved to the point that the entire IMF loan was disbursed without cancellation and a new Extended Fund Facility program was initiated in 1981.

After limited compliance with the 1981 agreements, Mobutu reverted back to the policies of the 1970s and the accompanying diplomatic intransigence. The EFF was cancelled in 1983. Zaire returned to minimal standards of performance required to continue to receive IMF assistance through the mid-1980s, but did not improve its international and domestic financial and economic situation. Young concluded that "Zaire thus appears locked in a crisis without end or solution." (1983, 129)

Many analysts conclude that Zaire is a case of "dependency reversal" in that Mobutu has been able to assert significant control over his financial condition and over the terms of international borrowing. Among many factors that might explain this is his political role as Western ally in Sub-Saharan Africa (Young 1983; Callaghy 1984a; Turner 1985; Aronson 1977; Körner 1986). As will be seen in the following section, much of Zaire's behavior can be understood in terms of intense bargaining and what might be called economic "brinkmanship."

The Actors in the Zaire Case

Principal Actors

Mobutu and the Zairian Elite. The Mobutu administration has been described in largely disparaging terms by most analysts of Zairian politics. Nour (1982), Körner (1986), and Gould (1980) have described Mobutu's government as a "cleptocracy," meaning "rule by a corrupt, self-enriching state-class" (Körner 1986, 99). Specific elements of this governing style included: an overvalued currency which made capital flight especially profitable, bribery, control of economic ministries and export-oriented firms, urban bias, and shrewd negotiation tactics (Körner 1986, 99–100).

After the failure of Zairianization and radicalization, Mobutu recognized, as did a large portion of the international financial community, that emergency measures were needed to salvage what was left of his nation's economy and, more importantly, his regime. "By late 1975, virtually no one beyond the narrowing group of beneficiaries (of Zairianization) challenged the conclusion that Zairianization had been a total fiasco, and that radicalization had added insult to injury" (Young & Turner 1985, 357). Zaire's foreign debt, estimated at under $100 million in the late-1960s, was now over $2 billion (World Bank 1984).[2]

In this first round of discussions, Mobutu undertook several administrative reforms, creating in November 1975, at the urging of a senior IMF official, a new "stabilization committee," composed of senior administration officials charged with financial affairs, with himself at the head. The committee immediately proposed the first of several measures aimed at de-nationalizing industries affected by Zairianization. "Retrocession," as it was called, began by returning "40 percent equity in foreign-owned radicalized or Zairianized enterprises" (Young & Turner 1985, 357). In return, bankers began considering a rescheduling of interest of Zairian debt.

Finally, after Mobutu received technical assistance and advice, talks between the IMF and Zaire in 1976 brought about a one-year stand-by agreement. The loan coincided with a 42 percent devaluation and preceded a Paris Club rescheduling. Thus Zaire began a series of stop-gap measures to maintain financial solvency. This process has been described with some cynicism:

> The very bonds of economic dependency have been used with virtuosity. The regime adroitly trades on the premise that its creditors cannot afford either to see its fall, or to see Mobutu fall. Bankruptcy would be as inconvenient for the banks (and Western governments) as for Zaire; at each negotiating brink, a temporizing formula is found, the debt rolled over one more time, while all await the millenium of higher copper prices (Aronson 1977, 6).

Thomas Callaghy's previously mentioned contention that Mobutu did not intend to abide by the letter of intent is borne out by the comment by Blumenthal in his report to IMF officials after his one-year term: "Mobutu and his government regard the idea of repaying their debts as a joke. . . " (Körner 1986, 97).

While the program was both ordinary and feasible, its implementation proved elusive. Zaire improved its tax collection procedures and thereby reached IMF targets for government revenues, but nonetheless saw its budget deficit remain high at z321.7 million. The deficit relative to GDP had risen nearly three-fold, from 12 percent in 1976 to 32 percent in 1977 (Young & Turner 1985, 382). Given restrictions on foreign borrowing, this deficit was financed in large measure by domestic credit expansion, far above IMF targets, with the result of continued high inflation. As it reached 58 percent, the zaire became quickly overvalued although pegged to the SDR. Imports were drastically cut and repayment of debts was postponed, creating a modest improvement in the balance-of-payments position through 1977, which was reversed in 1978 (Young 1983, 122–123).

Mobutu, in November 1977, committed the nation to a far-flung recovery program, to include such platforms as an infusion of $1 billion in foreign aid, decentralization of the highly concentrated decision-making processes of the government, and improved public services and administration. Scholars have viewed with disdain these types of pronouncements (Turner, 1985; Young, 1983, p. 122). While it is true that some powers were shared to other officials and bodies after the Shaba I experience, "the credibility of this new program was nil" (Young & Turner 1985, p. 383).

By the end of 1977, Zaire had tried the patience of the IMF to its limit. It was determined that due to the government's failure to meet conditions and repay arrears, it would no longer be eligible to draw from its higher tranche until its house was put in order. A further consideration was the fact that financial information emerging from Zaire was so disjointed, uncoordinated, and confused that the Fund had "no notion of what Zaire was doing" (Young & Turner 1985, 383). Zaire's good faith efforts had completely stalled by the end of 1977; through 1978 delinquent payments mounted at the rate of $125 million per quarter and inflation climbed to 80 percent as domestic credit expanded in 1978 (Gran, 23, cited in Young 1983, 123). "Since 1975, Zaire has been effectively bankrupt," said one Western economist in 1978 (Ottoway 1978, cited in Kabwit, 400).

In 1978, when asked whether Mobutu would allow foreigners to reform its economic system directly, the answer came: "The answer is no, a categorical no. . . I do not interfere in the cases of prisoners of Sing–Sing, why do you accept they can interfere in my internal affairs?" (Pringle 1978, 50). By June 1978, the IMF, at the urging of creditor nations, began sending officials to replace local Zairian officials in top posts in each of the major financial agencies of the government (*Wall Street Journal* 1978b, 19).

Blumenthal became de facto director of Zaire's Central Bank while others occupied senior positions at the Finance Ministry, the Office of Customs, and the Planning Ministry (Gould 1980, 95). The Blumenthal team intended to carry out its mission of restoring Zaire's fiscal and financial viability by allowing the small number of competent Zairian technocrats to do their job without political interference. By so doing, the team attempted to rid the country of corruption—a task far beyond the capacity of a few dozen Western economists.

Blumenthal began by cutting off foreign currency credits to "some fifty companies tied to the politico-commercial class, including seven members of the Political Bureau and, most prominently, a Mobutu relative, Litho, who had long been the incarnate symbol of plunder" (Young 1983, 123). This policy would have done much to aid in minimizing the negative foreign reserves situation, as well as assure that as much as possible of the recently loaned Western money would be used for the proper purpose.

There is no doubt that such drastic measures were economically justified. However, such an approach struck at the heart of the deeply engrained clientelism of the Zairian political-commercial system. After all, the economic security of these people depended on their ability to expatriate hard currency rather than keeping even large sums in zaires in Kinshasa. Likewise, Mobutu would often use access to foreign currency as a political plum to be judiciously distributed between his various supporters. It is natural enough, then, that:

> most of those who lost their foreign currency status were 'rehabilitated' shortly thereafter by President Mobutu. Many of Blumenthal's reformist decisions were blocked by the bank director, the president, the bureaucracy, or what he himself—as quoted in a confidential, diplomatic cable—referred to as the 'hydra-headed dishonesty' of the regime (Gould 1980, 95).

Illustrative of the problems faced by Blumenthal and the foreign team in managing another country's government are the following:

> When one of the intercept channels placed into the pipeline carrying national resources is discovered and removed, another one is inserted elsewhere. Characteristic was the discovery that large amounts of the emergency rice aid provided by the United States in 1977 at once entered speculative channels via trading firms tied to the politico-commercial class. *Los Angeles Times* correspondent David Lamb asserted in March 1979 that some 12,000 tons of this rice shipment (acquired by a son of Mobutu) had simply been hidden for eventual speculative gain. In early 1979 the IMF discovered that 200 tons of cobalt had been transferred at $25 per pound by the state marketing corporation, SOZACOM, to a Swiss company created by SOZACOM director, Lukusa Mwanagula. This company then reaped a cool $8 million profit by reselling it at the spot market price of 442 per pound. (Young 1983, 124)

Blumenthal tried, is this later instance, to force repatriation of that $8 million profit back to Zaire, but he failed. Shortly after this incident,

Blumenthal and his team abandoned the effort and left Zaire entirely. Commenting on his experiences and his assessment of the Mobutu administration, Blumenthal wrote:

> [It is] alarmingly clear that the corruptive system in Zaire with all its wicked and ugly manifestations, its mismanagement and fraud will destroy all endeavors of international institutions, of friendly governments, and of the commercial banks towards recovery and rehabilitation of Zaire's economy. Sure, there will be new promises by Mobutu, by members of his government, rescheduling and rescheduling again of a growing external public debt, but no (repeat:no) prospect for Zaire's creditors to get their money back in any foreseeable future (Callaghy 1984a, 68).

Zaire obtained a $155 million stand-by arrangement after the departure of the Blumenthal team. The program called for a freeze of public sector wages, a withdrawal of private sector wage indexation and prompt repayment of arrears. (IMF 1979. 265)

At roughly the same time as the 1979 stand-by was arranged, Zaire hired the services of the well known "holy trinity" of financial consultants: Lazard Frères, Lehman Brothers' Kuhn Loeb, and S.G. Warburg. Acting as a financial and even diplomatic go-between, this group assisted Zaire in its dealings with foreign private and public financiers as well as the IMF. In 1979, it managed to coordinate a Paris Club rescheduling, and in 1980 it put together a London Club rescheduling of private bankers. Note that in 1982 the group withdrew its services on the grounds that the government was unwilling to cooperate with creditors. (Callaghy 1984a, 68)

In 1981 an EFF loan worth over one billion dollars was extended. This was provided in part because the Fund acknowledged in 1979 that continual support would follow the agreement at the time, and also because in 1980 Zaire's economic conditions improved. The currency was devalued several times from 1977 to 1981, declining as a result from equivalence to the U.S. dollar to being worth sixteen cents. Zaire remained roughly current on its IMF payments and was able to reduce its arrears thanks to rising copper prices. (Young & Turner 1985, 323–24) To further explain the apparent shift to fiscal responsibility in Zaire, Erwin Blumenthal commented in a confidential memo: "Mobutu was almost constantly abroad, and the new Prime Minister, Minister of Finance, and central bank director were able to work without constraint." Foreign officials continued their attempts at management of the economy.

Mobutu has remained in power in Zaire and has recently made political life more open, but the economy remains in a state of crisis. The total foreign debt swelled to $5 billion in the mid-1980s and Zaire's per capita income fell by an average of more than two percent each year from 1980 to 1985. Zaire is now among the ten poorest nations of the world in spite of a rich resource base. Exports declined an average of three percent per year during the same period and inflation average 55 percent. (World Bank 1987) In spite of repeated efforts by presumably well-meaning technocrats, the cleptocracy of Mobutu remains in force, to the detriment of Zaire's people. Only in 1990 was hope for democracy rekindled.

In terms of the models, it is clear that Mobutu's behavior is anything but passive, thus allowing us to reject the utilty of the functionalist model. The bargaining model is able to explain more effectively the efforts at manipulation of the Fund by the Mobutu regime as well as its success. Mobutu was able to use his nation's apparant vulnerability to persuade creditors to continue providing essential resources in spite of the very low prospect of receiving a return on their capital.

The IMF and the Blumenthal Team. As mentioned earlier, Mobutu received technical assistance and advice from the Fund in 1975 and initiated formal negotiations in 1976. The Executive Board agreed to a $47 million (35 percent of quota) one-year stand-by with the following objectives: "limitations on the expansion of domestic demand, stimulation of domestic production, and furtherance of exports," (American University 1979, 191) not to mention the obvious goal of restoring Zaire's international credit rating, which had fallen below 10 on a 100-point scale. (Körner 1986, 22–25) Specific policy instruments to be employed included:

(1) a 42 percent devaluation to align the zaire with the SDR, (2) a ceiling of twenty percent on wage increases, (3) a dramatic cut of government expenditures involving foreign exchange, (4) a limit on domestic credit expansion to 22 percent during 1976, (5) renegotiation of external public debt. (Young 1983, 119)

The IMF mission which visited the country in February 1977 to assess Zaire's compliance with the accord returned with a very critical report, pointing out that the huge budget deficit emerged only in part because of falling copper prices, in contradiction to Mobutu's claims. In particular,

Gecamines, was unable to meet its financial obligations [in tax payments]. . . . Additionally, presidential, army and educational outlays were well over budgeted amounts. . . [O]nly about $120 million of $400 million potential earnings generated from the fabulous coffee bonanza were re-patriated. The new national copper-marketing firm, SOZACOM, was also a major culprit—well-connected members of the inner presidential circle received huge, vague "consultancy" contracts, payable abroad. (Young 1983, 120–1)

The Fund extended further credit to Zaire at the completion of the first loan in April 1977 in the form of a $33 million compensatory financing package to offset declining copper prices. Further, $53 million was extended in the form of a stand-by arrangement to assist in reducing a balance of payments deficit that was calculated at SDR 442 million in 1975 and SDR 135 million in 1976. (IMF 1977, 127) This took the total holdings of Zaire to 186 percent of its quota.

General aims of the standby included the standard litany of IMF objectives:

> containing the estimated deficit in the balance of payments to an amount consistent with the available financing and, at the same time, considerably reducing the rate of inflation by making possible an upswing in economic activity and a sufficient supply of imported goods. (IMF 1977, 137)

In other words, the overall goals involved maintaining Zaire's credit worthiness and ability to trade. In more specific terms, the budget deficit was to be reduced from 313 million zaires to 160 million in 1977, government revenues were to increase in order to achieve this goal, and inflation was to be reduced from its 1976 level of 61 percent. (American University 1979, 192) This agreement in turn allowed Citibank to complete coordination of its promised $250 million consortium loan. (Young & Turner 1985, 382)

The economy failed to rebound in 1977–1978 as the government expanded credit to compensate for restricted access to foreign capital and a nearly sixty percent inflation rate. The public sector deficit expanded two hundred percent and debt repayments were further delayed. (Young & Turner 1985, 122–23) It had become clear to Zaire's creditors that the government had no intention of implementing the reforms of the IMF in order to repay arrears on its foreign debt. Even more important, it was widely assumed by 1978 that Zaire's economic data was fundamentally unreliable and probably even misleading. (Young & Turner 1985, 383)

Finally, in June 1978, the IMF, at the urging of creditor nations, began sending officials to replace local Zairian financial leadership. Mobutu was informed that he must accept this team in order to continue qualifying for IMF assistance, and so he grudgingly complied. (*Wall Street Journal* 1978b, 19)[3]

The team was to serve two purposes: First, it would attempt to control the hemorrhage of hard currency through official channels and parastatals, as well as create a political buffer between "a technocratic core of competent Zairian officials" and their corrupt political superiors. (Callaghy 1984a, 67) After one year of effort, Erwin Blumenthal abandoned his post. "The maneuvers of the political aristocracy to detour the controls have been creative, persistent, and, to a substantial degree, successful. The political aristocracy has both systematically harassed and 'worn down' the teams over time. . . ." (Callaghy 1984a, 68) This experince reveals that "[t]he IMF does not have the power, in a sovereign state such as Zaire, to control all the cleptocratic practices." (Körner 1986, 104) It is for this reason that the Fund was forced to return to traditional negotiating practices with Zaire.

In August 1979, in spite of a year of ineligibility and frustrated reform attempts, the IMF extended yet another credit arrangement to Zaire. In this case, roughly $155 million would be disbursed over an eighteen month period in the context of a stand-by arrangement. Using more dramatic language than is usual in its dry press releases, the IMF blamed the situation on: (1) inadequate price incentives in production, (2) expansionary monetary policy, (3) declining copper prices, (4) poor management of budget policies resulting in increasing deficits, and (5) "weakness in foreign exchange management." (IMF 1979, 265) Even more interesting is that in this staid and official announcement, typically aimed at allaying the fears and concerns of the international financial community, it is openly acknowledged that the standby will have to be followed by more lending:

> The present stand-by arrangement has been approved in support of the Government's short-term stabilization program. However, given the size and structural nature of Zaire's economic problems, the corrective process will need to be continued over the medium term [three to five years]. (IMF 1979, 265)

Among the policy instruments involved was a rather harsh wage policy involving the rescinding of wage indexation to inflation and a public sector wage freeze for 1979. Other aspects of the program included several initiatives to regulate flows of foreign exchange and begin "an orderly process of reducing outstanding external payments arrears." (IMF 1979, 265) Total Zairian holdings up to this point came to 136 percent of quota. The 1979 standby would take Zaire's obligations to the Fund to $500 million, or 255 percent of quota, one of the largest among Fund member countries at the time. This contrasts with the fact that Zaire's creditworthiness had further fallen to only six out of a possible 100— one of the five worst counry ratings in the world. (Körner 1986, 24)

In recognition of both the Fund's original statements in the 1979 press release and Zaire's relative success in 1980, Zaire was granted a medium-term loan by the Fund on June 22, 1981 to the tune of over $1 billion or 400 percent of Zaire's quota bringing her total obligations to the Fund to 471 percent of quota. Fund assistance on this scale has been matched in Africa only by Morocco, with a much larger quota, and Zambia, and neither of these received as much in a lump sum. (Zulu & Nsouli 1985, 4–5) That this assistance was available was made possible through a variety of institutional changes within the Fund itself, and set the tone for loans to come. That Zaire's compliance was a major factor is reflected again in the staid press release: "After some initial difficulties [in implementing the 1979 SBA], significant progress was made under the program in 1980, especially in slowing the high rate of inflation." (IMF 1981, 207)

Some of the policy objectives and instruments included further re-duction of inflation and a relative slowing of overall economic growth, while allowing for moderate increases in the budget deficits. A further devaluation of forty percent came a few days before the agreement was announced, bringing the value of the zaire to $US 0.16 (IMF 1981, 211) and in line with black market rates.

With increases in copper prices, Mobutu embarked on a restoration of policies of the past regarding foreign investment. As a result, the 1983 agreement was rescinded and Zaire was forced to renegotiate with the Fund. Its triumvirate of advisors quit in 1982 citing government intrasigence. Banks rescheduled uninsured debt with reluctance and a certain degree of resignation. Eventually, the IMF entered into yet another new agreement at the end of 1983 and has maintained the relationship in spite of the lack of prospect for improvement.

Within the IMF, it is difficult to determine exactly what factors influenced the decisions to continue support. It is clear that the idea of sending a team of experts to take over positions in the Zairian bureaucracy was not the IMF's, although it is a rather logical expansion of the concept of IMF teams that periodically undertake what are known as "Article 4" consultations and periodic monitoring visits while a stand-by is in force.

Because the IMF's support for Zaire was so extensive, even though the tone of the press release and memoranda betrays a high level of impatience with Mobutu, it leads one to search for non-economic factors. One of these could have been the role of the Managing Director, Jacques DeLarosière, who came to the Fund in 1978 with extensive experience in France's Organization for Economic Cooperation and Development's. He "was in charge of the development assistance programs managed by the Ministry of Economy and Finance" in France. (IMF 1978, 177) This extensive work in development, particularly in the latter post, brought the Managing Director into close contact with African states, especially the francophone region. As described by senior officials (active and retired) of the Fund, he has shown an enduring sensitivity to the special needs of African states as Managing Director of the Fund.* This may help to explain the ten-fold increase of Fund lending to African states from 1979 to 1981, especially since the difficulties of repayment illustrate the lack of strict economic justification for the loans. (*South* 1985, 31–40)

Another factor which may have had marginal importance in the process is the inherent weakness of the African Department in the Fund at the time. As mentioned earlier, it is common knowledge among Fund staff that the African Department is a relatively unattractive post to which those who lack the talent to secure a more prestigious assignment typically gravitate. As is seen in the case of Sudan, it is believed by some Fund officials that a relatively less capable (and confident) staff might find it difficult to debate the managing director's suggestions. The result is a more exact implementation of his opinions and preferences, including, possibly, expanded lending to unsafe debtors.*

More generally, it would seem that the Fund's tolerance of Zaire's manipulative behavior is most consistent with the bargaining model. The Fund did not have resources and assets required to overcome the impediments to stabilization in Zaire, even though it had the expertise to diagnose its problems. Mobutu was able to maintain ultimate control of the governmental machinery in spite of the IMF's both traditional and unorthodox efforts.

Secondary Actors

Paris Club. Zaire was yet another example of nations that many Western governments could neither tolerate nor abandon. The economic liabilities of working with the Mobutu government were extremely high—financial exposure and risk to private creditors, large numbers of man-hours to negotiate and reschedule debt, possible support for corruption, and risk of public humiliation for collapse of process. The economic rewards for those involved with Zaire were modest—avoidance of formal default and the hope of continued collection of debt payments. The political gains—of retaining a Western ally in Sub-Saharan Africa—were considered adequate compensation for the economic risks, however.

Some radical critics of the Fund have assumed that it was the United States that propped up the Zairian economy in the mid-1970s so that it could use Zaire's territory for covert attacks against Marxist rebels in neighboring Angola. (Körner 1986, 105) In fact, military and economic support for Zaire came from many different nations, including Belgium, Uganda, France, and even the PRC. (Kabwit 1979, 381) And the U.S.

Ambassador was expelled in 1975 because of his criticism of Mobutu's financial mismanagement. (Kabwit 1979, 395) Later, a senior CIA official accused Mobutu of embezzling $1.4 million in American aid for UNITA rebels in Angola. Finally, Americans were in the lead in the call for the Blumenthal team. (Kabwit 1979, 398) Although American support for Mobutu is understandable on strategic grounds, their day-to-day antipathy parallels U.S. policy in Sudan towards Nimeiri.

In 1975, the U.S. Export-Import Bank gave Zaire its lowest possible rating and urged Mobutu to sign an IMF agreement in order to restore the nation's creditworthiness. (Senate 1978, 11–16) Once the IMF was involved, the United States joined France, Belgium, and West Germany in Paris Club talks beginning June 1976. (American University 1979, 193) These talks resulted in a rescheduling of Zaire's publicly-guaranteed debt. The group met again in 1979 after Blumenthal's failure. (Callaghy 1984a, 68) This later rescheduling effort was orchestrated in part by the work of private consultants working for the Mobutu government. The Paris Club continued its role in 1981, 1983, and 1985 reschedulings. (Körner 1986)

The Paris Club in each case waited until Mobutu had concluded an accord with the IMF before dealing with debt repayment schedules. The IMF intervened in each case in part due to pressure from the Paris Club to instill greater financial discipline in Zaire. (IMF 1979, 265) This symbiotic relationship was critical in motivating Zaire to give at least a modicum of respect to international financial rules of creditworthiness. However, Paris Club members recognized the futility of their efforts in the long run. (Callaghy 1984a, 68)

Although there were purely economic reasons for the Paris Club members to protect Zaire's economy, political interests were at times a consideration in their activities. Note the response of Belgium, France, and the United States to the first of several separatist invasions into southern Zaire by anti-Mobutu exiles:

> Fifteen hundred Moroccan troops were ferried in French planes; the United States flew in $1.5 million of non-lethal weapons, Belgium supplied equipment and advisors, West Germany sent humanitarian aid including medicine, and additional support came from other nations as disparate as China, Egypt, Saudi Arabia, and Uganda. (Kabwit 1979, 381)

After yet another Shaba invasion in May 1978, French and Belgian troops succeeded in routing the enemy only after losing the mining town of Kolwezi for a long enough time to have copper and cobalt production disrupted. (*Wall Street Journal* 1978a, 14)

A Carter administration official justified continued American support for Mobutu's plans to construct the massive Inga-Shaba power line:

> It makes political sense, I think, because finishing the project would bolster our reputation as financiers and reliable partners. To do otherwise would harm our image in that regard and be harmful to the bilateral relations as well. Most importantly, we believe the project makes sense in terms of overall policy toward Zaire. Everything that we are doing as a government in Zaire in conjunction with our European allies and Zairians themselves, is designed to encourage economic and political stability in that part of central Africa. We think if we do not work toward that, the very basis and context of our interests and the interests of the West in general will continue to disintegrate. (Jones 1979, 25–6)

While the United States was most concerned with regional and strategic considerations, other European creditors had different goals in Zaire. Belgium was concerned with protecting the $6 billion in direct business investment in the country. This interest led Belgium to "placate Mobutu by toning down loud criticisms of his regime by Zairian emigrés in Brussels, and it has urged other western states to rally behind the current regime." (Kabwit 1979, 406) Likewise, the French government was eager to include Zaire in its growing "francophone" zone of Third World influence spanning the Caribbean, the Maghreb, and much of Sub-Saharan Africa. For these reasons of cultural affinity, "France was usually the soft underbelly of the phalynx of creditors." (Young & Turner 1985, 395)

How do these disparate interests and varying degrees of involvement take on meaning in the context of the political model of IMF decision-making? First, the Paris Club members appear to have made significant economic concessions to Mobutu in part because he promised to work as a pro-Western presence in what was becoming an increasingly radicalized Black Africa in the 1970s. This seems to be the dominant motivation for American intervention. However, even this attraction was not the supreme consideration, since the United States was willing to risk breaking diplomatic ties by criticizing Mobutu corruption during the Ford administration.

Second, the Paris Club worked to make Zaire's economy more open by urging IMF involvement and supporting all IMF agreements. Belgium was especially eager to see its assets protected and repariation of profits guaranteed—both of which were danaged by Mobutu's radical reforms of the late-1970s. The IMF acted in consort with the Paris Club by isolating Mobutu when he attempted briefly to re-impose a policy of nationalization in the mid-1980s. In these two dimensions, then, it would seem that the political model is a useful descriptor of IMF decision-making with regard to Zaire.

One might challenge the autonomy of Paris Club actors. Because Mobutu's tactics and strategy were clearly confrontational and risky, one might wonder who actually determined the course of events. The political model assumes major powers will behave autonomously and strategically, not reactively and out of desperation to salvage some semblance of success. In the case of Zaire, it would seem it was Mobutu who held the reins of negotiation.

London Club. Zaire's total private debt was difficult to estimate, since Zairian accounting techniques were not adequate for the task. Suffice it to say that it involved over one hundred banks in the United States, Japan, France, Belgium, and other Western nations. Citibank was perhaps the most active in lending to Zaire in the early-1970s. (Aronson 1977, 169) Mobutu's radicalization, combined with the fall of commodity prices, and excessive government expenditure on ill-advised and failed military incursions into Angola prompted private creditors to conteplate how to pressure Mobutu into an IMF agreement. "Citibank's Irving Friedman, who had previously worked with the IMF and the World Bank, became the private banks' chief negotiator." (Aronson 1979, 169)

This group, dubbed the London Club, debated whether to reschedule Zaire's debt over a fifteen-year period, in accordance with demands made by Zaire's Central Bank President Samba Pida. Under pressure by Citibank, however, the London Club opted for a refinancing plan involving fresh credit in order to make debt repayment possible and boost Zaire's credit rating. Private bankers demanded in exchange for their generosity a package of economic reforms on the part of Mobutu. In November 1976 a "Memorandum of Understanding" was signed and which released a loan of $250 million on condition of immediate repayment of outstanding interest ($40 million) and a pledge to seek an IMF stand-by arrangement by 1977. (Young 1983, 120)

Although Zaire remained generally current on private debt interest payments, Mobutu typically opted to pay the IMF first in the event of a shortage of funds. (Young & Turner 1985, 323) In 1979–1980, Zaire paid back $1 billion in arrears, although during the 1980s its performance deteriorated to the point that private bankers began slowly writing off Zaire's debt. (Callaghy 1984a, 72)

Paraphrasing a legendary concept, Brazilian economist Celso Ming once said: "If I owe a million dollars, then I am lost. But if I owe fifty billions, the bankers are lost." (Sampson 1981, 317) In more sophisticated language: "Once banks have extended substantial sums to borrowers, they are, for all practical purposes, committed to the borrower through thick and thin. . ." (Aronson 1977, 6) Thus it is simple enough to explain why the private banks and some public creditors were willing to continue floating new loans and rescheduling old debts to Mobutu: because to have done otherwise would have risked bankruptcy, or at least a precipitous loss in stock value. The case of Zaire in the early 1980s was in fact merely a harbinger of things to come, as will be seen in other cases found in this study. The bankers apparant powerlessness is generally consistent with the bargaining model. Bankers control extended only to what Mobutu did not.

Conclusion

The experience of Zaire and the Mobutu administration includes several very unsual elements. In addition to a surprisingly long string of significant loans by the Fund to a clearly undeserving nation, the IMF employed as radical a set of techniques as Mobutu in an effort to gain a handle on a collapsing economy and corrupt government.

Can the Zaire case be understood in terms of the functionalist model? Overall, it would take a significant stretch of the imagination to say that the IMF consistently applied rigorous standards of economic performance and IMF modelling to explain the general trend of IMF lending. Although there were moments when the IMF's programs could be termed "routine" (1977 and 1979), during the bulk of the period the IMF displayed at times remarkable tolerance of a clearly intransigent government, and at other times employed almost illegitimate devices to exert some discipline on the government. The willingness to come again and again with new offers of significant aid is startling in the context of Zaire's overall pattern of performance. It led us to speculate whether the Managing Director's personal affinity for Africa might have been a factor—certainly not a very technocratic element. Likewise, the Fund's injection of a team of Western technocrats to seize control of as much of Zaire's economy as possible far exceeds what could be termed normal Fund behavior and border on classic colonialism. Although it is understandable why the Fund was driven to such schizophrenic behavior, one cannot simply assume this was the result of normal technocratic decision-making.

The political model does address some questions left unanswered by the functionalist approach. The influence of Paris and London Club members on IMF policy is consistent with the model's assumptions. This extends to the unorthodox intervention of the Blumenthal team—a solution advanced by the Paris Club of official creditors. The motivations of these major powers and financiers is also rather clear, although one might wonder to what degree they acted out of long-term self-interest or short-term paranoia. The IMF's general passivity is regardless anticipated.

This analysis works rather well until one considers the period of radicalization of the late-1970s. At this juncture, Western powers became ambivalent, thereby losing their coherent leadership of the Fund. France and Belgium were concerned about protecting perishable financial and cultural ties. The United States was unsure whether the political benefits outweighed the economic costs of supporting Mobutu. The IMF was left to drift for a time, and reverted to a functionalist approach. This approach was vindicated by the success showed during Mobutu's absence.

One might question the wisdom of Western policy toward Zaire, especially since the country seemed to do better without Mobutu than with him. Perhaps the Western creditors are better advised to allow Mobutu and his cleptocratic regime to collapse under its own weight, on the assumption that anything will represent an improvement. But this question was never seriously asked by an overly nervous Western coalition. Instead, they continued to provide the minimum support necessary to allow Mobutu to retain his position.

While these two models complement each other and provide valuable insight into certain periods of Zaire's relations with the IMF, it is not possible to generalize about the entire experience without resort to a bargaining and negotiation model. Many have described the relationship between Zaire and the Western nations as a rare case of "dependency reversal" in which the exploitation moves in the opposite direction than is usually the case. As put by Turner, "What dependency theory does not indicate . . . is the extent to which Western governments and financial institutions have been ensnared and manipulated by Mobutu." (1985, 181–82) Mobutu's success in controlling the outcomes of his interactions with the IMF and the West in general stems from his shrewd and strategic use of bargaining assets: financial weakness combined with control of critical natural resources, pro-Western sympathies in the context of the radicalization of Africa generally, familiarity with financial rules and procedures added to a willingness to risk all to keep power and control national wealth personally. The experience of Zaire becomes coherent when analyzed in terms of bargaining, although one must not assume that bargaining leverage always flows to the most wealthy and powerful. Even relations between the Fund and the Western creditors was a function of the relative bargaining power of each, since the erosion of creditor unity was the opportunity the IMF needed to assert its own style of lending, which in turn was facilitated by Mobutu's removal from the process for a time. Conversely, while the introduction of the Blumenthal team would normally be a sign of weakness on Mobutu's part, it was ultimately turned in his favor by his use of tools at his disposal— an unwillingess to dismantle the cleptocratic regime he established and from which he benefitted, which in turn gave him control of all the lower echelons of Zaire's extensive bureaucracy. In sum, the bargaining model offers a coherent image of the dynamics at work in the case of Zaire and the IMF.

Notes

1. Part of the reason Zaire was able to obtain concessions from private creditors was due to Zaire's involvement of over one hundred banks in its external borrowing. Although it Citibank's portfolio Zare's debt was minor, it was seen as critical to the survival of numerous smaller institutions, who in turn pressed Citibank for resolution of the situation before Zaire defaulted. (Young 1983, 120; American University 1979, 193)

2. Note that capital flight was so high in Zaire that reasonable estimates suggest that a repatriation of hard currency held overseas by Mobutu's immediate family and protegés would have more than covered the entire Zairian external debt. When this fact was pointed out by several members of Zaire's powerless parliament, they were immedialte arrested for "subversion and incitement to rebellion." (Körner 1986, 100)

3. The IMF's role in organizing the Blumenthal team is somewhat unclear. While the task assigned the team would have fallen under the Fund's Fiscal Affairs and Central Banking Departments, the use of non-IMF staff was apparantly the Paris Club's idea.

Bibliography

Alexander, David. 1977. "Debt Rescheduling by LDCs: A Case Study of Zaire." Cambridge, MA: Harvard University, typescript.

American University. 1979. *Zaire: A Country Study*. Washington, D.C.: American University Press.

Aronson, Jonathan. 1977. *Money and Power: Banks and the World Monetary System*. Beverly Hills, CA: Sage.

Callaghy, Thomas. 1984a. "Africa's Debt Crisis." *Journal of International Affairs* 38 (Summer): 63–73.

———. 1984b. "The Ritual Dance of the Debt Game." *Africa Report* (Sept–Oct): 22–26.

———. 1984c. *The State-Society Struggle: Zaire in Comparative Perspective*. New York: Columbia University Press.

Cunha, Antonio-Gabriel M. and Joanne Donnelly. 1983. "Defusing Africa's Debt." *Africa Report* (Sept–Oct): 21–24.

Gould, David J. 1980. *Bureaucratic Corruption and Underdevelopment in the Third World: The Case of Zaire*. New York: Pergamon Press.

Gran, Guy. 1978. "Zaire 1978: The Ethical and Intellectual Bankruptcy of the World System." *Africa Today*. 25 (Oct–Dec): 18.

IMF Survey. 1977. May 2: 137.

———. 1978. June 19: 177.

———. 1979. Sept. 3: 265.

Jones, C. Robin. 1979. "Reappraising U.S. Policy." *Africa Report* (Nov–Dec): 22–26.

Kabwit, Ghilsan. 1979. "Zaire: The Roots of the Continuing Crisis." *The Journal of Modern African Studies* 17: 381–406.

Kaufman, Michael T. 1978. "Zaire: A Mobutu Fiefdom Where Fortunes Shift Quickly." *The New York Times* June 3: IV:4.

Körner, Peter, Gero Mass, Thomas Seibold, & Rainer Tetzlaff. 1986. *The IMF and the Debt Crisis*. London: Zed Books.

Ottaway, David B. 1978. "Zaire: Mobutu's Tactics Frustrate Efforts to Impose Order in Army, Economy." *The Washington Post* June 6: M-3.

Pintak, Lawrence C. 1978. "Can Mobutu Maintain His Grip On Power?" *The Washington Post* June 6: M-4.

Pringle, James. 1978. "Zaire: Sign of Life." *Newsweek* June 19: 53.

Sampson, Anthony. 1981. *The Money Lenders*. New York: Penguin Books.

South. 1985. July: 31–40.

Turner, Thomas. 1985. "Zaire: Stalemate and Compromise." *Current History* 84 (April): 179–183.

United States Senate, Committee on Foreign Relations, Subcommittee on Africa, *Security Supporting Assistance for Zaire*. Hearing, October 24.

Young, Crawford. 1983. "Zaire: The Politics of Penury." *SAIS Review* 3 (Winter–Spring 1983): 120–134.

——— & Thomas Turner. 1985. *The Rise and Decline of the Zairian State*. Madison, WI: University of Wisconsin Press.

Wall Street Journal. 1978a. May 18: 14.

———. 1978b. June 14: 19.

World Bank. 1984. *World Development Report–1984*. Washington, D.C.: World Bank.

———. 1987. *World Development Report–1987*. Washington, D.C.: World Bank.

Zulu, Justin B. & Saleh M. Nsouli. 1985. "Adjustment Programs in Africa: The Recent Experience." *Occasional Papers* #34 April.

5

The Case of Sudan: 1979–1985

The case of Sudan does little to uplift and inspire, in that it illustrates the degree to which a debtor nation can lose both its economic stability and its political autonomy. The IMF dealt with Sudan in a very autocratic fashion, handing down conditionality that exceeded even its own economic models. The Western powers, while at times providing essential financial support to Nimeiri, ended by allowing his overthrow—something which later proved to be very much against the interests of the West. Perhaps the only model that provides a complete explanation is the bargaining model, which focuses on the fact that by 1985 the Sudanese government simply had no more "chips" left with which to negotiate concessions from its creditors.

Background

Sudan is a large, diverse country which has yet to industrialize. Its economy, in the period under consideration, was based on cash crop exports (particularly cotton for which it ranks second in world production). Food produced for local consumption was sustained by price subsidies and irrigation programs. Sudan was successful in reducing its food import bill during the 1970s, as seen in table 5.1. (Nelson 1982, 187)

Sudan has consistently run a trade deficit and made up the need for hard currency with foreign borrowing, given the lack of foreign investment in Sudan. As early as 1969, structural impediments became apparant when the debt service ratio reached ten percent.

Sudan's government has been authoritarian for a generation, in that Jaafar al Nimeiri, a colonel at the time of his seizure of power in 1969, instituted military rule and divested the civilian parliament of its authority. The general governing system is based on patronage, with a large proportion of the population either disenfranchised or inarticulate. In particular, the North-South cleavage in Sudan (which follows Moslem-Christian religious differences) has been especially violent and volatile,

TABLE 5.1   Changes in Agricultural Output in Sudan, 1973-1979 (1973=100)

	1973/74	1974/75	1975/76	1976/77	1977/78	1978/79
For Export						
Cotton	100	93.7	45.6	62.3	82.1	60.3
Sesame	100	97.1	99.6	84.6	102.1	89.2
Groundnuts	100	171.3	171.5	129.8	186.4	148.1
For Local Consumption						
Wheat	100	117.9	112.3	128.1	134.9	75.3
Sorghum	100	104.6	124.3	105.5	124.1	148.2
Dukhn	100	149.6	150.4	174.3	182.1	205.2

Source: El-Khouri 1978, 267.

although Nimeiri went far in resolving it with a treaty in 1972. (Mawson 1984, 521)

In imitation of its neighbors and in order to shore up political support among the masses, the Nimeiri regime instituted many large-scale development projects during the early 1970s. Major irrigation and transportation projects to the North were complemented by rather extravagant food processing programs in the South. The goal was to turn Sudan into the "breadbasket" of Africa. (Nelson 1982, xxv) However, these projects failed because no major reforms were made in the structure of agricultural pricing and distribution. These structures tended to discourage cotton production among farmers and encourage corruption among the military elite. (*Wall Street Journal* 1985, 36) Also, the system of price subsidies on locally-consumed food was retained, which was used primarily as a political tool by the government.

Sudan's agricultural expansion was highly vulnerable to external shocks. Not only did it rely on foreign markets and finance, but it relied heavily on imported equipment and energy. When the 1973 oil crisis erupted, Sudan's agriculture suffered, both because transportation costs rose and because foreign markets and financing were withdrawn. As can be seen in Table 5.1, cotton production fell from 1973 to 1975 by more than half. Government expenditures dramatically rose to compensate for the lack of foreign loans, resulting in a near doubling of public spending in both 1974 and 1975. The fiscal deficit increased by the amount of seven percent of GDP each year from 1974 to 1979. (El-Khouri 1978, 269) As put by Nelson:

Sudan's economic position deteriorated alarmingly in the late 1970s, owing largely to earlier efforts to complete projects beyond the country's financial ability, ill-advised borrowing to meet the domestic insufficiency, widespread bureaucratic weakness, and general public apathy about the need to work hard to produce economic transformation. (Nelson 1982, xxv–xxvi)

Sudan's overall trade deficit fell from nearly $500 million in 1974 to over $600 million in 1978. (El-Khouri 1978, 269) Foreign currency reserves dwindled to only two weeks' worth of imports. Sudan's foreign debt grew to over $2 billion in 1978, and it was increasing its arrears— especially to foreign governments. (Nelson 1982, 90, 190) Even before the second oil crisis, Sudan was in dire straits.

Sudan's Relationship with the IMF

Sudan, much like Zaire, has had very many programs with the IMF. In fact, during the period January 1983 to July 1984 there were at least three different letters of intent signed, although it is not possible to determine precisely what the programs entailed in detail. The total number of programs entered into between Sudan and the IMF from 1979 to 1985 was five—one Extended Facility arrangement and four stand-by arrangements. Of these, three were cancelled due to non-compliance and accumulation of arrears.

An unusual feature of Sudan's IMF relations is the fact that Sudan was almost always expected to conceive and implement an austerity program on its own, prior to receiving funding from the IMF. Even Zaire was not always expected to do this. In the case of Jamaica, the IMF accepted mere pledges to reform from the Manley administration in 1977. This anomaly clearly deserves further investigation.

To be more specific on the IMF agreements with Sudan, the first and most significant loan can in 1979 in the form of a three-year, $260 million Extended Facility arrangement. The terms were based on a June 1978 reform program which included a variety of policies aimed at promoting exports (20 percent currency devaluation in particular) and financial stabilization (removal of certain subsidies, cap on domestic credit and cessation of on-going development projects). (Haggard 1984, 24; El-Khouri 1978, 269) The Fund allowed a concession to Sudan: establishment of a preferential exchange rate for Sudanese workers overseas to encourage wage remittances. The signing of a letter of intent paved the way for a rescheduling of roughly $500 million of Sudan's debt that was guaranteed by OECD nations (organized ad-hoc in the "Paris Club"). (Nelson 1982, 190)

Implementation of the first IMF loan was successful, in that the GNP began to grow, reversing a previous pattern, and the public sector deficit declined. (*IMF Survey* 1982, 68) This relative success came at great political cost, however, in that riots ensued following the removal of price subsidies (This pressure prompted Nimeiri to reinstate the subsidies). (*Africa Contemporary Record* 1982, 96) In response to Nimeiri's good faith efforts, the Fund expanded the total resources available to Sudan via the EFF in November, 1980 to $455 million, or 400 percent of Sudan's quota.

From 1981 on, however, the Nimeiri regime was unable to satisfy the terms of its IMF loans and remain in power. By mid-1980, economic performance had already begun to slip, especially in the area of the fiscal deficit. The EFF was "effectively cancelled" in late-1981 (Haggard 1984, 26), and in October the IMF laid down for Nimeiri a set of minimal standards of economic performance as prerequisites to obtaining further assistance. (*Africa Contemporary Record* 1982, 103)

Nimeiri announced an 18-point austery plan in early 1982, which included devaluation of the pound, gradual removal of food subsidies and new taxes on imports. The IMF provided $225 million in February 1982 to support a one-year stand-by agreement. (Zulu 1985, 5) Nimeiri implemented his program with abruptness rather than tact, and was met with more riots in the streets.

The government did not keep up its payments of interest on previous loans, even though it did pay $440 million back to the IMF. In September, the 1982 agreement was cancelled, although only seven months old. In 1983 and 1984, the Sudanese government concluded several agreements, each of which provided roughly $100 million. Sudan attempted to make at least token payments on its debt and was able to restore good relations with the Paris Club. By the end of 1984, Sudan's total foreign debt exceeded its GNP and its debt service was more than double the value of its export earnings. (*Africa Report* 1984, 57) In spite of the precariousness of the situation, Sudan seemed to have begun a new phase in its relations with its creditors. The United States provided $25 million to cover Sudan's debts in June 1984 and oil was being produced in Southern Sudan.

In late 1984, however, civil war in the South erupted and cut off oil flows, leaving the government with no viable means of obtaining hard currency. The Nimeiri regime fell even more hopelessly into arrears (it owed $110 million to the IMF alone) and was cut off entirely from foreign capital. In a last effort to persuade foreign creditors, from the Paris Club to the Fund, to restore funding, Nimeiri carried out another major devaluation, froze all hard currency accounts in Sudan and completely removed all price subsidies. (*Africa Research Bulletin* 1984, 7607) The results were yet again violent protests which this time resulted in a military coup and Nimeiri's ouster. Roughly one year later, in late 1986, Sudan's arrears totalled $250 million and its foreign debt had swelled to $10 billion. Sudan had become a case study in economic collapse.

Analysis of Actions of Actors Involved

In the case of Sudan's relationship with the IMF, the principal players were, as usual, the IMF and the Nimeiri government. In addition, because it worked in consort with the IMF, the Paris Club will also be considered a primary actor. Secondary actors included the collective opposition to Nimeiri in Sudan (ranging from professional and labor groups to unorganized students crowds), the Moslem Brotherhood, and the Reagan Administration of the United States.

Primary Players

Nimeiri. By the time Nimeiri went to the IMF, his political power base was relatively weak. Many of his actions encountered stiff resistance, as will be seen later. Additionally, he was pulled toward an Islamic fundamentalist governing style by the Moslem Brotherhood which significantly increased resistance to his rule by Christian groups. In the end, when he had also to satisfy the demands of the IMF, Nimeiri was in an untenable position. It is also clear from reviewing the history that Nimeiri himself was aware of the risks he faced.

In June 1978, before the first request for IMF and Paris Club assistance, the Nimeiri regime instituted major reforms. The government made a commitment to open Sudanese markets and promote exports (El-Khouri 1978, 269) in order to repay mounting arrears with foreign creditors. (Haggard 1984, 24) Nimeiri carried out a large devaluation, the first of many, and a partial removal of price subsidies, particularly on fuel, both of which had a negative effect on inflation control.

These actions had the desired effect. The IMF came forward with a large loan package. The loan itself was worth roughly three times Sudan's quota—certainly a generous amount by any measure—and the conditions were not particularly stringent (considering they merely built on the reform programs that had already been implementerd. One could say that Nimeiri had successfully prepared for negotiations with the Fund up to this point. It would be difficult to call the interaction up to this point a true "negotiation," however, since there was very little compromise involved. The Nimeiri regime simply did what it expected the IMF would have told it to do—and it guessed correctly.

The first year's experience with the extended fund arrangement yielded very small fruit, but fruit nonetheless. The Fund conceded that "progress was achieved in several important areas during the first year of the program. . ." (IMF 1980) More specifically, the GDP turned around and showed positive growth after two years of decline, and the public sector deficit declined slightly. (*IMF Survey* 1982, 68) This good faith effort was enough to win a major concession from the Fund in 1980. In November, the Fund agreed to expand the resources to be made available to $455 million, or four times Sudan's quota. This put the country among the top borrowers from the Fund in Africa, ranking only behind Egypt. The only additions included in the 1980 program relative to the 1979 programs were: "the authorities have introduced additional incentives to encourage the production of cotton. The exchange system has been further reformed, and credit expansion is being limited. . ." (IMF 1980)

During the next year, Nimeiri increased the severity of his governing style, jailing striking workers and adopting the Islamic sharía law system to placate the growing Moslem Brotherhood. His "popularity" was clearly at an all-time low (see later sections). Additionally, the government had failed to produce the results expected by the IMF. In spite of the fact that some of Nimeiri's difficulties were unavoidable for reasons of drought and the second oil crisis, the IMF cancelled the large EFF on the immediate grounds that Sudan was too far in arrears on its Paris Club debt payments. (Haggard 1984, 26)

Nimeiri, out of "desperation" rather than as "a calculated gamble to restore the fading fortunes of the government," as put by a *Guardian* editorial, announced an eighteen point plan for economic adjustment. Included in the plan were the traditional devaluation and removal of subsidies, as well as a new tax on imports of ten percent and an oil tax of forty percent. Specifically, Nimeiri announced his intention to gradually phase-out the subsidies on wheat (flour), cooking oil and sugar. The new value of the pound was listed at US$1.11 and the dual exchange rate was unified. Some free-market exchange trading was still allowed, however. It is interesting to note that government military expenditures were not specifically targeted, although it was clear to Sudanese scholars that they were excessive.

Nimeiri continued to implement the conditions of the stand-by through late-1981 and early-1982. In December, rather than phasing out sugar subsidies as promised, the subsidies were "abruptly" removed and the retail price of sugar soared 62 percent. Petrol prices were increased by 30 to 40 percent and petrol was rationed at the rate of five gallons for three days. Lack of petrol impeded the sorghum harvest. (Haggard 1984, 55) His cabinet reassembled (with largely the same individuals), he dismissed twenty-two senior military officers to preempt a coup in January. Student riots erupted in Khartoum in response to the removal of subsidies, and the violence left 45 dead.

The Nimeiri regime appears at this stage to have very little room for maneuver. The government's support in Sudan was too fragile to sustain a comprehensive austerity program, unlike Turkey, India or Argentina under Ozal, Gandhi and Alfonsín, respectively. On the other hand, the IMF required nothing less than dutiful implementation of its rather strict conditionality for Sudan to retain even minimal access to IMF funding. The Nimeiri regime was forced to deal with the IMF because of its large foreign debt ($4 billion in 1982) and its inability to generate foreign exchange earnings through trade and investment (unlike Argentina in 1984 which still had sizeable foreign exchange reserves). Sudan did not even have the strategic location or resources of Zaire or Britain, and could therefore not expect special concession from the Western powers on purely political grounds. In terms of its bargaining assets, the Nimeiri regime had none. It is therefore not surprising that his administration and his relationship with the Fund ended in collapse.

The 1981 stand-by lasted roughly one year, but was cancelled before nearly two-thirds of the loan was even disbursed. Sudan paid back to the Fund in 1982 nearly as much as it had withdrawn. (Zulu 1985, 5–6) Part of the reason for the IMF cancellation was the discovery by the Paris Club that Sudan's total foreign debt was not $5.2 billion as expected, but nearly $8 billion.

It is difficult to fault the Nimeiri regime for not putting forth a sincere effort to adjust Sudan's economy. As put by Mohammed Hashim Awad:

> the Sudan is known to have gone much farther than most countries in implementing the Fund's measures. Yet, as most independent observers state, the internal and external balance, or rather imbalance, has increased instead of shrinking. . . . (*Sudanow* 1982, 21)

In 1985, Sudan's currency, once valued at three dollars, was worth roughly 70 cents. Its total foreign debt, estimated at $2 billion in 1978, was listed at $10 billion in 1986. The debt service ratio climbed from less than twenty percent in 1978 to over two hundred percent in 1985. Clearly, there was little evidence that austerity, in and of itself, was not bringing about the results that had been anticipated.

While the Nimeiri regime only went part-way with the Fund regarding devaluation in its final agreement with the Fund, (the IMF had again pressed for a float), (*Wall Street Journal* 1985, 36) it went all of the way in the removal of food and petrol subsidies, as it had in the past. And again, as in the past, the prices of these essentials shot up, by 60 to 75 percent on petrol and 33 percent on bread and sugar. Again, students rioted in the streets and were joined eventually by professionals and physicians. In this case, after leaving the country, Nimeiri was unable to return and was overthrown by a military junta. Given the deterioration of Sudan's economy and political life since 1986, it is difficult to see a way out for a nation that went from "breadbasket" to "basket case" in such a short time.

The IMF. For some of the cases that will be included in this study, it will be possible to identify with precision and document the internal dynamics of the IMF staff-Managing Director relations, Managing Director-Executive Board relations, etc . . . In the case of Sudan, however, there is very little material (either published, unpublished or oral) that describes these internal dynamics. Much can be inferred, however, from the behavior of the Fund staff and Executive Board that is known.

As was discussed in chapter two, the Fund only recently went into Africa in a significant way. Its lending had been limited prior to the 1980s for reasons of the low creditworthiness of nearly all African economies. However, perhaps in part because of the personal predelictions of the Managing Director, DeLarosière, in part because of the pressures of the NIEO, and in part because of the absence of private credit, the IMF became a major lender in Africa in the 1980s. The inability of the IMF to pull Africa out of economic dependency has been one of its most serious failures to date, and has led it to create special lending facilities. (Zulu 1985; *South* 1985, 35) The experience with Sudan represents a more extreme case of the failings of IMF lending in Africa.

A three-year extended fund arrangement finalized with the IMF on May 4, 1979 consisted of the same policies as proposed by Nimeiri himself in June of 1978, with the exception of the value of the pound, which was further lowered to US$2.00 in March. In addition, a preferential exchange rate was established for the benefit of Sudanese working abroad in order to encourage remittances. This preferential exchange rate was especially low, which allowed Sudanese working abroad to earn more in Sudanese currency equivalent—as long as they repatriated the earnings. The other principal difference between the programs was the $260 million that accompanied the agreement. The IMF disbursed $39 million by the end of 1979, which of course represented only a fraction of the total needs of the country. In spite of the slow disbursal, one could say that the 1979 EFF was quite generous, providing as it did nearly three times Sudan's quota. (Haggard 1984, 26)

Sudan made additional drawings from the the Fund, including a drawing of $46.5 million from the compensatory financing facility in November 1979 (IMF 1979) and a first tranche regular drawing of $22.3 million in September. Total borrowing from the Fund by Sudan at the end of 1979 was listed at $152.8 million, or 174 percent of quota. (Zulu 1985, 5–6) However, Sudan did not keep up on its repayments to either the IMF or the Paris Club creditors in the late-1970s, and it has never able to regain a viable position. Sudan's arrears hovered near $200 million. (*Economist* 1982, 55)

The economic performance of the country did not improve during 1981. As described by the IMF:

> During . . . 1979/80 and 1980/81, performance proved to be below the objectives (of the EFF) . . . the production of cotton fell to the lowest level in twenty five years, the balance of payments remained under severe pressure, and, after some initial improvement, the public sector deficit as a percentage of GDP widened. (*IMF Survey* 1982, 68)

It appears that in October 1981, the IMF team laid down its minimum acceptable program and told Nimeiri to begin implementing it. (*Africa Contemporary Record* 1981, 103) The IMF finally agreed "after months of haggling," to a one-year stand-by (more cautious than a three-year commitment) of $225.75 million on February 21, of which the first payment could be drawn in April. This was an unusual clause in that most stand-bys provided for immediate disbursement of significant portion of the loan. (Zulu 1985, 5, *Economist* 1982a, 55, 1982b, 57) The process of laying down minimal performance standards is perhaps not so unorthodox, but merely a measure of how passive the Sudanese government had been rendered. This decision-making process is clearly consistent with a functionalist model.

Relations with the IMF soured in 1982 as demand for imports remained high and exports sagged in spite of the devaluations, resulting in a continuing increase in the balance of payments deficit. Local economists were quick to point out that since imports were made up in large part of essential fuels and foodstuffs, demand was highly inelastic relative to price. Also, cotton failures were due to poor agricultural techniques, labor shortages and the poor transportation resulting from fuel rationing.

With the collapse of yet another arrangement with the Fund, Sudan again went through the process of proving itself worthy of Fund assistance by announcing a currency devaluation in November 1982 and the withdrawal of subsidies it had failed to remove earlier. Sudan devalued the pound, but stopped short of allowing an unrestrained float, which the IMF had demanded. In a rare concession, the IMF proceded with the 1982 stand-by anyway. (*Africa Contemporary Record* 1983, 86–88)

The new stand-by amounted to $150 million and lasted one year. For the first time, Sudan was able to placate the Fund for the duration, and even scored some respectable marks in the area of repayment of arrears: "repayment of obligations to Club of Paris and commercial bank creditors have been met—although at a total of $50 million, they represent no more than a gesture of intent." (*Africa Contemporary Record* 1984, 68)

The question of Sudan's arrears was clearly one of the dominant concerns of the IMF, since it was at least a major factor in the decision to cancel the 1979, 1981 and 1982 accords. This can be explained in part from the fact that Sudan owed much of its debt to public creditors, rather than private banks (as was the case in Jamaica, for example). Because these public creditors are represented directly on the Fund's Executive Board, it is easy to imagine that their short-term interests would express themselves more clearly in IMF decisions. There is little empirical evidence of Executive Board machination, but based on the general observations made during interviews with Fund staff, the potential for direct interference by the Board is clearly high (see chapter 2). The attitudes of these creditor nations was doubtless mirrored by the IMF staff, given the fact that Sudan had also fallen in arrears to the IMF itself—a cardinal sin which has been punished with threats of expulsion (see the case of Peru in 1987).

From January 1983 to June 1984, Sudan signed three letters of intent, and it is unclear exactly what became of each of the programs. It can be presumed that some were cancelled while other were expanded. Suffice it to say that Sudan seemed to be dancing the debt game adroitly in 1983. Each of the agreements were for small amounts (between $90 million and $150 million) and for short durations, indicating the great caution with which the Fund viewed its African client.

As the civil war heated up in 1984, the Nimeiri regime became unable to protect foreign investments and personnel. In this context, U.S. support waned rapidly, as did the IMF's. In September and December 1984, both laid down ultimata to the Nimeiri regime. The United States froze $194 million in economic and military aid to Khartoum until it complies with IMF conditions. "Meanwhile, the Executive Board of the IMF is understood to have rubber-stamped the de facto suspension of Sudan's 1984-5 standby arrangement, and its reactivation still looks a long way off," as one Western journalist put it in February 1985. He was describing the extent of the Board's actions regarding the Fund's ultimatum to Sudan in late 1984. (*Africa Research Bulletin* 1983, 7607) The IMF laid down a demand for a further 48 percent devaluation and repayment of part of the $110 million is arrears owed the Fund as conditions for the resumption of the June 1984 stand-by that had been frozen in September. In addition, the Fund demanded that the pound be left to float in the case of foreign exchanges, and that there be a general crackdown on foreign exchange flight.

An IMF team was in Khartoum as late as March 26, 1985, "negotiating" with the Nimeiri government at the time. In fact, according to the account, the Fund was not really "negotiating" with Sudan, since the Articles of Agreement forbid interaction with a country in arrears. Instead, the team was simply determining whether the regime had "come to grips" with the problem. (*Washington Post* 1985, A23)

In chapter two, it was found that the IMF's dealings with Africa suffered from several institutional weaknesses. First, the IMF had very little experience with chronic, agrarian debtor nations. The problems of crop vulnerability to weather and price fluctuations, low price elasticity of demand for imports, and high levels of political instability—all common to many African debtors—were all quite novel to the Fund. The Research Department of the Fund had spent some time administering the Compensatory Financing Facility, but its knowledge had not spread throughout the institution (Note the scarcity of articles on the subject in *Staff* Papers). Certainly ETR and the Treasurer's Departments had not incorporated these factors into their routine calculations as of 1980. (Assetto 1988)

Second, the institutional advocates for debtor nations—the area department staff—were less prepared to press a strong case. Based on interviews with Fund staff, it was found that the African department was one of the least attractive assignments for upwardly mobile IMF professionals. Because Fund staff have a certain amount of flexibility in selecting their posts, the Africa deparment tended to be staffed by the less ambitious—although highly qualified—IMF personnel. While difficult to demonstrate, many in the Fund have concluded that this bureaucratic quirk resulted in a more tentative role for the Africa department when negotiations among Fund staff took place. In the absence of a strong, assertive government (as in Zaire), such tentativeness would naturally result in the dominance of the more rigid elements of the Fund—ETR and the Treasurer's department. The net result was a strict appication of the IMF's monetarist models to African debtors, without significant consideration to the unique circumstances that made many of these principles counterproductive. Several staff members agreed with this general notion, although they were not permitted to say whether this pertained to Sudan specifically.

Finally, Sudan's representation in the IMF was (and is) very weak. Not only is Sudan's representation diluted amoung a large number of other African nations, but Sudanese nationals have few personal ties to IMF staff (as opposed to Indian officials). There were no Sudanese on the staff of the IMF—and very few Africans aware of the problems of Sudan first-hand. Compared to a country such as Argentina or the United Kingdom, Sudan was essentially disenfranchised.

The net result of these and other forces was a fairly rough treatment of Sudan and a rigid application of conditionality. This is important in relation to the three decision-making models. It would appear that the functionalist model applies quite well. However, this is only because the Nimeiri regime has none of the typical bargaining chips to exert a greater influence over the process.

The Paris Club. Because much of Sudan's foreign debt was guaranteed by industrialized nations, the Paris Club became heavily involved in Sudan's debt crisis from the start.

The 1979 EFF arrangement with IMF led led the way to the first of many Paris Club reschedulings of $400–500 million in debts guaranteed by Western export credit agencies in November 1979. (Nelson 1982, 190) By late 1981, however, additional credit was unavailable. (Haggard 1985, 26) The Paris Club waited until Nimeiri had undertaken new adjustment programs and signed a letter of intent with the IMF before providing additional funding. Even the World Bank cut off loans to Sudan because of arrears. (*Africa Contemporary Record* 1982, 103)

As the reader will recall, a new, one-year stand-by was signed in 1982. In addition to providing limited resources directly to Sudan, the new program was respected by the Paris Club and other, private creditors. They agreed to reschedule $100 million in interest (payable in three years) and $400 million in principal (due in seven years). In private, however, bankers recognize that "no manufacturer in his right mind is prepared to do business with Sudan on a credit basis anymore." (*The Economist* 1982, 55)

When Sudan's debt total was recalculated at $8 billion, a banker and government consortium was formed in early 1983, the "Consultative Group for Sudan," and was given the task of coordinating creditor strategy. Sudan had drawn only $79 million of the total stand-by of $226 million. In 1982, Sudan had paid roughly $40 million back to the Fund. (Zulu 1985, 5–6)

After that agreement failed, yet another attempt was made by Sudan to implement an austerity package. Most important, as it would appear, was Sudan's repayment of some of its arrears. The Paris Club agreed to yet another rescheduling in January 1984 and a new stand-by was finalized.

As Sudan's circumstances took another turn for the worse in 1985, many of its creditors were pulling out. Even Saudi Arabia demanded repayment of arrears as a condition for further disbursement of its budgeted loans. The Khartoum government responded by closing down currency shops in February 1985 and freezing all hard currency accounts a few days later. As part of the final collapse of the Nimeiri regime, the IMF, the United States, and other creditors declared Sudan ineligible for further loans pending yet another adjustment program and arrears payment schedule.

It is clear that both IMF and the Paris Club worked in consort throughout the period under consideration. One could just as easily say that the IMF and the Paris Club were sychronized in their approach to Sudan. This differs from the case of Argentina, for example, where the banks clearly hoped to extricate themselves from the relationship while the Fund pulled them into deeper commitments. Likewise, in the case of Zaire, the United States in particular seems to have shown a greater tolerance for Mobutu's behavior than either the Paris Club or the Fund. In the case of Sudan, there is no apparant tension between the two institutions. The Paris Club and the Fund are both, simultaneously preoccupied with Sudan's arrears on its interest payments and both sought to use the other to exert pressure on Sudan.

Part of the reason for this may be that Sudan had the unfortunate problem of getting behind to all of its creditors. Peru under Alain García, for example, was careful to stay current with the InterAmerican Development Bank and the World Bank, while falling behind with the Fund, and Argentina under Alfonsín made a point to make token payments from its plentiful reserves at least every quarter. The result was that neither of these nations was ever completely denied credit. Sudan, on the other hand, was delinquent on all of its accounts, and for this reason, in part, received very similar treatment.

Another possible explanation for this is the politicized nature of the Paris Club and the Fund. As mentioned earlier, the major creditor nations of the Paris Club are the dominant actors on the Fund. Although there is no direct evidence of interference with staff policies on the part of the Executive Board (if anything, there is evidence of its passivity), the staff may have felt pressure to press hard on Sudan to force it to remain current on its debt payments. In this sense, it is possible that the Fund played the part of "debt collector" for the Paris Club. Note that this conclusion is not supported by the outcomes of IMF policies. Sudan's debt increased, its debt ratio mushroomed, its arrears grew, and it ultimately became more of a threat to political stability in the Horn of Africa. After Nimeiri's fall, the generals who replaced him established warmer ties with Quaddafi's Lybia and failed to resolve the civil war in the South, which dramatically increased hunger and famine for thousands of refugees and peasants. It is possible that in the case of Sudan, both the IMF and the Paris Club were guilty of remarkable short-sightedness, and so a "bad" outcome may not have been intended. It does tend to make one question whether Sudan was the victim of a Western conspiracy, since the West is perhaps the primary loser in the end.

Secondary Players

Although Sudan did not have an open democratic form of government, there were several major opposition movements during the Nimeiri regime. In particular, the Moslem Brotherhood, a fundamentalist group, pushed Nimeiri toward religiously-based policies similar to Iran's. Also, there were a variety of labor unions and student groups that were mobilized by specific policies of the Nimeiri regime.

The Moslem Brotherhood. In the regional politics of Sudan, the Northern peoples were generally Moslem, of Arab descent, and tended to be more powerful. In the South, Black African Christians were dominant, although they were relatively disenfranchised with regard to national policy. As Nimeiri's support dwindled in the South, he sought out support from radical groups in the North to strengthen his hand.

The Moslem Brotherhood was growing in strength during the years following Khomeini's rise to power in Iran. By 1982 they were dominant in the newly created regional parliaments in the North. Their demands for the institution of sharía law multiplied in the following years until in 1984, in order to avoid a coup attempt, Nimeiri relented.

With its rather brutal punishments for civil and "religious" crimes alike, the sharía was applied to Moslem and Christian alike, although the government denied that Christians were being tried according to it. The Catholic minority and Southern political leadership were outraged, and nearly all of Sudan's moderate Arab and Western allies expressed outrage. The South, on the defensive, had little access to Nimeiri, although it was clear the Moslem Brotherhood in the National Assembly were behind the new order. Southern unrest broke into terrorist violence as the dreaded "anyanya" terrorist organization of the 1960s was reincarnated to form a more violent and radical alternative to the more conventional Sudanese People's Liberation Army.

The relevance of the Moslem Brotherhood to Nimeiri's relations with the IMF is simply that its efforts and pressure further undermined the viability of the Nimeiri regime, which in turn weakened its bargaining position relative to the Fund. The fact that the Moslem Brotherhood increased the regional polarization of Sudanese politics also had a direct bearing on instability in the South, which in turn affected foreign investment in that region.

General Sudanese Opposition. The groups that were most active in opposing Nimeiri were various student organizations (some of which were not "organizations" at all but merely spontaneous mobs), and various worker organizations.

Students protested each time subsidies were removed from basic foods and fuel. These demonstrations often spilled into riots, as in 1982 when 45 were killed. (*Economist* 1982, 55) In some cases, these spontaneous demonstrations included more than students, such as in 1978 when taxi and bus fares increased by roughly 60 percent following the removal of fuel subsidies (Haggard 1984, 25–26) and in 1985 when riots could not even be quelled by a reinstatement of subsidies.

The Nimeiri regime typically responded to these activities by either postponing or cancelling the subsidies in question. This happened in 1978, 1982 and 1985. (*Africa Contemporary Record* 1982, 96) However, whereas Manley of Jamaica was able to get concessions from the Fund because of political strife, Nimeiri either never asked for special consideration or was denied the privilege. Perhaps his government's status as a military dictatorship was a hindrance (Note the IMF's willingness to grant concessions to democracies such as Argentina, India and Jamaica to prevent political unrest).

Perhaps more serious in terms of its destabilizing effects were reactions by various trade unions to Nimeiri's efforts at austerity. In 1978, for example, Nimeiri postponed automatic wage increases for railway workers and some professionals. This was met with a general strike by railway workers that brought the country's transportation to a halt. This strike was augmented by walk-outs of physicians and bank workers. Later, in March 1981, 1,000 civil servants were mysteriously purged from the bureaucracy. This provoked a June 1981 strike of 8,000 railway workers.

In the first instance, rather than "stand tough" against the railway strikers, the government placated their demands with 33 percent wage increases. However, consistent with his generally more intransigent style of government after 1980, Nimeiri declared the 1981 strike illegal and brought in the army to operate the nation's rail system. The army proved incapable of performing the task. Nimeiri, rather than yielding to the rail workers' demands at this point, took the unprecedented step of banning the union itself, threatened to cut off public benefits of the striking workers (including their homes) and to hang the strike leaders for treason. (*Africa Contemporary Record* 1982, 94–95)

Without going into detail, it should be mentioned also that the Southern opposition was growing daily by 1983. Terrorist movements sprang up to complement (and in some cases replace) the more cautious Sudanese People's Liberation Army that had been fighting for Southern independence since the 1960s. It was these terrorist groups that ultimately chose foreign businessmen as their targets and brought to a halt oil exploration and extraction in the region. These events in turn precipitated the withdrawal of aid to Sudan from most Western creditors and the final collapse of the Nimeiri regime in April 1985. (Mawson 1984, 526)

This is not the place to ask whether Nimeiri could have handled the various opposition movements, or whether the political system itself was at fault. What is more important is that Nimeiri never came to grips with the political question of how one implements austerity in a nation that refuses to support it. In a few countries considered in this study, even democratic regimes have been able to set in motion austerity packages that resulted in significant hardship and sacrifice, without jeopardizing their political survival (See Argentina in 1985, India in 1981 and Jamaica in 1977). One would expect a military government to have an even easier time of it. Doubtless the sources of Sudanese resistance lies deep in the political culture and economic circumstances of the Sudanese people. Suffice it to say that Nimeiri clearly did not understand how to deal with this, except to leave the country to receive medical check-ups immediately after removing price subsidies! This political weakness on the part of Nimeiri clearly prevented him from implementing IMF conditionality and retaining power simultaneously.

United States. Although Nimeiri made a formal state visit to the United States in 1981, the direct influence of the government of the United States in Sudan's economic stabilization is not observable until the mid-1980s, a time when Nimeiri's power was already severly undercut. The United States provided $25 million in short-term loan to cover part of Sudan's private debts in June 1984. Because this took place within a year of the Reagan administration's air attacks on Tripoli, one can surmise that the loan was intended to shore up an unstable ally in an unstable region. (*South* 1985, 31–40)

If the United States was serious about sustaining Nimeiri, it committed a serious miscalculation in late-1984 when the United States froze $194 million in aid to Sudan in order to coerce it into compliance with IMF conditionality. (*South* 1985, 31–40) When Nimeiri left for the United States in April 1985, it was to describe the country's latest austerity package and request a renewal of American aid. However, the coup had already taken place.

In the case of the U.S. role in Sudan's IMF relationship, it appears that the United States either miscalculated the degree of deprivation Nimeiri could sustain, or valued repayment of arrears more than maintaining a loyal ally in the region. In either case, the United States ended by simply reinforcing IMF and Paris Club policy.

Conclusion

The experience of Sudan between 1978 and 1985 illustrates the extreme vulnerability of certain Third World nations in dealing with the Fund. While some of Sudan's problems were the fault of its own arguments, it is also clear that international circumstances and flaws within the IMF's logic itself conspired against the success of the country's adjustment.

Like many countries, Sudan's problems arose in the late 1970s after a period of enthusiastic expansion. Just as in the case of Zaire, some projects were more extravagant than prudent, although most of the projects made good economic sense. Unlike Zaire, Sudan's borrowing came primarily from official public sources. This made Sudan more vulnerable to changing political policies of new administrations in various countries. After the arrival of the Reagan, Thatcher and Kohl administrations, as well as growing economic conservatism in Saudi Arabia, Sudan was caught in the general contraction of aid from the West.

There is some disagreement among scholars over whether Sudan had an easy or a difficult experience with the Fund overall. Local officials naturally blame external factors in their failure to meet IMF conditions, while the Fund tends to blame administrative incompetence and political cowardice. Other observers argue that the IMF was especially lenient toward Sudan because of pressure from the United States and Saudi Arabia. This last view is valid only during the brief period from 1979 to 1983, when U.S. assistance to Sudan became dependent on Sudan's compliance with IMF conditions. However, neither the United States nor other Western nations ever came through with the type of aid package necessary to fully complement the small amount of assistance coming from the Fund. The Western nations contented themselves with a series of reschedulings which were themselves being dependent on Sudan's compliance with IMF conditions. But they only served to increase pressure on the government rather than to give it the breathing space it needed.

Most important, it seems that the policies advocated by the Fund were highly insensitive to the realities of Sudan's political system. As was mentioned at the beginning of this study, the subsidies on basic products that were the target of so much IMF effort were essential to the political stability of the regime. It should have become apparant after repeated attempts to remove them provoked increasingly severe responses from the urban masses, that these subsidies could not be removed without seriously threatening the regime itself. The IMF had other policy instruments at its disposal in dealing with the persistent problems of government debt and trade imbalance that were not used, such as limiting military expenditures, and it did not need to push so hard on this issue. A plausible explanation for this stubbornness on the part of Fund officials is the lack of expertise in Sudan to counter the proposals advanced by Fund teams. Sudan has for many years been suffering from a "brain drain" of top experts to better-paying jobs in Saudi Arabia and other Gulf Coast nations. This has left the government bereft of intellectual talent of the type needed to effectively debate IMF teams on their own terms.

It also seems that the persistent demands for devaluation on the part of the Fund were misguided. Devaluation, it was expected, would increase cotton exports and reduce sugar imports, however, these trade flows were tied not to prices but to non-monetary factors such as energy supply for production and inelasticity of demand for imports relative to prices. The IMF seems to have fallen prey to its own economic theories and world-view in demanding monetary solutions to Sudan's economic problems. Sudan's problems seem to have had little to do with the kinds of imbalances the IMF is accustomed to dealing with. The result of trying to implement these policies was a deterioration of political as well as economic conditions, as crowds increased in violence and the control of economic variables required more and more centralization of power. Even IMF officials themselves admit that "an institution designed to help countries overcome temporary economic imbalances was never going to resolve the long-term problems of Africa. . . ." (*South* 1985, 31)

How does the experience of Sudan relate to our overall bargaining model of IMF decision-making? It simply reveals that, in fact, when one country lacks any important bargaining chips, it loses badly. Sudan lacked crucial support from Western creditors, economic expertise, political stability and the political sophistication to effectively use what little resources it had in the first place. Perhaps Sudan would have fared better if it had kept up its payments of arrears more than it did. Perhaps Sudan could have stalled the Fund missions better than it did by failing to provide complete information, or by hiring a consulting firm, as did Zaire. Perhaps Sudan did not play up the foreign threat enough—perhaps Nimeiri should have invented a massive Soviet conspiracy in the South with the claim that the SPLA and Anyanya were Communist fronts in order to gain more support from the United States. When all is said and done, it is clear that not only did Sudan fail in its interaction with the IMF, but the IMF itself lost prestige and credibility in the process.

While Zaire might be considered a "success story" of debtor relations with the Fund, from the government's point of view, the case of Sudan illustrated the difficulties inherent in borrowing from a position of weakness. Nimeiri, following a relatively prosperous period in the early 1970s, over-extended his government with recycled oil money in order to expand agricultural production and industry. Unfortunately, the bottom fell out of the cotton market and Sudan's export earnings plummeted as its import requirements swelled. Destitute and desperate, Sudan approached the Fund in 1979, hoping that a newly announced austerity plan would increase its chances for a suitable package. It did, and the next two years were relatively easy ones for the Nimeiri regime.

However, the honeymoon ended in 1981 as Sudan failed to maintain complete compliance and was pressured into a new and far less generous stand-by. Over the next three years, Sudan would receive only token support from the Fund and the West in general, while it struggled to maintain solvency. With serious threats from elements within the government, urban mobs and public workers each time fiscal austerity was attempted, Nimeiri had little room to maneuver. Finally, in 1985, after an attempt to solidify support from radical Moslem elements backfired and a new round of austerity measures provoked unrest, Nimeiri essentially retired and was ousted in a coup. But the coup leaders were incapable of maintaining cordial relations with the Fund, and Sudan was declared ineligible to receive further loans in 1986.

This case is complex, and our models can only explain features of it with difficulty. To begin, the functionalist model would have correctly predicted the gradual tightening of conditions as Sudan's economy deteriorated, since more drastic measures would be required to correct the deteriorating situation. The Fund's suspension of programs in 1980 and 1983 is consistent with this economic reasoning. The fact that successive Fund programs were nearly identical attests to the application of the uniformity principle. All this leads one to believe that Fund policy was drafted by a process of cold, objective reasoning.

However, some events are not explained so neatly by the functionalist model. For example, in 1980 Sudan's extended fund arrangement was dramatically expanded, apparently as a reward for compliance. It is extremely rare that programs be thus expanded in mid-stream, although cancellations are rather common. It seems as though the original arrangement was drafted with the expectation that the government would not comply. Otherwise compliance would not provoke such exuberance and apparent gratitude. Our information on the transaction is obviously only partial, but it would appear that some rather "non-economic" factors were taken into account in the drafting of either the original 1979 or the expanded 1980 agreement.

The same reasoning applies to the suspension of the 1981 agreement in 1982. The grounds given were inability to pay arrears on Paris Club debts—a reasonable enough complaint—and the discovery that Sudan's total debt was far greater than originally estimated. This second cause is rather odd. If the staff underestimated Sudan's obedience, it would seem that Sudan's need for assistance was all the greater. If Sudan had agreed to limit the growth of its total debt to a certain proportion of its 1981 debt, then the discovery of the error should not have resulted in punishment of Sudan, since the original target would have been in error as well. In either case, suspension of the agreement does not appear justified. Perhaps the government had deliberately submitted falsified debt records—a difficult thing to do, considering the fact that every foreign debt is recorded in at least two countries. But even if this were the case, cessation of the program as punishment for deception hardly seems rational from an economic perspective. Clearly, processes outside of the economic realm were at work in this decision, although it is unclear exactly what these processes consisted of.

The political model explains the Fund's desire to maintain relations even with an unreliable and recalcitrant Sudan for strategic and economic reasons. Ten billion dollars in debts could hardly be ignored, although they were not of sufficient magnitude to provoke panic in the West. Sudan's strategic situation and pro-Western foreign policy placed it in good stead with creditors, and they responded well from 1979 to 1985. However, the collapse of the Nimeiri regime, coming on the heels of Fund-sponsored austerity, leaves questions regarding the degree of complicity between the Fund and Western powers. In fact, it appears that the Fund attacked those economic policies that were precisely the most threatening to Nimeiri's power. Granted, there were few reliable alternatives, given the state of Sudan's economic and political system, but it does seem that if political considerations were dominant, political factors would have figured into the Fund's cost/benefit analysis. It may be that the Fund merely miscalculated and did not want Nimeiri to fall. This argument does not take into account the Fund's extensive experience with Nimeiri, however, especially the 1981 near-collapse. May the Western powers have miscalculated? It does seem that the Reagan administration was pushing especially hard, perhaps on the grounds of faulty intelligence estimates of Nimeiri's power. Mistakes do happen, after all, and it is always difficult to determine, in retrospect, whether a particular chain of events was in fact predictable or not. It seems reasonable, however, to think that political policy-makers would attempt to err on the side of caution, however, and the argument that the Fund simply over-reached is not satisfying.

From the perspective of the bargaining model, new factors can be brought into that discussion that greatly elucidate the processes. First, the Fund has an interest in encouraging sound economic policies. It can be expected, then, that it would be willing to offer some "rewards" for compliance with its conditions. These rewards would come, in the case of Sudan and other countries, in the form of enlarged access to resources and the softening of conditions. This would explain the enlarged access in 1980. Likewise, the Fund seems to have punished the Sudanese for non-compliance and irresponsibility during the 1980s, rather than responding to progressively deteriorating economic problems. Logically, deteriorating economic circumstances should have inclined the Fund toward for increased, rather than restricted, access, since more resources would be needed to pay the arrears and purchase the imports, etc. The 1982–1984 experience resembles more a "dance of the debt game" than the thoughtful and systematic resolution of Sudan's financial difficulties.

Sudan's difficulties can be explained in part in terms of political tensions and restriction at home which naturally inhibited Nimeiri's ability to comply with the Fund's terms and stay in power. It can also be explained in terms of a lack of expertise in economics. The Fund's arguments notoriously dominate discussion in the poorest developing nations, and Sudan had been suffering from a brain drain during the 1970s. Just as Great Britain was strengthened by her ability to rebut the Fund's arguments, Sudan seems to have been weakened by its inability to overcome Fund suggestions.

Nimeiri did not use his position as strategic linchpin to Northern Africa and the Middle East as effectively as Mobutu, and this might have cost him some time and maneuvering room. Skill in negotiation seems to have been lacking in Nimeiri's administration. In addition, Sudan's heavy public, as opposed to private, indebtedness meant that it had few external advocates, outside the Fund/Paris Club clique. And finally, Nimeiri seems to have mastered the art of alienating the maximum number of constituents. Although he could have lifted price subsidies gradually or reduced wage increases over time, he chose more often than not, to make more rapid adjustments, which resulted in a maximum reaction from disaffected elements in society. Sudanese society was too resistant and the Sudanese military too ambivalent to allow such programs to stick. Nimeiri emerged from rounds of removal and restoration of subsidies weakened politically at home and abroad. His credibility was very low. All these factors account for Sudan's inability to maintain a productive relationship with the IMF. That many non-political and non-economic factors need to be included in the analysis to make it complete attests to the relevance of the bargaining model in the case of Sudan.

Bibliography

Adedeji, Adebayo. 1985. "Foreign Debt and Prospects for Growth in Africa During the 1980s." *The Journal of Modern African Studies* 23 (January): 53–74.

Africa Contemporary Record. 1982. "Sudan." New York: Africana Publications 13: B90–B106.

———. 1983. "Sudan." New York: Africana Publications 14: B70–B91.

———. 1984. "Sudan." New York: Africana Publications 15: B56–B71.

Africa Report. 1984. (Sept–Oct): 57.

Cunha, Antonio-Gabriel M. 1985. "Toward a New Deal," *Africa Report* (May–June): 21–24.

——— and Donnelly, Joanne. 1983. "Defusing Africa's Debt." *Africa Report* (Sept–Oct): 17–21.

DelaMaide, Darrell. 1984. *Debt Shock: The Full Story of the World Credit Crisis*. New York: Doubleday & Company.

Economist. 1982a. February 20: 55.

———. 1982b. August 21: 57.

El-Khouri, Samir. 1978. "Sudan Carries Out Broad Program of Reform, But Faces Further Problems in Medium Term." *IMF Survey* September 1: 267–269.

Haggard, Stephen. 1984. "The Politics of Stabilization: Lesson from the IMF's Extended Fund Facility." Paper Presented at the Annual Meetings of the American Political Science Association, Washington, D.C., September.

IMF Survey. 1980. March 8: 68.

———. 1982. March 10: 71.

Mawson, Andrew. 1984. "Southern Sudan: A Growing Conflict." *The World Today* December: 520–527.

Nelson, Howard D., ed. 1982. *Sudan: A Country Study* Washington, D.C.: U.S. Government Printing Office.

Oesterdiekhoff, Peter and Wohlmuth, Karl. 1983. "The 'Breadbasket' is Empty: The Options of Sudanese Development Policy." *Canadian Journal of African Studies* 17 (January): 35–67.

South. 1985. July: 24–25.

———. 1985. July: 31–40.

Sudanow. 1982. May: 21.

Wai, Dustan M. 1979. "Revolution, Rhetoric, and Reality in the Sudan." *The Journal of Modern African Studies* 17 (January): 71–93.

Wall Street Journal. 1985. February 20: 36.

Washington Post. 1985. March 28: A-23.

Zulu, Justin and Nsouli, Saleh. 1985. *Adjustment Programs in Africa: The Recent Experience.* Occasional Paper #34 Washington, D.C.: International Monetary Fund.

6

The Case of India: 1981

While displaying some similarities to the experience of Turkey, the case of Indian borrowing from the IMF is *sui generis*. Never before, and probably never again, did a nation draw such a large sum from the IMF. The Fund committed to providing $5.5 billion via the Fund's relatively new Extended Fund Faciliy. The conditions of the loan were uncharacteristically "soft." In the executive board, the U.S. Executive Director took the extremely rare action of registering an abstention as an expression of indignant protest for such institutional generosity. How did such an unusual set of events come about? What circumstances gave India the privilege of such a bargain?

Background of the Indian Loan

The period leading to the Indian loan request was rather turbulent, although the nation's economy prospered. Amid regional and religious conflict, the government carried out agricultural reforms and industrialization with the help of large loans from international lending institutions. In particular, India received the lion's share of the World Bank's International Development Association's loans. While the results in the agricultural realm were spectacular—even after the historic drought of 1979 India's granaries were still stocked with surpluses (*Economist* 1981a, 8,9)—industrialization progressed at a sluggish pace. The Indian economy grew at a fast six percent average rate during the 1960s and slowed only slightly in the following decade. Factory employment grew by an annual average of three percent in 1950–1965, and by nearly two percent in the next decade. (*Economist* 1981a, 16) This expansion was offset, however, by a nearly three percent average annual population growth.

The government of Indira Gandhi was criticized for many years as a source of bureaucratic corruption and inefficiency. Catherine Gwin noted that the Indian economic system was "rampant with corruption" during the 1960s and 1970s; this contributed in no small way to the poor productivity and growth of industry. (Gwin 1983, 513) Even in the late 1970s the average capital-output ratio was 6:1. (Gwin 1983, 515) Some impediments to industrialization included: (1) production licenses which were geared toward stopping bad projects rather than promoting good ones; (2) the Monopolies and Restrictive Practices Act—aimed at inhibiting the expansion of any firm reaching a certain size, regardless of the firm's productivity; and (3) import controls (in place since Nehru) to protect India's "infant industry." (*Economist* 1981a, 31) Prices of essential products were heavily subsidized, which encouraged both stagnation and inefficiency, while promoting the goal of equalizing the distribution of income in the country.

In addition to internal impediments to growth, the Indian government limited foreign participation in development to the provision of soft loans. Annual foreign direct investment did not increase over the decade of the 1970s, in major part due to legal limits. As put by B. Bhattacharya,

> [I]n the case of India, foreign capital has contributed only a minor proportion of domestic investment. In fact, in the seventies the net capital inflow from abroad became almost insignificant and in some years even negative, whereas the domestic savings rate increased steadily, from about five per cent in the early fifties to about 20 percent in the late seventies. (Bhattacharya 1984, 20) [1]

In part because of the success of the government's agricultural policy, India's balance of trade and balance of payments positions were relatively healthy during the 1970s. The current account balance showed a slight deficit during the early 1970s but went into surplus by 1976, in part with the help of a World Bank sponsored debt rescheduling and IMF urged stabilization in 1974. (Frankle 1978, 515-517; see Table 6.1)

Reserves of foreign exchange were extremely healthy throughout the period, averaging roughly six to nine months' imports. IMF staff point out that reserves increased more than five-fold from March 1975 to March 1979, reaching the equivalent of 10.5 months' imports. (*IMF Survey* 1981a, 374–5) Even the first oil shock was absorbed with relative ease. Although the domestic inflation rate rose three-fold in 1974 over 1973, from six to eighteen percent, it returned to pre-shock levels the next year. Not until the next oil shock did inflation exceed ten per cent. (*IMF Survey* 1981a, 374)

It was in part because of the healthy international position of the Indian economy that calls came for increased opening in the economy in the 1970s. The Gandhi administration resisted these initiatives. Eventually, for more than merely economic reasons, the government of Indira Gandhi's Congress Party was defeated at the polls in mid-1977 and

TABLE 6.1   Indian Foreign Exchange Transactions, 1972-1980 ($US billion)

Fiscal Year (4/1-3/31)	1972	1973	1974	1975	1976	1977	1978	1979	1980*
Trade Balance	--	--	--	-1.5	0.2	-0.7	-1.3	-3.2	-6.5
Exports	--	--	--	5.1	6.5	6.9	7.1	8.1	9.1
Imports	--	--	--	-6.7	-6.4	-7.7	-8.4	-11.2	-15.6
Oil Imports	--	--	--	-1.6	-1.8	-2.1	-2.2	-3.9	-7.3
Current Account Balance	-0.5	-0.9	-2.1	-0.6	1.4	1.2	0.8	-0.4	-3.3
Official Aid	0.9	1.5	2.2	2.5	2.1	1.4	1.4	1.8	3.4
IMF Transactions	--	0.2	0.5	0.3	-0.5	-0.5	-0.3	-0.2	1.1
Foreign Reserves	0.6	1.1	1.1	1.4	3.4	5.3	7.4	6.5	6.5

*Projected
Source: IMF Survey 1981a; The Economist 1981a.

replaced by a broad coalition under the banner of the Janata party. The Janata government, in power for three years, promoted economic liberalization while continuing the goals of agricultural development, self-sufficiency and income-redistribution of Gandhi government. Imports of essential industrial inputs were liberalized, while exports were deliberately promoted, in part to cope with the 1979 drought and the second oil shock. (Gwin and Veit 1985, 81)

Although the Janata regime was unable to prevent India's economy from deteriorating, it has been described as an effective and stable government. (Gupta 1979, 150) Due in part to divisiveness in the Janata coalition at the time, and adept political maneuvering by Indira Gandhi, the Congress party was returned to power in late 1979. Gandhi encountered several crises left unresolved by the short-lived Janata regime, (1) drought, resulting in lower food exports and severe energy shortages, (2) unrest in the oil-producing region of Assam, and (3) the second oil shock. These events combined to produce a twenty percent inflation rate in 1980, a sixteen percent decline in agricultural output, a drop in the current account from $800 million in March 1979 to minus $3,300 million in March 1981, and a decline in foreign reserves to only three months' worth of imports.

The drought, while clearly affecting agricultural output, had a very serious impact on all economic activity. Declines in hydro-electric power production had a negative impact on production in such basic industries as coal, steel and iron, with predictable results on other types of industrial production. Overall real growth fell by four and a half percent. (*IMF Survey* 1981b, 375)

However, rather than revert to the protectionist policies of the past, the Gandhi administration in 1980 opted for a policy of internationalizing the Indian economy, in part due to the momentum created by the Janata government. "Since 1980 . . . the government has chosen not to retrench but to adjust by taking measures to improve resources, foster investment, and maintain growth with the help of outside resources." (Gwin and Veit 1985, 82) In April 1980 imports were further liberalized and in July a new industrial program was announced which would include export promotion, partial removal of price subsidies and promotion of foreign investment in oil production. These policies were preceded by expansion of state control over the banking industry, perhaps in preparation for the massive foreign borrowing to come and to placate segments of the Congress Party opposed to liberalization. (Ram 1980b, 64)

The government's new program of adjustment and expansion was codified in the sixth five-year plan, which was overdue by one year when it appeared in late 1980. It covered the fiscal years 1980/81 to 1984/85. It included policies to liberalize foreign investment and trade, as well as projecting real growth of 5.2 percent for the GNP and an eventual decline of the balance of payments deficit. The plan provided for a dramatic increase in foreign borrowing: seven and a half billion dollars in external assistance or ten percent of the plan's requirements would be borrowed from a variety of foreign sources. One fifth of India's $6.25 billion in foreign exchange was earmarked for use by the government in meeting the rest of the plan's needs. (Ram 1981a, 44)

More important than this general acceptance of the need for foreign resources was the willingness of the government to increase private borrowing rather than rely solely on concessional aid from the IDA and other World Bank sources. This effort at diversifying creditors anticipated the IDA's reduction of funding to India following the accession of the People's Republic of China and U.S. lessening of its contributions. Not only were the prospects for concessional lending dim in 1980, but India's foreign debt position was healthy enough not to be jeopardized by increased borrowing from private sources. The World Bank estimated in 1981 that India's debt-service ratio was only 9.4 percent, which led many Western bankers to view India as "under borrowed." (Ram 1981b, 109)

In summary, then, the Indian economy suffered primarily from inefficiency rather than a lack of resources. After years of relative autarky, India was experiencing strong pressures from abroad and from many powerful groups within to liberalize and internationalize its economy. It is important to understand that India did not have a "debt crisis" to contend with when it approached the International Monetary Fund for the first time in 1980. This situation allowed India to explore many policy alternatives that are typically not feasible for debtor nations.

The Role of the IMF

As early as mid-1980 rumors began to surface in the Fund concerning a major loan to India. For example, in July, India's Finance Minister said that "India's balance of payments will enter an extremely difficult phase and that phase will not be temporary." (Ram 1980a; Patri 1980, 48) In another instance, a "senior Indian official" indicated the possibility of borrowing from the IMF's compensatory financing facility. With oil prices increasing to the point of absorbing 60 percent of India's export earnings, it was clear something had to be done. As early as August 11, 1980, India began drawing on the Fund's resources, borrowing SDR 266 million ($345 million, or 23.2 percent of quota) to compensate for the oil crisis. (*IMF Survey* 1980, 259) In addition, the Gandhi regime secured a $660 million loan from the IMF's Trust Fund and a two billion dollar nonconcessional loan from the Asian Development Bank. (Patri 1980, 49; Gwin 1983, 517)

In late-1980 India and the IMF began negotiations in earnest regarding a large drawing. Fund officials also worked closely with World Bank officials during the period. According to Catherine Gwin, Fund officials and Indian officials agreed on a considerable number of essential premises: (1) the root problem of India's economy was not circumstantial, but structural, with the implication that demand constraint ought not be a major element of any adjustment strategy (*IMF Survey* 1981b, 375), (2) domestic oil production needed to be dramatically expanded to reduce oil imports, and (3) India's difficulties were not out of proportion to the size of the Indian economy and its capacity to adjust. (Gwin 1983, 518–19) To illustrate India's capacity to adjust, note that in the very early stages of the negotiations, the government was able eliminate imports of two million tons of cement and major amounts of aluminium, steel and paper almost overnight, thereby cutting imports by over $1.5 billion. (Patri 1980, 49)

Sticking points in the negotiations also arose early on, in that India and the IMF differed on the timing and the specific policies to be used in reaching these goals. The Indian government was concerned about losing face by giving in too easily to the dictates of the Fund, while IMF officials worried that the upcoming adjustment would consist of empty promises with no authentic reforms. "The Fund, therefore, pressed the Indian government hard for specific commitments" and suggested that its five-year plan be broken down into annual goals, something the Indian government was reluctant to do. (Gwin 1983, 519) The negotiations stalemated. The Fund used its leverage of control over resources and suggested the advisability of a one year stand-by arrangement rather than a large scale, three year loan. The Indian government felt strongly that such a short-term arrangement would not be advisable, because it had projected balance of payments difficulties through 1984. In addition, it needed the enlarged funds that could come through an extended arrangement in order to make new investments in oil production.

In order to demonstrate the sincerity of its intentions, the government of India further liberalized industry in July 1981, months before the negotiations with the Fund had ended. It removed subsidies on many basic goods and allowed prices to rise to near-market levels. The result was a tripling of domestic prices of crude oil and major increases in fertilizer prices. Following other such demonstrations of good faith, the cumulative reforms undertaken by the Indian government prior to the signing of the IMF letter of intent combined to provide 90 percent of the resources required in the sixth Indian five-year economic plan. (Gwin 1983, 519) Thus, in the early stages of the negotiation the Indian government made a fairly significant concession in order to get access to a large-scale IMF package, rather than postpone reform and settle for a more modest loan.

Finally, on August 11, a letter of intent was signed by the Indian government and submitted by the Minister of Finance, Rawaswami Venkatarman, requesting $5.65 billion over a three-year period. In addition, the program committed the Indian government to carrying out all of the various liberalization policies outlined in the government's plan: prohibition of price subsidies on basic goods, export incentives, increased oil production to reduce oil imports, imposition of limited price controls to counteract the inflationary pressures of the removal of subsidies, a relatively high ceiling on domestic credit, deregulation of foreign investment in oil, banking and industry, and expansion of foreign borrowing. Most of these objectives were stated in rather broad terms without the explicit targets—a break with other IMF programs.

In addition to providing unprecedented levels of assistance, this program differed dramatically from other IMF programs because there were no provisions to restrict consumption. As mentioned earlier, the IMF staff felt that the Indian economy was not yet in a crisis, and therefore could easily remedy its problems with minor liberalization of its economy. There were no arrears on interest payments to foreign banks, no unsustainable budget or balance of payments deficits, and therefore no urgent need for austerity. When in July 1981 India took the initiative to implement the last of a series of major industrial and trade liberalization reforms, "the government not only avoided the appearance of submitting to Fund conditions, but it also took the teeth out of the arrangement it eventually submitted to the Fund." (Gwin, p. 520) Just as Turkey before had successfully negotiated the Fund's largest loan to that point in June 1980 by implementing most of the Fund's favored policies before completing the loan, India had discovered a way to render the Fund's "medicine" nearly powerless. In addition, not only had India implemented the Fund's most pressing goals, but by coming to the Fund early, it did not need to adjust in the traditional ways. Its exchange rate was realistic relative to the changing values of other major currencies, and its savings rate and reserve position were adequate.

The package was quickly approved by the Fund's senior staff and the Managing Director Jacques DeLarosière and passed on to the Executive Board in late September. The highly publicized program was a major topic of discussion at the annual meetings of the IMF and World Bank in the last week of September 1981. The most controversial dimensions of the package were its scale and its leniency. U.S. Treasury Secretary Donald Regan criticized the plan in his speech to the assembly, stressing that such a loan should come from private banks because of India's credit rating and the Fund's limited resources. (Nations 1981, 60) These points were echoed even by more sympathetic officials and would be brought up after the fact by opposition leaders in New Delhi. Both the IMF and the Indian government were quick to counter these criticisms, noting that the loan amounted to only 290 percent of India's quota, a small proportion by African and Latin American standards. Regan also criticized the loan plan on the grounds that not enough reform was expected of the Indian government in return for the funds. "We don't think the IMF should become another International Development Association—a soft loan window." (*Facts on File* 1981a, 712) The Interim Committee, an IMF policy advisory body of finance ministers and central bank presidents from developed and developing nations, endorsed this view of the Fund's role, as did the Managing Director in principle. Clearly, the concern went beyond the advisability of this particular loan and focused on the precedent this loan would set. The U.S. and most officials did not want to see the IMF become a lender of "first resort," but desired that it instead remain a safety net for the financial community.

The executive board discussions were more lively than usual when the Indian loan was discussed. The U.S. Executive Director Richard Erb argued that the loan was not needed and expressed concern over the plan's "lack of specificity." (Gwin 1983, 529) Indeed, many standard elements of Fund packages were not included, such as minimum performance criteria which, if breached, would trigger suspension of loan disbursement. Elaboration of such criteria was deferred until the end of the loan's first year. Not mentioned by Erb but also an unusual element of this loan was its intended use: the $5.65 billion was to go "to increase investment in such vital sectors as coal, oil, rail transportation, and agriculture." (Andersen 1982, 125) The IMF had never before funded oil exploration and production. In fact, given the requirement of the Articles of Agreement that the Fund provide money only for balance of payments adjustment, it is possible that the terms of this loan—due to their development orientation—violated at least the spirit of the Articles. This is certainly how the U.S. delegation assessed the situation.

Nonetheless, in spite of U.S. opposition, the SDR 5 billion ($5.65 billion) credit was approved by the Executive Board on November 9, 1981. The IMF planned to disburse the money over a three-year period, in increasing installments starting with $390 million through March 1983 and $780 from April to June 30, 1982. In the two following years, the Fund released $2.07 billion and $2.64 billion, respectively (Note that 46 percent of the total was held back until the third year—indicating a high degree of caution on the part of the Fund with this first-time borrower). Forty-eight percent of the loan came from internal IMF sources, and the rest was secured through international contributions under the umbrella of the General Agreement to Borrow, a program developed during the 1970s to enhance IMF lending capacity on a case-by-case basis through developed nation lending.

When the United States realized that it did not have enough support to block the transaction, the U.S. Executive Director abstained as a gesture of protest. (*Facts on File* 1981b, 389) It is very unusual for any executive board members to register votes because of its consensual decision-making process. To register an unfriendly vote is politically dangerous since it invites diplomatic rebuttal. As discussed in chapter two, no country wants to risk retaliation for opposing one country's loan in the form of that country's executive director opposing a loan in the future to the former country. (Eckhaus 1985) In practical terms, very few executive directors could dramatically alter Fund policy at the level of the Board meeting at any rate. Only a major, coordinated effort of major creditor nations could muster the votes required to block a loan.

The results of the IMF loan have been almost universally applauded. India recorded remarkable economic growth and adjustment in the three years following the signing of the letter of intent. To begin, India's inflation, which had reached 25 percent in 1980, declined to twelve percent in 1981, and further to seven percent in 1984, in part due to Fund-sponsored price controls. (Nations 1981, 61; Hardgrave 1985, 138) India never fell out of compliance with the agreement: "Thus far, all of the performance criteria established under the arrangement have been observed," noted the IMF after the crucial first-year test (IMF Press Release #82/30). India also stayed current on all of its debt repayments:

In October [1984] foreign exchange reserves reached a record $5.3 billion. In avoiding the 'debt trap', India, with a relatively low external debt and manageable debt service ratio, stands in sharp contrast to many nations of the Third World. (Hardgrave 1985, 138)

India's financial stability was further evidenced and in turn enhanced by the government's decision not to draw the portion of the IMF loan slated to be disbursed in the third year. By so doing, the government in fact drew only 54 percent of the total $5.65 billion agreed-upon, meaning of course that it would only have to repay that proportion. Although no economic analysis can afford to be too rosy, it is interesting to note that India was described as an economic "miracle" in 1985. (Gwin & Veit 1985)

Analysis of Interactions

Although the Indian loan is a relatively simple transaction compared to the complex relationship between the Fund and Zaire, several different actors became important players in the process nonetheless. In particular, the Gandhi regime, the IMF staff, the IMF Executive Board each played a major role in influencing the content of the conditionality of the loan. Additionally, the World Bank staff, the U.S. government, and various Indian opposition parties also had an indirect influence on the agreement.

Primary Actors

Gandhi Administration. As the leader of India at the time, Indira Gandhi was responsible for formulating the substance of both the 1980 sixth plan as well as the 1981 letter of intent to the Fund. Although the Gandhi governments of the past were associated with a strongly nationalist, quasi-autarchic economic program, it seems that by 1980 the Congress party and the Gandhi administration had changed their ideology. Factors accounting for the liberalization carried out by the newly reelected Gandhi administration include the fact of a severe balance of payments crisis in India and a heritage of liberalization begun under the preceding administration. Economists in the finance ministry seem also to have pressed for liberalization, given comments and quotes in the media. (Patri 1980; Ram 1980b)

The IMF and Indian economists at the time predicted that India's balance of payments deficit would not only persist, but would become chronic. (*IMF Survey* 1981b, 375; Gwin 1983, 519) The possibility of alleviating the balance of payments pressure through significant foreign borrowing was probably attractive to the Gandhi administration since this allowed it to forego a painful (and no doubt politically hazardous) austerity program. Finally, opposition to liberalization was rather small (although vigorous), in part because the principal opposition party (Janata) had itself set in motion the liberalization programs which Gandhi merely expanded.

All things considered, the IMF loan was a pragmatic choice on both political and economic grounds for the Gandhi administration. The fact that Gandhi was able to develop and implement much of the program prior to the signing of a letter of intent further strengthened the government's resolve and autonomy. From all indications, the Fund staff made very few changes in the sixth five-year plan, except to urge more rapid implementation than originally anticipated.

IMF Staff and Managing Director. The IMF had only recently created the Extended Fund Facility when the IMF loan request came. The original intent of this lending facility was to provide large-scale assistance to countries with chronic balance of payments difficulties. It resembles the structural adjustment loans of the World Bank, in that it was intended to provide not only large-scale assistance aimed at adjustment, but also to provide enough resources to allow the borrower to direct other resources to purely development purposes.

Because the Indian loan request was based on solid arguments presented by Indian economists and confirmed by Fund studies that the Indian economy would not cure itself, the negotiations commenced without hesitation by the Fund. The total amount of the Indian loan request was also consistent with IMF expectations, in that it amounted to only 290 percent of India's quota (at a time when countries like Sudan and Jamaica were borrowing up to 400 percent of quota). In this sense, the Indian loan was broadly consistent with the purposes of the EFF. The fact that some of the loan was intended for use in oil exploration and drilling was a departure from IMF tradition, however. The more fundamental issue is whether the EFF itself was a departure from the more strict IMF standby arrangement. It was for this reason (among others) that the Reagan administration expressed the concern that the Indian loan was overly generous.

A serious issue that was never resolved by Fund officials was the effect of the loan on general Fund liquidity. The loan represented roughly 30 percent of the Fund's total resources, and therefore greatly increased both the Fund's exposure and significantly reduced the resources left for other members. The fact that India repaid its loan faithfully allowed the Fund to continue operations without disruption. The danger of Indian default existed nonetheless.

Because the procedures and rules applied in the Indian case are so far removed from normal IMF experience, it is difficult to say that the Indian loan was merely "business as usual" for the Fund. The implication of this is that the functionalist model alone does not adequately explain the decision-making process in the Indian case.

IMF Executive Board. The executive board, as usual, was brought in at the last moment to approve the loan that had already been agreed to between the Fund and India. However, rather than merely "rubber stamping" the letter of intent, the board discussions were quite lively and pointed. As mentioned earlier, the U.S. delegation opposed the loan on the grounds that it departed too far from IMF customs, it was insufficiently precise in its elaboration of conditionality, and it unnecessarily exposed the IMF. These consideration were amplified by the fact that India was still credit-worthy and could have obtained large amounts of private credit for the asking. Other members of the Board pointed out the right of India to borrow from the Fund as long as it fulfilled the expectations of the staff (de Vries 1985). The staff also pointed out that for a nation to approach the Fund *prior* to the emergence of a debt crisis was actually a sensible policy, and that India's example should be encouraged.

It should be pointed out that the general attitude of industrialized nations in 1981 was still generally sympathetic to development lending and balance of payment assistance. The massive debt crisis and recession of 1982 had not yet taken place, and therefore the leaders of most industrialized were generally well-disposed toward multilateral international lending. One should recall that it was in part this spirit of generosity that led to the creation of the EFF in the first place.

The executive board ultimately played a relatively passive role, in spite of the vigor of the debate and its legal decision-making authority. There was the potential for significant influence.

Secondary Actors

The United States. The U.S. reaction, already described in the body of the text, was strong and obstructionist. What is most interesting about the U.S. role is that the Reagan administration did not respond to the IMF-India negotiations until they were complete and the letter of intent had been signed. Unlike other cases, such as the United Kingdom, Jamaica and Sudan, the United States waited until the critical decisions had been made before attempting to influence the outcome. It is possible that the Reagan administration was surprised by the Indian loan. It is certainly true that Third World economic conditions were not a priority for the incoming Reagan administration, but the fact that the negotiations lasted nearly a year makes this explanation unlikely. Also, the fact that the United States has a prominent role in both the IMF and the World Bank leads one to believe the Reagan administration likely knew many of the details of the program before it was formally submitted to the executive board. Finally, the attention that the Indian loan received at the ministerial level in the United States indicates that it had probably already been the focus of considerable sub-ministerial scrutiny.

It is possible that the United States felt confident it could persuade other creditor countries to oppose the Indian loan once it came before the Board, and therefore did not take the negotiations seriously. This explanation is borne out by the observation that the U.S. Executive Director was surprised at the lack of support in executive board meetings and chose the abstention option only when it was clear he could not alter the outcome of the vote. (Gwin 1983, 529; Andersen 1982, 125; *Facts on File* 1981b, 383) If this explanation is correct, then it illustrates the declining stature of the U.S. delegation in the Fund and the Bank— a development consistent with the larger theory of "hegemonic decline" (Gilpin 1987; Keohane 1984). Before concluding that the United States has lost its economic preeminence, however, one should recall the significant influence the U.S. has had in the many debt renegotiations since 1981. Perhaps it would be more plausible to conclude merely that the United States erred in overestimating its capacity to alter IMF decisions—a natural enough mistake for a new administration.

Indian Opposition. Opposition politicians and economists expressed concern that India was being pushed around by the Fund. Venkatachalam and Singh, two Indian economists, noted that "the conditionality imposed by the IMF on this loan have redirected the country toward free market philosophies. . ." (Venkatachalam & Singh 1982, 124) The opposition parties were almost all against the loan. The nationalist Bharatiya Janata Party's Paliamentary Board condemned Gandhi for 'unceremoniously' abandoning the objective of self-reliance. The communists charged the government with mortaging the Indian economy to the West." (Andersen 1982, 125) Parliamentary opposition groups threatened a motion of censure against Finance Minister Venkataraman and stormed out of the chambers at one point. (*Facts on File* 1981c, 897) [2]

The Gandhi administration was little influenced by these objections, countering each one in turn. Gandhi pointed out that the liberalization was ultimately a nationalist approach because it would benefit India directly. She favored pragmatism over dogmatism. (Andersen 1982, 124) To the criticism that the Fund was too intrusive and powerful, Gandhi retorted that the IMF had added nothing to India's previously adopted five-year plan. (Gwin 1983, 522) To the objection that Indian did not require foreign borrowing, Gandhi responded that foreign borrowing would make the inevitable adjustment process more tolerable and less expensive, given the relatively low interest rates charged on multilateral loans. (Gwin 1983, 523) Indian economist Mammen concluded that, on the basis of his studies, the IMF loan would be used productively by India and would not result in a long-term debt burden. (Mammen 1984)

Gandhi had established fairly firm control of the Congress Party by 1981, placing her son Rajiv in the General Secretary's post (Andersen 1982, 124), and had filled the cabinet with loyal ministers. The result was a strong resistance to motions of censure and a high degree of flexibility in policy formation. This in turn gave the Gandhi administration great strength in negotiating with the IMF. The immediate success of the reforms even more firmly established Gandhi's credibility with the mainstream opposition parties. Of course, this economic success was not directly helpful in settling the Punjab dispute which ultimately cost Indira Gandhi her life.

World Bank/IDA. An important institutional factor helps further account for India's success in its IMF negotiations. India had already carried on a long, successful relationship with the World Bank. India was becoming too wealthy to continue qualifying for IDA credits in the late-1970s, however. China's accession to the IDA put great pressure on the available resources of the World Bank system of institutions. India had traditionally borrowed very large proportions of the IDA's total resources (roughly 40 percent—leading some to call the IDA the "India Development Association"), but China would now be eligible to attract some of the funding previously ear-marked for India. In sum, India could no longer expect continued support from the IDA.

The sixth plan called for diversification of lending sources. In order to support the goal of diversification of public funding sources, the Fund would have to be involved. The World Bank staff worked closely with IMF officials, participating in the mission and acting as consultants to the IMF staff. Although Fund staff are extremely loyal to Fund principles, in a world where "confidence" is of the essence, it was certainly to India's benefit to have economists of high professional repute personally acquainted with participants on both sides of the table, confirming the credibility of the regime's intentions. Moreover, the Bank officials could provide friendly advice to Indian officials unfamiliar with procedures and rules of the Fund. While it is certainly difficult to document specific cases of Bank staff involvement, such a scenario is certainly plausible and helps to explain the outcome. In Gwin's words: "Given the kind of adjustment problems India faces, this contribution by the Bank was key." (Gwin 1983, 529) Finally, India was well-equipped with economic analysts, many of whom had extensive experience in the Fund and the Bank. One of the most persuasive arguments in the negotiations, it will be recalled, was not that India needed the resources for current needs, but that the three-year projections of financial crisis by Indian economists, later confirmed by Fund staff, demanded prompt action. One can scarcely imagine the same chain of events in Sudan or Zaire.

Conclusion

The Indian loan was a case of "pre-emptive reform" on the government's part. By carrying out many of the liberalization policies that normally make up a Fund program prior to completion of negotiations, India was able to take the "teeth" out of the IMF package. Because of a high quota, a new lending facility, and evidence of a need to prevent future shortfalls in the balance of payments, the Indian government was able to obtain a large disbursement of funds.

Does the functionalist model explain the process and outcome of the Indian loan? First, the active role of the Indian government in shaping conditionality undermines the functionalist predictions in the most significant way. Clearly the IMF neither initiated nor conceived the Indian adjustment program, although the Fund did accelerate India's implementation of the reform program.

On the other hand, the staff dominated the Executive Board in the final analysis, although the United States attempted to expand the Board's influence. In terms of the dominant players within the Fund, it is not possible, given the information available, to determine whether exchange and trade relations department and the managing director were dominant. One can only surmise that, because traditional lending terms were dramatically altered in the context of the Indian loan that either ETR was uninvolved or quiescent.

More troublesome is the question of whether the conditionality applied to the Indian loan was consistent with the economic circumstances of the country. Because India was in a very unique situation relative to other IMF borrowers, it is not surprising that its loan terms were unique as well. Ultimately, it is this uniqueness that leads one to conclude that, based on traditional IMF lending arrangements, the Indian loan is inconsistent with the monetarist model of the Fund. This is to say that, as the *Articles of Agreement* had been interpreted and applied over the Fund's history, the Indian case is an anomaly. This also points to the possibility that the Extended Fund Facility provisions were inconsistent themselves with Fund traditions. The fact that the EFF has never again been used as a large-scale development program since the Indian loan indicates that this possibility has been recognized and corrected. The U.S. reaction to the loan has also likely had a chilling effect on Fund staff.

In conclusion, then, the functionalist model is quite inadequate to explain the development in the case of India. The program was simply more innovative than usual and the role of the recipient government was far too assertive to be consistent with the functionalist model.

The political model would have been the most useful interpretation had the United States succeded in reversing the Fund's decision to lend to India—or even if the United States had managed to "tighten" the lending terms themselves. However, this did not transpire, and the result is a decision-making process that is inconsistent with the provisions of the political model. The fact that India was a non-aligned political actor was never raised as an issue—even by U.S. representatives—is inconsistent with the predictions of the political model. The fact that the executive board did not dominate decision-making likewise undermines this interpretation.

One dimension of the IMF loan to India that is somewhat consistent with the political model, however, is the fact that India had liberalized its economy prior to approaching the Fund. As would be expected, from the perspective of the political model, India received kind treatment. However, the IMF did not immediately commit to a large-scale loan. As will be recalled, the Fund attempted to persuade the Indian government to accept a one-year stand-by while implementing the provisions of its reform package. This prompted the Indian government to implement its reforms more quickly than it had originally hoped.

In conclusion, then, the political model does not completely explain the Indian loan, although its predictions regarding liberalization and leniency are borne out. This implies that the "liberal culture" of the IMF is a more significant force than the direct actions of major creditor nations acting on either political or economic logics.

The bargaining model identifies important features, such as the timing of the request, and the intellectual talent and persuasive ability of Indian and sympathetic World Bank economists. More significant, the active role of the Indian government is consistent with the bargaining model, as are the rather unorthodox outcomes this activity engendered. One can see rather clearly the contrary pressures of various actors, each attempting to manipulate the institution to their own ends. The Indian government wanted maximum support at minimal cost, the Fund wanted to press India into major economic liberalization and send a message to the larger community of nations (the message being: "It is better to come to the Fund *before* the crisis has erupted."), and the executive board was torn by the conflicting desires of the majority of major creditors to display tolerance and generosity on the one hand, and to be firm and fair on the other. The result was a unique and even unexpected chain of events leading to a novel outcome.

Notes

1. IMF studies indicate domestic savings peaked at 24 percent of GDP in 1978/79. See *IMF Survey* 1981b, 374.

2. Shortly after this outburst the Finance Minister was reappointed to head up the defense ministry. See Andersen 1982, 123.

Bibliography

Andersen, Walter K. 1982. "India in 1981: Stronger Political Authority and Social Tension." *Asian Survey* 22 (February): 119–135.

Bhatia, H.L. 1981. *Does Foreign Aid Help?* New Delhi: Allied Publishers.

Bhattacharya, B.B. 1984. *Public Expenditure, Inflation and Growth: A Macro-Economic Analysis for India.* New Delhi: Oxford University Press India.

Das Gupta, Jyotirindra. 1981. "India in 1980: Strong Center, Weak Authority." *Asian Survey* 81 (February): 147–161.

Deb, Kalipada. 1982. *Foreign Resources and Development in India.* New Delhi: Heritage Publishers.

"Derailment." 1981c. *The Economist* September 19, 1981: 85.

Eckhaus, Richard. 1985. "How the IMF Decides on its Conditionality." Paper Presented to the Annual Meetings of the International Studies Associations, Washington, D.C.

The Economist. 1981a. March 28: 7–47.

———. 1981b. August 1: 40.

Facts on File. 1981a. September 30: 712.

———. 1981b. November 30: 838–39.

———. 1981c. December 4: 897.

Frankle, Francine R. 1978. *India's Political Economy, 1947–1977: The Gradual Revolution.* Princeton, N.J.: Princeton University Press.

Gilpin, Robert. 1987. *The Political Economy of International Relations.* Princeton, N.J.: Princeton University Press.

Goldsmith, Raymond W. 1983a. *The Financial Development of India, 1860–1977.* New Haven, Conn.: Yale University Press.

———. 1983b. *The Financial Development of India, Japan, and the United States: A Trilateral Institutional, Statistical, and Analytical Comparison.* New Haven, Conn.: Yale University Press.

Gupta, Suraj B. 1979. *Monetary Planning for India.* New Delhi: Oxford University Press.

Gwin, Catherine. 1983. "Financing India's Structural Adjustment: The Role of the Fund." in John Williamson, ed. *IMF Conditionality.* Washington, D.C.: Institute for International Economics: 511–531.

——— and Veit, Lawrence A. 1985. "The Indian Miracle." 58 *Foreign Policy* (Spring): 79–98.

Hardgrave, Robert L., Jr. 1985. "India in 1984: Confrontation, Assassination, and Succession." 25 *Asian Survey* (February): 131–144.

Keohane, Robert. 1984. *After Hegemony: Cooperation and Discord in the World Political Economy.* Princeton, N.J.: Princeton University Press.

Mammen, Thumpy. 1984. "A Trade Gap Model and IMF Loan to India." 31 *The Indian Economic Journal* (January-March): 45–52.

Mukherjee, Pranab. 1984. *Beyond Survival: Emerging Dimensions of Indian Economy.* New Delhi: Vikas Publishing.

Nations, Richard. 1981. "Cowboys Attack Indians." *Far Eastern Economic Review* October 9: 60–61.

Patri, N. 1980. "India Turns to the IMF For Aid." *Far Eastern Economic Review* July 25: 48.

Ram, Mohan. 1980a. "Turning to the IMF for Aid." *Far Eastern Economic Review* April 18: 72.

———. 1980b. "Indira Mounts New Takeover." *Far Eastern Economic Review* May 9: 64.

———. 1981a. "New Delhi Banks on Aid." *Far Eastern Economic Review* February 13: 44.

———. 1981b. "Knocking at the Door." *Far Eastern Economic Review* October 16: 109–110.

Seiber, Marilyn. 1982. *International Borrowing by Developing Countries.* New York: Pergamon Press.

Venkatachalam, Viswanathan and Singh, Rajiva K. 1982. "The Political, Economic, and Labor Climate in India." 8 *Multinational Industrial Relations Series* Philadelphia, PA: Wharton School, University of Pennsylvania.

7

The Case of the
United Kingdom: 1975–1977

The case of Britain illustrates in vivid colors the capability of both the IMF and certain borrowers to bargain over terms of lending. Britain, as a hard currency country, had certain policy options unavailable to other debtors, such as the ability to attract foreign capital by increasing its interest rate. On the other hand, Britain attracted far more attention and was subjected to far more international pressure to adjust than other borrowers, given the significance of the pound to the international financial system. The Callaghan government made very careful use of its assets and attempted to nullify its liabilities throughout the negotiations with the Fund. The process and outcome bear detailed examination and explanation.

Background: The "British Disease"

Britain's economic collapse in the 1970s was of historic proportions. Britain's productivity declined relative to its European and Asian counterparts, the result being a decline in export volume. In 1962 over fifteen percent of the trade of the eleven top trading nations involved Britain. In 1974 the figure was down to less than nine percent. (de Vries 1985, 461) Britain's current account fell into deficit in 1973, dipped to a 1.5 billion pound deficit in 1973 and fell further to 3.4 billion pounds in 1974. (de Vries 1985, 463–4) Pressure on the pound led to a decision to float in 1972. From this point on the pound began to fall in value. After 1973 the British inflation rate rose from ten percent to over twenty percent in 1975.

Government policies at first involved manipulation of monetary policy in order to find an interest rate that stimulated both the economy and the pound. Failing that, it adopted more traditional Keynesian measures to stimulate employment. The increased government expenditures were financed in part through foreign borrowing and an infusion of OPEC deposits. (Crawford 1983, 425–6; Porteous 1976, 781) The Wilson administration attempted to reduce inflation with wage restraints and stimulate investment with tax incentives. Neither proved entirely successful, however, and in mid-1975 a brief run on the pound led the government to seek a short-term loan from the Fund. Britain was not alone in doing this (the Carter administration would later follow suit), and it was relatively easy for Wilson to obtain a $2 billion lower-tranche loan to stabilize the pound. (de Vries 1985, 464)

Britain and the IMF

Chancellor of the Exchequer Denis Healey signed a letter of intent with the IMF in December 1975 and thereby pledged to refrain from imposing import controls and reduce the public sector deficit that had built up since 1973. (*Economist* 1975, 18, de Vries 1985, 465) The public sector borrowing requirement (PSBR or fiscal deficit) was to be reduced through increased revenue (28 percent in 1976 and 25.5 percent in 1977) and reduced spending. (*Economist* 1976a, 89) The executive board approved the program on recommendation of the staff in December 1976.

The Callaghan government did not have time to wait for the effects of the stand-by to make themselves felt. The continuing balance of payments decline required immediate action. However, the more radical members of the Cabinet, supported by large numbers of rank-and-file Labour party supporters, opposed the use of fiscal instruments to deal with the crisis on the grounds that this deprived the poor of essential government services. (McLellan 1976, 42) It was at this point that the Bank of England Governor, Gordon Richardson, and others orchestrated a gradual decline in the pound. (Fay & Young, 1978a, 34; de Vries 1985, 468) The strategy backfired, however, and in March the pound fell below two dollars. Attempts were made to shore up the collapsing pound. A total of roughly $4.6 billion from Britain's hard currency reserves was used to buy back pounds, leaving the country with only $5.4 billion in the coffers at the end of May. (Crawford 1983, 428; Porteous 1976, 761)

The United States then organized a short-term emergency loan of $5.3 billion from the Bank for International Settlements. However, the loan had a repayment deadline of December 1976—just six months' duration. American Treasury officials insisted that Britain be required to seek out IMF assistance if it failed to pay back the loan on time. (Fay & Young 1978a, 33) The result was a short reprieve for the Callaghan government during which it was forced to consider the possibility of IMF-imposed austerity.

Within the British Cabinet a crisis erupted between Tony Benn of the radical wing of the party and Denis Healey of the Exchequer regarding the advisability of austerity. It was only after nearly six months of difficult negotiations with the Fund that the Callaghan administration ultimately struck a compromise. Many unusual events took place during the negotiations, including obstructionism by British bureaucrats, vigorous debate on the matter at the annual Labour party conference, a visit to 10 Downing Street by IMF Managing Director Johannes Witteveen, and a collapse of the pound to under $1.50. More will be said about the details of the negotiation below.

The January 1977 IMF program provided roughly $3 billion over two years and required the government to reduce its PSBR by 3 billion pounds over two years and freeze government expenditures in order to reduce by fifty percent Britain's current account deficit and lower both unemployment and inflation. (*IMF Survey* 1977, 1–5)

The Bank for International Settlements provided an additional $3 billion days after the IMF loan was concluded. Britain abided by IMF conditionality for at least the year 1977, but in 1978 Britain unilaterally cancelled the loan and drew no more in 1978. (de Vries 1985, 476–7) By this point, Britain's current account was in surplus and the PSBR had actually fallen more than called for by the Fund. In 1979, the Executive Board issued a post-mortem of the package, praising it as "the most successful [adjustment program] ever implemented." (de Vries 1985, 477) One could further observe that this IMF experience may well have signalled the end of an era of British politics and the beginning of Thatcherism.

Analysis of the Players

Principal Actors

Prime Minister Callaghan. Prime Minister Callaghan was caught between the urgent need to adjust Britain's imbalanced international economic position and the desire to retain the support of all elements of the British Labour party. In the P.M.'s favor was the British tradition of collective responsibility which required of Cabinet ministers to either support the government's policy or tender their resignations. (Macintosh 1984, 62–74) Ultimately, Callaghan anticipated the support of the Cabinet once a final decision was made.

Callaghan allowed Denis Healey to dominate policy-making in the area of balance of payments adjustment. During the 1975 negotiations and the initial phase of the 1976 negotiations, Healey dominated. Callaghan, however, initiated negotiations directly with U.S. and West German financiers with the assistance of Anthony Crosland of the foreign ministry. His goal was to create a sterling "safety net" through the Bank for International Settlements whereby the pound could be replaced as a reserve currency by other hard currencies. (Fay & Young, 1978b, 23) Two year's experience with a falling pound had convinced the administration that it could no longer serve as a hard currency in the full sense. (Bray 1976, 583) Additionally, it was hoped that an emphasis on the purely monetary dimensions of Britain's balance of payments crisis could avoid the need for austerity.

By late November, however, it became apparant to Callaghan that the conditionality proposed by the IMF was unavoidable. On November 29, Callaghan conferred with German Chancellor Helmut Schmidt. At this occasion Schmidt affirmed his support of the IMF package, reversing a position taken in October when he implied that he would try to soften Fund terms. Callaghan realized he must adopt a pro-IMF view. Upon his return from the discussion, which had shaken his resistance, Callaghan was surprised to be met by Johannes Witteveen on December 1. Witteveen, unaware of the Schmidt meeting, was very bold with Callaghan and the ensuing discussion was quite acrimonious. Callaghan, although personally committed to a pro-IMF plan, argued that to impose the IMF terms would threaten the foundation of stable democracy in Britain, a claim that had been well-received in Washington and in Bonn in previous weeks. Witteveen responded that the credibility of the Fund and the stability of the international monetary system were also at stake, as well as Britain's financial survival. Callaghan finally conceded to the need to pare back the PSBR and otherwise accept IMF terms. Witteveen stayed on for the rest of the day until Callaghan accepted a set of modified conditions from Witteveen:

> That done, Witteveen offered his concessions: the Fund, he said, would be content with public spending cuts of 2.5 billion pounds, over two years, as long as the economy did not overheat, which, with the BP sale [of 500 million pounds worth of shares], was 25 percent lower than 4 billion, the sum Whittome's team had first thought of. Before this decisive accord, Healey had in fact prepared the final Treasury paper, also proposing 2.5 billion. After it, according to reports received in Washington, Witteveen and Callaghan shook hands on the bargain. (Fay & Young 1978c, 33)

All three of the principal chroniclers of the U.K. loan agree that this tête-à-tête was the principal turning point in the negotiations. (Crawford 1976, 431, de Vries 1985, 472) This colorful description illustrates the extent to which bargaining was a crucial part of this negotiation.

Callaghan made the Cabinet aware of his decision to side with Healey and the Fund. At this point, in the spirit of collective responsibility characteristic of British government, the members of the Cabinet fell in line behind the Prime Minister and the political struggle was all but won. The Labour backbenchers fell behind their P.M. when the vote to support the adjustment program came before the Commons. (Fay & Young 1978c, 33)

The sterling safety net was established by the BIS, as requested by Callaghan and Crosland, shortly after the letter of intent was approved by the IMF Executive Board. Two billion dollars was set aside for use by the British government for two years, conditioned on continual compliance with IMF conditionality. (de Vries 1985, 475)

Ultimately, the experience with the Fund strengthened Callaghan's position for several years. However, one could argue that the rejection of democratic socialism implied in the IMF program was the first step in the conservative reforms in Britain in the 1980s.

Because Callaghan did not take a firm position regarding austerity in the initial phases of the negotiations, it is difficult to say whether or not he was "coerced" by the Fund. It appears that he was successful in securing most of the concessions he sought—a compromise on the PSBR and a sterling safety net to name two—and that he achieved these through traditonal bargaining tactics. The experience of the Prime Minister, therefore, would tend to support the bargaining model, at least superficially.

Denis Healey and the Monetarists. Denis Healey conducted the negotiations between the IMF and Britain. He was a strong advocate of austerity in the Callaghan Cabinet, and eventually persuaded the government to implement IMF conditionality. His success was so significant that even after the Fund program had lapsed in 1978, the Callaghan administration continued to support IMF objectives and policies. (de Vries 1985, 477)

Prior to conducting the 1976 negotiation, Healey concluded an agreement in 1975. The letter of intent signed by Healey on December 18, 1975 included relatively few adjustment measures.

However, the program would not prove adequate to support the pound. Because of the great expense involved in propping up the currency, officials at the Bank of England and the Treasury decided to allow a managed fall. As put by Fay and Young, the strategy involved "backing into" deflation, meaning that efforts would be made to give the appearance of fighting a falling pound while in fact encouraging it: "We intended to shout 'Rape!', but not loud enough for anyone to hear. . ." (Fay & Young 1978c, 34) Beginning on March 4, 1976, the authorities allowed the sale of sterling on the open market. On March 5, the Treasury announced a fall in the minimum lending rate from 12 percent to 9 percent. (*Economist* 1976b, 9) Coincidentally, the Nigerian authorities, holding, as did many OPEC members, a large sterling balance, had sold off much of the country's assets on March 4th, pulling the rug out from under the carefully laid plan of the government. The value of the pound fell by five percent in one week. (Crawford 1983, 427)

During this rapid depreciation, the value of the pound fell below $2.00, what was described as a "psychological barrier," although, as Crawford points out, this was true only to the extent that traders ignored the signals betraying the government's intentions. The timing of the actions was significant, since it was decided to allow the lending rate to drop after the Nigerian sale had already taken place, so that the government sold pounds on a falling market. (Fay & Young 1978c, 34) The Government, recognizing that the pound was falling far faster than planned, decided to reverse course and attempt to buy back pounds in order to restore its value. From a total of $6.5 billion available in reserve, $1.3 billion was spent in March alone to shore up the pound. Over the next two months, with an addition of $2 billion from the IMF in May, another $3.3 billion was spent, leaving total reserves of $5.4 billion at the end of May. (Crawford 1983, 428, Porteous 1976, 761) In addition, the minimum lending rate was raised to 11.5 percent in May in order to attract more foreigners to buy pounds. (Crawford 1983, 429)

During the tense months before a loan was offered by the Bank for International Settlements (BIS) in June, the British Cabinet under Callaghan was split on economic policy. While the Treasury and the Bank were generally in favor of deflation, most other Cabinet members, and even some Treasury officials, urged avoidance of IMF conditionality at all costs. More will be said later about opposition in Britain to the IMF.

After receiving the BIS loan, conditioned on quick repayment, the government decided to spend part of it. This use of the loan, though limited, was enough to force the British to obtain further credit from the Fund in order to meet the December 7 pay-back deadline. With the recently expanded access as agreed by the executive board in early 1976, the U.K. would be able to draw a full 245 percent of its quota, or SDR 4.06 billion. Since the government had already drawn SDR 700 million via the late-1975 stand-by, this left SDR 3.36 billion available. Naturally, since her needs were considerable, Britain was interested in drawing the maximum.

Although talks had begun informally in August, British officials were not eager to have the IMF involved in their problems. As would happen at several junctures, British officials seem to have deliberately delayed the negotiating process by setting up bureaucratic impediments. In the early stages, U.K. officials informed the Fund staff that essential economic forecasts would not be available until late-October. Once the Fund mission actually arrived in London, on November 1, they would be asked to wait yet another few days for these elusive projections. (deVries

1985, 467, Fay & Young 1978c, 34) Such obstructionism, while irrational in the face of Britain's financial deadline of December 7, was politically practical, given the divided state of the Cabinet on the issue of IMF lending and conditionality.

Annual IMF/World Bank Board of Governors' meetings were about to begin in Manila when action by the Labour Party conference precipitated a new run on the pound, pushing it down by eight percent in two days. (Fay & Young 1978a,35) Healey was already at the airport, looking forward to important private discussions with Managing Director Johannes Witteveen, when he learned of the pound's further decline. He was forced to remain in London. Wass went in his place, but was not able to confer with senior Fund officials in as effective a manner. DeVries points to this unfortunate chain of events for an explanation for the subsequent difficulty of U.K. negotiations: the lack of "frank, face-to-face talks at this stage. . . may have added to the difficulty of later negotiations." (de Vries 1985, 468) Some British observers considered the failure to attend the meetings as an embarrassment, at best. (*Economist* 1976d, 85)

When the IMF negotiating team arrived in London, economic forecasts were still not available. Many hours were spent by the team members in the confines of their hotel rooms. Once the projections were finally available, it was obvious the Treasury had inflated its PSBR, and so the team cut it down from its original 11.2 billion pounds to a more realistic 10.5 billion. (Fay & Young 1978b, 34)[1] In addition, Treasury and Bank officials had not been authorized to discuss departures from the government's economic program: "Mr. Healey had stated that he believed existing U.K. policies would suffice as a basis for a stabilization program and had so indicated to the Managing Director." (de Vries 1985, 469) American and German officials and observers deplored this intransigence, calling upon the United Kingdom to tighten its belt as a signal to currency markets. The negotiations were bogged down by a larger-than-usual cavalcade of experts presenting conflicting images and predictions of Britain's economic health. (*Economist* 1976g, 95, Vasiliou 1977, 77–79) This wealth of competing expert opinions had the effect of undermining the Fund's proposals. Within a week the negotiations were at a stand-still, each side posturing. Bargaining poles were as follows: the U.K. officials demanded a PSBR of well over eight billion pounds for the 1977–79 period (relative to projections of nearly 12 billion) while the Fund insisted on a maximum of 7 billion pounds; the United Kingdom wanted roughly two billion more credit expansion allowance than the Fund was willing to give; the Fund team wanted to limit the initial amount available from the loan to be roughly SDR 1 billion, while the U.K. team wanted as much as possible in the first installment, considering its need to repay the American-European loan. (de Vries 1985, 471) It should be recognized that not only did the U.K. negotiators stake out an extreme position, but the Fund mission itself began by demanding "ten percent" more than they felt was necessary in order to at least give the appearance of flexibility. (confidential interview with Fund staff)

The British continued obstructionist tactics, however, leaking stories to the press denouncing the strong-armed pressuring of the IMF and a conspiracy between Healey and Simon. The British also continued to carry on parallel negotiations for a sterling safety net, attempting to pull the teeth out of the Fund negotiations, leaving the team in limbo. It was at this point that Witteveen and Callaghan negotiated directly to resolve some of the last obstacles to agreement.

After the Callaghan-Witteveen encounter, the negotiations were all but complete. Denis Healey detailed more specifically the provisions of the program before Parliament and in his letter of intent, forwarded to the Managing Director on December 15: policy objectives included lowering the current account deficit by fifty percent over the next two years (with the hope that North Sea oil revenues would push the balance into surplus by 1979), and lowering both unemployment and inflation. Policy instruments included: lowering the PSBR from 10.5 billion in 1976/77 to 8.7 billion pounds in 1977/78, and maintaining a stable figure on total government expenditures over a two-year period until mid-1978. (de Vries 1985, 472; *IMF Survey* 1977, 1, 4–5)

More will be said about the role of the monetarists in the internal debates in the Cabinet. At this point, it is possible to conclude that although Healey and others acted as advocates for the Fund's suggestions, they utilized every conceivable method to prevent making significant concessions to the IMF team itself. This behavior is the epitome of bargaining and negotiation, and it would seem to reinforce the assumptions of the bargaining model.

The United States and Germany. Although there was some debate over whether harsh austerity was appropriate to remedy the British problem (American officials were more convinced of the necessity of austerity than German officials at the beginning of the experience). There was also some question as to whether the pound should be preserved as a hard currency. By the end of the negotiating process, there was a consensus on the creation of a sterling safety net.

Edwin Yeo, American Treasury Under-Secretary for Monetary Affairs, and Treasury Secretary William Simon favored a conditional loan to Britain in consort with Germany and other EEC countries. American observers and officials viewed the British problem as one of over-consumption and over-spending on the part of the public sector. The solution was simple from this perspective: austerity. (Fay & Young 1978c, 34)

In early June, 1976, Western bankers under the auspices of the BIS arranged a $5.3 billion short-term loan for Britain to shore up its still-declining pound (it reached $1.77 in June—a 15 percent decline since March 3rd.). Since $2 billion of this loan was to be provided by the United States, American policy-makers were insistent on limiting the loan to six-months: by December 7 the loan must be repaid or else the U.K. would have to go to the IMF. This put Britain in the unusual situation of having resources needed to shore up the pound, but without the freedom to spend them in the effort. Anything spent would have to be almost immediately repaid. (Fay & Young 1978c, 33) It was hoped by U.S. authorities, in particular, that the U.K. would in fact use up some of the loan, since it was their ultimate aim to bring the British to the Fund. That the United States would desire to use the IMF as the financial watchdog illustrates the emerging importance of the Fund in the international monetary and political system. In days previous, the United States would have filled this role itself, as was the case in the early post-war years. On the other hand, this also illustrates the politicized nature of the U.K. loan.

Although the United States stayed aloof from the talks between Britain and the IMF, at various junctures it provided encouragement to Whittome and the IMF mission. In particular, in November 1976, when the negotiations came to a deadlock, U.S. officials were advised of the IMF's intentions to allow the Managing Director to involve himself directly in the negotiations. The initiative received President Gerald Ford's approval. (de Vries 1985, 471–2, Fay & Young 1978c, 35) The visit of Witteveen followed closely the discussions between Callaghan and Schmidt during which the German Chancellor advised the British Prime Minister that the austerity program proposed by the Fund had the support of the major creditor nations. With the Germans and Americans united in their support of the Fund, Callaghan recognized that he could not obtain sufficient external funding to sustain adjustment without austerity.

Whether the United States and Germany simply used the Fund to carry out the distasteful tasks of negotiation and enforcement while still controlling events from behind the scenes is difficult to determine. At any rate, the Fund was successful in pushing Britain into difficult adjustments—with some help from the Germans and Americans. (de Vries 1985, 478–9)

Whether this process is consistent with the political model is not as clear-cut as it first might seem. It is evident that the United States and Germany had a significant role in the process under consideration, but were the policies and positions advocated by these creditor nations consistent with the political model? One would have expected, given Britain's prominent role in the NATO alliance and the Cold War generally, that the United States in particular would have treated the British with sensitivity and consideration, rather than the rather rough bullying that in fact took place.

Additionally, one would have expected the British, with their very open economic system, to have been encouraged and sustained rather than coerced into austerity. One could argue that other nations in similar economic circumstances might have been treated even more kindly, but this is not apparant at first glance. It is possible, rather, that Britain's position as a weakening hard currency holder in fact made it more vulnerable than one would have expected. The United States and Germany recognized the volatility the pound had introduced into international currency markets by 1975 and set about to exert the necessary influence to persuade the British to remedy the situation. Note that these countries were still pursuing their self-interest, and therefore their behavior could be construed as broadly consistent with the political model. One would need to alter the political model to take into account more economic interests than merely maintenance of open economic systems for it to "fit."

Johannes Witteveen. Witteveen was nearing the end of his second term as Managing Director of the IMF in 1976. He was held in such high regard by many Executive Directors that there was talk of an unprecedented third term. (Southard 1985) Witteveen was acutely aware of developments in the British loan situation, although he made a point of allowing his mission as much latitude as possible, avoiding direct involvement in the early stages. (Whittome 1985)

In October, Witteveen took advantage of the annual IMF/World Bank meetings which took place in Manila to meet with Healey. However, as mentioned earlier, Denis Healey cancelled his appointment in order to deal with a currency crisis at home. The subsequent talks between Wass and Witteveen failed to produce resolution in part because Wass lacked the authority to change British monetary policy. (de Vries 1985, 468)

Whittome left the negotiations in London in mid-November to confer with Witteveen regarding the negotiating deadlock that had emerged. He urged the Fund mission to be patient and allowed them to stay in London a total of six weeks rather than the traditional two. He felt that the British government should be permitted to formulate policy in its traditional, deliberative fashion. (deVries 1985, 470–1)

With the December 6th deadline for the BIS loan looming nearer, Callaghan had begun to dig in his heels in late-November. Given this major obstacle, it was decided, at Whittome's urging, and with U.S. President Gerald Ford's blessing, that Witteveen inject himself directly into the negotiations. (de Vries 1985, 471–2; Fay & Young 1978c, 35) [2] Witteveen then made his trip to London to "strike a deal" with Callaghan.

The aftermath of this trip was interesting from the point of view of the models, in that the Executive Board reacted very negatively to this event. Even though Witteveen's mission was successful, it took place without the prior knowledge or approval of the Board members (although presumably the U.S. Executive Director knew since Gerald Ford had given his approval). Both de Vries and Southard acknowledge that it was at least in part in reaction to this unilateral tactic that the Board denied Witteveen a third term. (de Vries 1985, 472; Southard 1985)

The relatively heavy involvement of the Managing Director in the negotiations is consistent especially with the functionalist model, although his behavior is more consistent with the bargaining model. The reaction of the Board can be explained in terms of the political model, however. Part of the problem in explaining Witteveen's behavior is the uniqueness of the pound crisis, in that its outcome had implications for the health of the international financial system as a whole—something the Managing Director of the IMF would be expected to follow closely. One would therefore have anticipated a heavy role for the managing director in the British loan negotiations based on the Articles of Agreement (functionalist model). An additional problem is that the British loan represents a turning point in the role of the Fund in international crises. The United States clearly had a strong interest and a coherent plan in this situation, but chose not to intervene unilaterally. Instead, consistent with the post-hegemonic world conceived by Keohane, the United States chose a multilateral vehicle (Keohane 1984). Because of the unusual U.S. approach in this case, there appears to have been some ambiguity regarding role definition—something which was sorted out during the process rather than à priori. In a sense, the role of the managing director itself was the result of compromise between the Americans, the British, the Executive Board and Witteveen himself. In this way, the Managing Director's role could be considered consistent with a bargaining model of decision-making.

Secondary Actors

The IMF Mission. The IMF mission to Britain was quite well prepared and professional. Alan Whittome, the mission chief, had served in Britain's banking system prior to working at the Fund and David Finch is widely respected as the current head of ETR. They were joined by a German, a New Zealander and a Greek. (Fay & Young 1978c, 33) The team arrived on November under a cloak of secrecy (They registered under assumed names and used the telephone sparingly to prevent leaks).

Malcolm Crawford released a story as early as October 24 that summarized fairly well the position of the Fund. These terms, which were of course vigorously denied by the Fund, included: (1) devaluation of the pound to an "equilibrium level" of $1.50, (2) PSBR limit of eight billion pounds for FY 1977/78 (vs. 10–12 billion projected), (3) limit on domestic credit expansion to 6 billion pounds (vs. 10 billion expected for FY 1976/77), and (4) limit on money supply growth of 10 percent for FY 1977/78 (vs. 12 percent for 1976/77). (Crawford 1976, 1) This news of a possible devaluation was enough to push the pound further to a low of $1.555 on October 28, 1976. The twelve-month forward market used by international traders drawing up sales contracts, set the pound below $1.50. This would be its lowest point of the decade.

As negotiations proceeded, complete with delays and manipulation by British officials, a deadlock arose over several issues. The Fund insisted on a maximum of seven billion pounds in additional public credit, Britain sought roughly nine billion; the Fund team wanted to limit the amount available initially from the loan to roughly SDR 1 billion, while the United Kingdom wanted as much as possible in the first installment, considering its need to repay the European-American loan. (de Vries 1985, 471)

Throughout the early stages of the negotiations (through the middle of November), both Britain and the Fund were negotiating from unreaslitically extreme positions. According to IMF staff, the Fund estimated targets it considered adequate to remedy Britain's ills, and then deliberately adjusted its figures away from the current British positions by ten percent. It was these exagerrated figures that the team took with them to London. This was done to provide the mission some room to compromise (or at least appear to compromise!) during the negotiations. This type of behavior is not anticipated in the functionalist model and is more characteristic of the bargaining model.

Johannes Witteveen praised the Fund team for successfully conducting "the largest, longest, most difficult, and, perhaps, most momentous negotiations in the history of the Fund." (de Vries 1985, 472)

Tony Benn and the Keynesians. As perceived by the lower classes in Britain, the mid-1970s was the worst of times. Unemployment reached a new post-war high in January 1976, at 1.4 million, or 6.1 percent of the workforce. Harold Wilson, in late 1975, put it well: "Britain has suffered, suffered severely, and is still suffering. . . some pretty bleak months lie ahead." (McLellan 1976, 42) Throughout the negotiations with the IMF, Tony Benn and other liberal members of the Cabinet took it upon themselves to protect the interests of the lower classes by protesting all moves to implement austerity.

The new Callaghan government was faced with a near-crisis situation in 1975. Harold Lever, the Prime Minister's adviser in economic and financial matters, began urging a quick request to the IMF while the need was not yet so great, in the hope that the severest of IMF conditions could be pre-empted. Other cabinet officials split in terms of Keynesians, who wanted to expand the PSBR and impose import restrictions, and monetarists, who argued for cutting the budget and limiting wage hikes. (Fay & Young 1978a, 34) In response to Denis Healey's July 1976 partial budget, Tony Benn developed a comprehensive program which included subsidies for incentives for industry as well as import restraints. The Cabinet was evenly split on the issue of allowing the pound to fall further. (*Economist* 1976c, 101) This indecisiveness of the Cabinet tended to undermine Healey's position vis à vis the IMF, since he could not guarantee that any of his concessions would receive the support of the government.

At the annual Labour Party convention at the end of September, Healey was required to report to the group regarding the government's actions vis à vis the Fund. The delegates were sceptical of Healey's efforts, as were other senior officials. By the end of the negotiation period, this internal split had swelled to a crisis. Healey resorted to accounting devices to gain the advantage in the internal discussions. He deliberately inflated his PSBR estimates for 1977 in order to convince his undecided colleagues that the economy was overheating. The ploy was effective, and the radical members of the Cabinet were placed on the defensive. (Crawford 1983, 432)

However, in spite of this tactical move, Foreign Secretary Crosland posed a serious threat with his proposal for a more moderate form of import controls and "cosmetic" expenditure cuts in order to shore up confidence in the currency markets. As of November 25, Healey's plan to cut £3 billion from the 1977 PSBR, in line with Fund demands, was in jeopardy again. Whittome could do nothing to influence the outcome of these internal negotiations. (Fay & Young 1978a, 35)

The internal dissention of Cabinet members clearly complicated the negotiation process. As mentioned earlier, it extended the negotiations themselves by about a month, and also increased the uncertainty surrounding the outcome of the process. Whether Healey gained any advantages over the Fund because of the reluctance of the government to carry out austerity is unclear. In other cases (see Argentina), the government has even exagerrated the intensity of public opposition to IMF programs in order to convince the mission to lessen their demands. In Britain's case, however, this process is not apparant.

What is most interesting about the internal British debate is the ease with which it was ultimately resolved. Once Callaghan made his decision, based on input from Healey, the United States, Schmidt as well as opponents to austerity, the radical voices were quieted. Britain's tradition of collective responsibility is rarely so well demonstrated. It is also likely that Cabinet members were aware of polls which showed a majority of citizens favoring fiscal and monetary restraint in late-1976. (Fay & Young, 1978c, 33) Even without the support of all Labour backbenchers, the Healey/IMF plan was destined to pass the Commons because it had the support of Tories and Liberals.

The dissent in the Cabinet helps to show the significance of the IMF's influence, although it was clearly mitigated by conservative voices within the government. Had Healey not been supportive of the program, it is plausible to assume that the program would not have been approved by the government. This tends to support the functionalist model, although a more sophisticated version which allows for indirect IMF influence.

The BIS. Much more so than the Fund, the Bank for International Settlements (BIS), known as the "central bank of Central Banks," carried out the immediate wishes of the United States and Germany. This is largely because of the supportive role of the BIS, providing as it does hard currency to member banks rather than developing global policy or acting as a mediator in North-South negotiations. The relatively passive role of the BIS allowed the U.S. and Germany to carry out large-scale, multilateral lending which exerted significant influence on British policy.

In early June, 1976, Western bankers under the auspices of the Bank for International Settlements arranged a $5.3 billion short-term loan for Britain to shore up its still-declining pound (it reached $1.77 in June— a 15 percent decline since March 3rd.). As will be recalled, the terms of the loan provided a very quick repayment schedule. If the British could not repay the loan in full by December 7, they would be required to undertake an IMF adjustment program. In July a full $2.5 billion, of which $1 billion of the $5.3 billion loan, was used to bring the pound from its low of $1.71 to $1.79. (Crawford 1983, 430) This made it impossible for the government to repay the BIS loan, and therefore tentative negotiations were initiated in August.

Soon after the IMF negotiations were completed, the BIS coordinated the creation of a hard-currency pool that would act as a safety net for the pound. Three billion dollars was set aside for two years, although use of the fund would be conditional upon Britain's continued compliance with IMF's conditions. Such compliance would be monitored by Witteveen himself. Interestingly enough, this safety net did not have the effect of weakening Fund conditionality, as was originally hoped by Callaghan. (de Vries 1985, 475)

The role of the BIS is interesting because the institution dramatically magnified the influence of the major creditor nations by synchronizing their actions. The BIS and the IMF have rarely been so closely intertwined in a major loan negotiation. The influence of the United States over both of the institutions explains much of this coordination. The role of the BIS is generally consistent with a political model of decision-making, since it served as a support to the OECD countries.

IMF Executive Board. Even though the Americans and the Germans were heavily involved in the UK loan outside the Fund, there is no evidence that either nation manipulated the executive board. In fact, the Board tended overall to behave in a fairly passive manner, approving both loans with little objection.

For example, when the first British loan package was approved by the Board in 1975, various executive directors merely urged Fund staff to enforce the wage restraint elements of the package with vigor. (de Vries 1985, 465)

On January 3, 1977, the Executive Board met to decide on the major 1976 loan. The agreements were ratified without amendment. Much praise was spread to the Fund mission, to the Managing Director, and to the British authorities. All were praised for their political courage and good economic sense. Only a few cautious words were spoken regarding the political risks of wage restraint to the Callaghan government on the one hand, and regarding the high exposure of the Fund on the other. These comments aside, the Board approved the action: SDR 3.36 billion would be gathered from various sources (SDR 945 million from United States, SDR 785 million from Germany, SDR 555 million from Japan, SDR 300 million from Switzerland and SDR 500 million from normal Fund resources. *IMF Survey* 1977, 1,5) The funds would be disbursed at the rate of SDR 1.95 billion available in 1977 and SDR 1.4 billion in 1978 (Note that Fund team originally hoped to limit 1977's disbursement to SDR 1 billion). (*IMF Survey* 1977, 1, 5)

The Executive Board offered a final statement of praise for the British experience as "the most successful [adjustment program] ever implemented." (*IMF Survey* 1977, 1) De Vries agrees with the assessment, pointing out that the U.K. loan was the first of its kind to be negotiated by the Fund and represented a "coming of age" for the institution. (de Vries 1985, 472) Comments from Fund staff support the view that the Executive Board, even in the historic case of the U.K. loan, contented itself largely to their now-traditional post-hoc decision-making style. This, in and of itself, cotributed to the "coming of age" of the institution as well.

The only activity of the Executive Board which is not consistent with the functionalist model was its decision not to reelect Witteveen for a third term. This action, which sent a strong message to Witteveen's successors, clarified the relationship between the Managing Director and the Board by limiting the MD's latitude to actions previously approved by the Board. Note that the Board did not object to the outcome of the

Witteveen initiative, only to the style. Overall, the Executive Board's behavior is consistent with the functionalist model.

Conclusion

The British experience with the IMF is useful in illustrating how the Fund employs a more bargaining-oriented decision-making style when dealing with an industrialized, hard-currency country.

The functionalist model explains the behavior of the Executive Board fairly well, in that its relative passivity is consistent with functionalist assumptions. The terms of the loan themselves were largely consistent with IMF monetarist theory, in that they were deflationary and promoted economic openness and competition. The participation of the state in private sector investment was reduced (BP shares sold), import restrictions were avoided, the domestic credit ceiling was lowered, wage increases were kept in check and the public sector deficit was reduced. An exception to the traditional loan package in Britain's case was the lack of currency devaluation (presumably because the pound was already dangerously low by historical standards) and the high level of absolute indebtedness that was allowed (Britain borrowed nearly $4 billion from 1976 to 1978). Further, the Fund exposed itself to a great extent by concentrating roughly thirty percent of its total lending during the 1976–78 period in one country. (IMF 1981, 80) Finally, because the BIS came forward with a $3 billion fund, much of the effort to impose conditionality to shore up the value of the pound was not needed. In fact, given the quick restoration of value to the pound and ease with which Britain attracted foreign exchange during 1977, it would seem that much of the problem in Britain's circumstances was one of perceptions—financiers overseas simply did not have confidence in Britain's economy and they sought a sign of good intentions. (Crawford 1983, 436)

All things considered, then, it would seem that the British loan was more generous than necessary in terms of total resources made available, and perhaps more strict than necessary in terms of conditionality aimed at remedying Britain's balance of payments crisis. An explanation for this is the functionalist model, in that the Fund followed rules and principles rather closely in the British case, even though this might not have been appropriate. For example, although the Fund lent large sums to Britain in relation to its total assets, the British loan was not large relative to Britain's quota. Also, although it appears that much of the British problem was one of perception, the Fund conditionality employed a set of relatively standard austerity measures ostensibly to remedy the British balance of payments crisis. Perhaps a more innovative and creative institution could have developed a more suitable and refined program for the British case. This is something the left-leaning members of the Cabinet tried to say all along.

The bargaining model offers a good set of explanations for the processes at work in the British case overall, as well as for the behavior of most of the significant actors specifically. The behavior of the Managing Director, the Prime Minister, the monetarists in Britain and the Fund mission were all described as bargaining behaviors. Each actor had a particular set of objectives and self-conciously perceived the decision-making process as a bargaining experience. The IMF mission and Witteveen develop a set of policy recommendation for Britain which were "ten percent" more severe than they judged appropriate, and likewise Callaghan and the British monetarists promoted a set of options that were more lenient than they felt they could politically justify. Between the two sets of actors, a compromise program emerged which ultimately satisfied both by splitting the difference between the initial positions.

Further, most of the actors consciously employed bargaining tactics in their negotiations. The British officials, for example, deliberately delayed the provision of data, the review of proposals and the discussion of alternatives. They employed such tactics as the "OZ method" (delaying a compromise by referring the decision to a "higher power"—real or contrived), countering expert testimony with more expert testimony, and exagerrating the political costs of IMF proposals. To a great extent, the division of the Cabinet allowed the Healey team more time to pressure the Fund team to make concessions.

Finally, both sides of the negotiation attempted to use outsiders to influence the positions of their opponents. In particular, the IMF made use of the U.S. and the German finance ministries to influence British positions (or perhaps the American and German manipulated the Fund . . .). The British likewise carried on parallel negotiations with the Americans in order to influence the outcome (or at least the significance) of the IMF negotiations. These types of behaviors point to a multi-actor, multi-level negotiation process not anticipated by the functionalist paradigm, but entirely consistent with a bargaining model.

The political model explains to a degree the behavior of the United States and Germany, in that they attempted to influence the process of negotiation (including its initiation) through both unilateral and multilateral (BIS role) means. What is surprising about the political dimensions of the British negotiation is that the objectives and outcomes are both inconsistent with the political model. Where the political model would have anticipated generous treatment for Britain due to its Western alliance position and its generally open economy, the Americans and Germans are especially rough with Britain. This implies that the political model does not take into account such sophisticated systemic political and economic objectives as "stability of the financial system" and "advocacy of liberalism at the domestic level." The British case illustrates how major industrialized nations operate against a higher standard of behavior than traditional debtor nations.

Overall, the functionalist model explains to a degree the outcome of IMF-U.K. negotiations, although the bargaining model explains more successfully the process through which these outcomes were achieved. The political model, although useful in principle, requires significant amendment to be applicable to the British case.

Notes

1. Note the importance of economic forecasts as a bargaining tool. Crawford cites recollections by the Chief Secretary of the Treasury at the time: "I thought I had done a fair amount of juggling with figures as an accountant, but when it came to the sort of sophisticated 'massaging' and 'fudging' I learned as chief secretary to the Treasury, I realized I had been a babe in arms by comparison. It was a case of changing this and that assumption, and—abracadabra—the PSBR is about the figure you first thought of." (Crawford, p. 432)

2. It is important to remember, also, that these U.K. negotiations were being conducted simultaneously with equally important negotiations with Italy, Mexico and Portugal. A recurrent thought among Fund staff was the importance of holding firm in London in order to prevent a debacle in the three other countries.

Bibliography

Bray, Jeremy. 1976. "Carter, Callaghan and the Pound." *New Statesman* October 29: 583–4.

Crawford, Malcolm. 1976. "The Price Britain Pays for IMF Aid." *The Sunday Times* October 24: 1.

———. 1983. "High-Conditionality Lending: The United Kingdom." in Williamson, John. ed. *IMF Conditionality* Washington, D.C.: Institute for International Economics: 421–439.

de Vries, Margaret Garritsen. 1985. *The International Monetary Fund, 1972–1978: Cooperation on Trial.* vol. 1. Washington, D.C.: International Monetary Fund.

The Economist. 1975. November 13: 18–20.

———. 1976a. January 17: 89.

———. 1976b. March 13: 9–10.

———. 1976c. October 2: 11–12.

———. 1976d. October 9: 85–86.

———. 1976e. October 16: 97–106; 127–129.

———. 1976f. November 13: 106.

———. 1976g. November 27: 95–96.

Fay, Stephen and Young, Hugo. 1978a. "How the Hard Money Men Took Over Britain." *The Sunday Times* May 14: 33–35

————. 1978b. "The Callaghan Offensive." *The Sunday Times* May 21: 33–35.

————. 1978c. "How the Cabinet Embraced the IMF." *The Sunday Times* May 28: 33–34.

International Monetary Fund. 1981. *Annual Report: 1981.* Washington, D.C.: International Monetary Fund.

IMF Survey. 1976. January 10: 1–5.

Keohane, Robert. 1984. *After Hegemony: Cooperation and Discord in the World Political Economy.* Princeton, N.J.: Princeton University Press.

New Statesman. 1976. October 29: 581.

Mackintosh, John. 1984. *The Government and Politics of Britain.* London: Hutchinson University Library.

McLellan, Gordon. 1976. "Pressing problems of Britain." *World Marxist Review* 19 April: 42–56.

Porteous, John. 1976. "Mr. Healey's Ninety Days." *New Statesman* June 11: 761–2.

Southard, Frank. 1985. Interview with the author. IMF Headquarters, Washington, D.C. June 26.

Vasiliou, Sheilagh. 1977. "Economic Decline and the UK." *Futures* 9 February: 77–79.

Whittome, L.A. 1985. Interview with the author. IMF Headquarters, Washington, D.C. July 17.

8

The Case of Turkey: 1977–1982

The case of Turkish foreign debt and IMF experience is instructive for several reasons. First, the 1980 IMF loan of over $1.5 billion was the largest of its kind up to that point, and therefore the case of Turkey is interesting in terms of IMF history. Secondly, the case of Turkey has often been cited as an IMF "success story" because of Turkey's dramatic economic recovery of the 1980–1982 period under the able leadership of Turgut Ozal, then Minister of State. We will see that other lessons may be drawn from Turkey's experience, but we will leave these more minor points until later.

Background to the 1977 Crisis

In 1977 Turkey's short-term arrangements for dealing with massive public expenditure in the context of a closed economy came crashing in on it, requiring the government to scramble for assistance from abroad.

The Turkish economy is sophisticated, much like Argentina's, complete with a well-developed infrastructure, banking systems and agricultural production which exceeds the needs of the domestic Turkish market. (*Institutional Investor* 1984, 144–5) Since the 1950s, Turkey has had less economic interaction with the rest of the world than countries of comparable economic development. Total 1977 exports amounted to only four percent of its GNP, as compared to 20 percent for most newly industrializing countries (NICs). (Pesvner 1984, 18) In a recent World Bank study, Turkey of 1977 was described as "virtually a closed economy." (Lewis & Urata 1983, 17) Turkey, however, preserved a reasonable balance of payments position throughout the 1960s and much of the 1970s, maintaining a small balance of payments deficit by keeping imports low and financing abroad at long-term (ten year), low interest (3.5 percent) rates. (Cohen 1981, 218; see Table 8.1) In 1974, total foreign reserves hit a high point of $2.4 billion. (von der Bay 1983, 339)

TABLE 8.1   Turkey's Balance of Payments, 1971-1977 ($US million)

	1971	1972	1973	1974	1975	1976	1977
Short-term Capital	57	35	-590	-189	-294	-585	842
Long-term Capital	217	697	360	404	1315	2334	1988
Merchandise Balance	-378	-522	-560	-1831	-2834	-2605	-3406
Total Net Balance	24	124	615	-634	-1848	-1964	-3325

Source: IMF 1978, 374.

Turkey's economy grew at a healthy rate overall in the 1960s and much of the 1970s. Annual increases in its gross national product (GNP) averaged 6.9 percent throughout the period from 1962 to 1976, with industrial output leading the way at 9.8 percent. (Carvounis 1984, 85) Turkey was integrated into the European economic system through its large guest-worker program in Germany and other Western states. These Turkish workers abroad sent home $1.4 billion in 1973—nearly as much as was earned from exports that year. (McCauley 1979, 142) Roughly 1.5 million Turks participated in this program, and another million were prepared to leave when the program was aborted in 1973. (Pevsner 1984, 12)

The state has been an important economic actor in Turkey. In the 1960s, several State Economic Enterprises (SEEs) were created to promote weak industries in Turkey. Given the right to price final goods below cost, they fell into debt within ten years and have since been supported by the government. SEEs' losses ran at 13 percent per year from 1974 to 1977. In support of these SEEs, the government deficit grew from 1.5 percent of GNP in 1974 to 4 percent of GNP in 1977. (von der Bay 1983, 339) It was difficult to enforce stringency on the SEEs because along with their vast economic size (SEEs accounted for over one-fourth the total fixed investment in Turkey in the 1970s), they were run by a "powerful self-perpetuating technocracy." (Pevsner 1984, 20)

Turkish political life in the 1960s and 1970s can be described as troubled. The Turkish military took control of the government three times in twenty years from 1960 to 1980. The principal reason for each of the coups was fear on the part of the military that civilian politicians could not cope with the growing disorder and unrest in society and in the economy. Each of the coups coincided with a crisis in external payments, interestingly enough. (Pevsner 1984, 19) For example, in 1971 the military leadership simply handed a memorandum to the Prime Minister indicating its concerns and inviting his resignation. In 1980, the debt crisis and subsequent austerity program precipitated violent outbursts and widespread strike activity. As will be seen, a show of force by the military was enough to topple the government.

Turkish democracy has nonetheless survived. Suleyman Demirel and Bulent Ecevit have long dominated two democratic parties in Turkey, the Justice Party (JP) and the Republican People's Party (RPP), respectively. The JP is somewhat similar to the centrist/conservative parties of Western Europe and the United States in its platform and support, while the RPP is similar to moderate labor parties and found in Britain and the United States. (Carvounis 1984, 85) Turkish unions were organized à la française in two broad union groups, DISK (Revolutionary Confederation of Labor) and Turk-Is (Turkish Confederation of Labor Unions), the former more militant and pro-Communist than the latter. We shall see that in general Turkish unions constrained politicians' attempts at imposing austerity. Various splinter groups of extremists operate outside the constitutional framework, employing terrorist tactics against government targets.

The Crisis of 1977

The most immediate cause of the debt crisis of 1977 was the CTLD crisis of short-term debt that had been building since the first oil shock.

The first oil shock and the 1973–74 global recession, European hosts to Turkish guest-workers revised their immigration policy and began sending Turks home. With the reversal in European, and especially German, policy, Turkey saw its foreign exchange earnings from worker remittances fall by $400 million in 1974 and a further $300 million in 1975–76. (McCauley 1979, 143; von der Bay 1983, 339–340) In addition, a decline in the profitability of SEEs forced the government to finance increasing government debt, resulting in an increased money supply and its twin evil, inflation. The overall government deficit grew from 1.9 percent of gross domestic product (GDP) in 1976 to 5.7 percent of GDP in 1977. (*IMF Survey* 1982, 229) The money supply grew by 24–30 percent annually from 1974 to 1977 (von der Bay 1983, 339), and the annual inflation rate rose from 17.4 percent in 1976 to 26.1 percent in 1977. (Cohen 1981, 220)

The value of the turkish lira remained at its 1974 level throughout the period, resulting in a highly overvalued exchange rate and a further dampening of worker remittances. This overvalued exchange rate also led to large increases in imports, which grew by 38 percent from 1970 to 1975, and which precipitated a nearly ten-fold increase in the trade deficit. (Bogdanowicz-Bindert 1983, 67) All of these events helped precipitate a fall in the real growth rate from 7.7 percent in 1974–1976 to five percent in 1977. (McCauley 1979, 145) A statistic that summarizes the predicament is the investment-savings gap, which increased from 2.5 percent of GNP in 1972 to 9.4 percent in 1977. (Lewis & Urata 1983, 9) Thus, a combination of German and Turkish decisions produced acute foreign exchange shortages in Turkey in the mid-1970s.

These shortages were in part compensated for through short-term borrowing schemes developed by the government with the help of Turkish banks. The term "convertible lira deposits," known by the acronym CTLDs, refers to the banking system through which Turkish private banks offered short-term investment packages which were guaranteed by the Turkish government, similar to the modern "certificate of deposit," to foreign banks and individuals. The government would in turn use lira to buy the foreign exchange used in the preceding transaction from the private bank with lira. The private banks would then lend these lira on the domestic market while the central bank would lend the hard currency to Turkish importers. The advantage of this scheme was that it allowed for short-term management of the need for foreign credit without going through the politically unpalatable means of passing debt legislation or undertaking massive, highly-publicized loans from private, foreign banks. This scheme also provided an incentive for Turks working abroad to return their paychecks. (McCauley 1979, 143–5)

Further advantages of the plan accrued to foreign bankers. Not only was the German government investing heavily in its traditional ally and protector of the Eastern flank of NATO, but it was urging American bankers to do the same. The latter obliged, and "by 1976 . . . [using the CTLDs], the big American banks, with Citibank and the Bank of America in the forefront, soon rushed in to take advantage of the quick profits." (Sampson 1981, 328) In addition, the CTLD plan offered increased convenience for subsidiaries of multi-national corporations and inter-national traders, since it was possible to "earmark" the foreign exchange provided through a particular "deposit" for eventual use by a particular importer, subsidiary, or turkish investor. "In fact more than half of all CTLDs which were established were made on behalf and in the interest of customers and tied to the granting of TL credits to designated borrowers in Turkey." (von der Bay 1983, 340)

Offsetting these advantages, most of which were of a very short-term and political nature, were several major dangers of the plan. The principal disadvantage of the scheme was that it provided short-term capital for a long-term need. Since the funds went to finance imports, and the need for these foreign funds was due to deep-seated problems in the Turkish economy, as discussed above, it was dangerous to finance these needs with CTLDs, most of which had maturities of only 12 to 24 months. By April 1977, banks began defaulting on repayment of CTLDs, and by the fall of 1977, transfers were at a complete standstill. Nearly two billion dollars of the funds which had flowed into the country through this mechanism was now due in full. Secondly, in addition to the problem of short maturities, the CTLDs brought in foreign currency at much higher interest rates than could have been obtained through the more traditional medium-term loan. Thirdly, CTLDs were poorly accounted for, and the total debt accumulated through CTLDs was unknown. As described by the director of the Deutsche Bank at the time:

> Neither the Turkish central bank nor the Turkish commercial banks used to report any figures about CTLD operations concluded or the accumulated volume. Only banks with closer business relationships with Turkey, visiting there frequently, has the possibility to follow developments by obtaining verbal statements from central bank officials or from their Turkish correspondent banks. (von der Bay 1983, 340)

Finally, the CTLDs naturally increased the Turkish money supply at a time when the foreign reserves of the central bank were declining rapidly. As early as October 1976, the central bank began approaching "several of its closest correspondent banks abroad to supply substantial emergency assistance." (von der Bay 1983, 342)

By mid-1977, as smaller lenders were bailed out by larger banks, "large banks became more committed to Turkey than they wished." (Aronson 1977, 193) "In March, Wells Fargo floated the last syndicated bank loan," due within only six months. (McCauley 1979, 145) By the end of 1977 the private banks refused to deal with Turkey any further. They demanded an arrangement with the IMF and OECD countries prior to rescheduling, "less for the financial impact involved than for the visible approval of the IMF for new economic, fiscal and financial policies." (von der Bay 1983, 343)

It can be debated whether foreign banks were wise or even behaving ethically in their massive use of CTLDs. Carvounis implies that the private banks expected eventual assistance from the Organization for Economic Cooperation and Development (OECD) states of the West in the eventuality of a crisis in Turkey. (1984, 86) When the OECD and the IMF eventually stepped in, the banks began pulling out of Turkey as quickly as discretion would allow. Even with that, the bankers attitudes provoked frustration and indignation from IMF officials, one of whom is reported to have exclaimed, "The banks overlent when the going was good, and now they show no responsibility. . . The IMF cannot act as the banks' debt collector—we didn't go in to let them get out." (Sampson 1981, 329)

In July 1977, amid increasing political violence in which over 300 died, Demirel of the right-of-center Justice Party organized a new government, even though his party polled fewer votes than did the RPP, under Ecevit (37 vs. 41 percent). He organized an unlikely coalition government with the help of the Islamic fundamentalist National Salvation Party. (Pevsner 1984, 67–8)

Enter the IMF

Demirel sought IMF advice regarding the implementation of austerity measures to deal with Turkey's foreign exchange crisis. Formal negotiations began in November 1977 amid popular and labor unrest in Turkey. During the period, the Demirel administration was replaced by Ecevit and the RPP, which was politically opposed to austerity. (Williamson, 54–5) Ecevit nonetheless devalued the lira by 23 percent, reduced domestic credit and implemented progressive taxation. (McCauley 1979, 146–8)

The Organization for Economic Cooperation and Development (OECD) began to work with Turkey's private creditors to reschedule Turkey's $6 billion debt in early 1978. In mid-1978 the IMF approved a $370 million, two-year stand-by and the OECD and private creditors rescheduled $3.9 billion of Turkey's long-term and short-term debt. (McCauley 1979, 148)

The Ecevit administration complied only partially with IMF lending terms, and the 1978 agreement was suspended. After careful intermediation by German officials, talks between Turkey and the IMF were renewed in 1979 and a more stringent program was signed in the form of a $320 million, one-year stand-by with more ambitious demand management provisions. (Lewis & Urata 1983, 171) The Ecevit administration was careful to legislate the IMF conditions prior to signing the letter of intent, apparently to avoid the appearance of making significant concessions.

Another OECD-coordinated rescheduling took place which provided nearly $1.5 billion in fresh loans to Turkey. (*IMF Survey* 1979b, 195–6) Private banks rescheduled $2.6 billion in long-and short-term debt, thereby removing the most urgent demands on the Ecevit administration. (Pevsner 1984, 77–8) However, Demirel won reelection in late-1979.

As the economy continued to stagnate and the debt crisis persisted, the Demirel administration, under the leadership of Turgut Ozal, conceived and implemented a dramatic reversal of economic policy. The "January 24 (1980) Program" was a "radical departure with the country's long-standing tradition of state socialism," surpassing even the IMF's policy recommendations for austerity and liberalization. (*Institutional Investor* 1984, 144) The currency was devalued by 33 percent, dramatically higher interest rates, export incentives were introduced, foreign investment was encouraged and the SEEs were released from government price controls. (Bogdanwicz-Bindert 1983, 67; Carvounis 1984, 95) The short-term results were dramatic in that export receipts grew by over thirty percent, inflation fell by nearly seventy percent, and government spending shrank from five to one percent of GNP in one year. (Carvounis 1984, 90–93; von der Bay 1983, 351)

In contrast to these positive developments, wages fell dramatically, resulting in DISK-organized strikes resulting in the loss of over seven million workdays in July and August of 1980. (Lewis & Urata 1983, 20) Terrorism and violence increased, leading to a military coup in September.

The IMF intervened in June 1980 with a massive $1.65 billion EFF program which simply endorsed the January 24 program already in progress. (*IMF Survey* 1980b, 177, 187–8) An OECD rescheduling followed shortly and delayed payment of three billion dollars of Turkey's debt. (Seiber 1983, 72) Private bankers were, however, quietly writing off their Turkish debts and attempting to withdraw from the situation. (Seiber 1983, 74–75)

In the years following the IMF loan and the military coup, Turgut Ozal would remain the most prominent political figure in Turkey. The OECD rescehduled Turkey's debt in 1981 and again in 1982, while the IMF provided new stand-bys in the years after 1983 for relatively modest amounts (roughly $200 million in 1983 and 1984). Economic conditions deteriorated in the years following the EFF expiration with inflation rising to 40 percent, interest rates falling (below inflation), the current account deficit rising by 80 percent and unemployment rising to 25 percent in 1983. (Pevsner 1984, 110–1)

While some dispute whether Turkey's experience should be emulated, there is no question that, at least in the short run, the IMF loan had dramatic, positive effects on Turkey's balance of payments crisis. (Cohen 1981, 219, Pevsner 1984, 109) In the section that follows, the activities of each of the major actors will be considered in the context of the three models of IMF decision-making.

Principal Actors and IMF Lending

Primary Actors

Turkey's Democratic Regimes. The Demirel and Ecevit administrations both shared the dual constraints common to many emerging democracies grappling with austerity: highly mobilized worker organizations and assertive military establishments. The balance of payments crisis of the late 1970s pitted the government against both of these forces. In an attempt to satisfy all parties, domestic as well as foreign, the governments attempted to set in place endogenous austerity programs which would have legitimacy at home and respect abroad. The delicate balance between satisfying the foreign creditors and the domestic working class at the same time could not be maintained, however.

In 1977, conservative Demirel attempted to carry out "painless" adjustment with the advice of an IMF mission, devaluing the lira by ten percent (the mission had stipulated 20–25 percent as a prerequisite for a stand-by in September). Even this relatively small ten percent devaluation was vehemently condemned by Demirel's coalition partner, Erbeken of the Islamic National Salvation Party, as a "plot of the Greek lobby." (*Journal of Commerce* 1977, 11) The tenuous JP-NSP coalition (nicknamed the "National Front") collapsed at the end of 1977, after only six months in office, to be replaced by an equally tenuous coalition of left-leaning parties led by Ecevit and the RPP.

Ecevit pursued Demirel's austerity plans and rescheduling negotiations. According to Williamson, these negotiations "started off with governmental reluctance to make policy changes on the scale the Fund considered necessary." (1982, 54–55) Ecevit nonetheless consented to carry out a further devaluation of the lira (23 percent) and tighten domestic credit along the lines the IMF mission advocated. (McCauley 1979, 146–8) By April 1978, the negotiations were nearing resolution. At this critical time, Ecevit, whose support came primarily from working-class and radical voters, gave several speeches in which he attacked the "neo-imperialist" bail-out attempts by the IMF and Turkey's creditors. Complaining that the measures proposed would lead to a "grave social and political crisis and eventually to upheavals, due to a slowing down of development or to increasing unemployment." Further, he told OECD nations indirectly that the Turkish people had "no intention of having our head chopped off by certain so-called solutions which fall foul of both contemporary realities and the economic and social realities of democratic Turkish society." (*Middle Eastern Economic Digest* 1978, 25)

It is interesting to note that these speeches were clearly aimed at Ecevit's supporters at home. It is likely that their content appealed to the voting groups that had supported Ecevit's campaign, in that they were likely going to endure sacrifices and costs in the event of an IMF-conceived austerity program. In addition, the NSP, Ecevit's coalition partner, was openly opposed to an IMF program on nationalist grounds. However, the speeches were given during the interval after the letter of intent had been signed, but before the stand-by had been approved by the executive board, and therefore had no effect on the content of the agreement itself.

As the program was implemented, inflation rose to 50 percent and other objectives were only partially achieved. The Central Bank president was removed under pressure from Erkaban of the NSP on the grounds that he tried too hard to comply with IMF conditionality. (McCauley 1979, 149) In December 1978, the IMF suspended negotiations for a new stand-by on grounds of Turkish non-compliance with the 1977 accords. (Carvounis 1984, 91) Ecevit had failed to maintain the fragile equilibrium between domestic and foreign demands.

A German representative of the Deutsche Bank, Walter Leisler-Keip, who "acted as an intermediary on behalf of the West German government and the other OECD countries, was able to bring the Turkish government and the Fund on to speaking terms again" in the spring of 1979. (von der Bay 1983, 349) In an attempt to both restore relations with the IMF and preserve the appearance of autonomy, the Turkish government adopted what has been described by World Bank scholars as a "stringent" stabilization plan in March 1979. (Lewis & Urata 1983, 17) The plan was further amended and strengthened in June and involved a roughly 40 percent devaluation of the lira (from TL26.5=$1.00 to TL47.1=$1.00). (*IMF Survey* 1979c, 217) The practice of presenting austerity programs prior to the adoption of the "official" Fund agreement became a pattern in Turkish dealings with the Fund, just it had with Sudan. An explanation offered by the Deutsche Bank president is that such an announcement preempted charges by extremist groups that the government was the slave of the Fund.

Unfortunately, the political clock had run out on the Ecevit administration, and in October 1979 Demirel and the JP won a "landslide" electoral victory on a platform of economic efficiency. (Pevsner 1984, 77–8) The new Turkish administration soon found itself required to ally closely with the military, which, as was mentioned, has never been far away from the political scene. In December, the military began offering "proposals" to the Demirel administration to deal with the rising political violence and economic crisis. The economy was not responding to the new administrations efforts, however, as inflation rose to 64 percent, exports stagnated, imports and other goods became scarce, and the government again fell in arrears on foreign debt payments. (Lewis & Urata 1983, 17, *Institutional Investor* 1984, 144) It was in this context that Turgut Ozal emerged as the dominant policy-maker, a massive austerity program was set in motion, and the military gained power in a coup.

With regard to the decision-making process at work in the democratic regimes of Turkey, one finds clear evidence of attempts at bargaining with the Fund. First, the Demirel administration delayed the initiation of talks until international credit was entirely cut off. Secondly, the government agreed on a compromise devaluation figure with the Fund. As will be seen later, the Fund also conceded to the government its traditional multiple exchange rate system. Finally, the government seems to have attempted to set the tone and pace of the negotiations by either refraining from implementing conditionality or carrying out unilateral reforms that took the "teeth" out of the IMF agreements. This style of decision-making is similar to that of India, Argentina and Great Britain. It is also indicative of a purposeful attempt at "bargaining" and compromise to arrive at acceptable conditionality and support.

The fact that the government was not able to go far enough indicates that the IMF had non-negotiable objectives of its own for Turkey which included at least minimal adherence to conditionality and repayment of arrears—something which has been found in nearly all of the cases thus far. One could consider these IMF objectives primarily technical and thus more consistent with the functionalist model. As will be seen later, the political forces in the case of Turkey seemed to be working in its favor, generally.

Turkey's Technocrats and the Military. The military intervened in Turkey when it perceived civil unrest and the economic crisis to be out of control. There is no deep-seated presumption of civilian control of the military in Turkey—as is typical of many LDCs and NICs. The possibility of military intervention was therefore generally accepted in Turkish political circles and was even expected in certain circumstances. For this reason, the Demirel administration began to work with the military in the months following the 1979 election.

Turkish technocrats in the Central Bank were on the defensive during early-1979 when the NSP, working with Finance Ministry officials opposed to IMF conditionality, removed Sadiklar from the Central Bank. (McCauley 1979, 149) However, when Turgut Ozal was elevated to Deputy Prime Minister under the new, conservative Demirel administration in late-1979, they found a sympathetic ear. The military also joined with the technocrats to recommend policy alternatives for dealing with Turkey's economic crisis by December. (Lewis & Urata 1983, 17) It is now known that the military had already begun planning a coup attempt that would eventually be put into effect in September, 1980. (Pevsner 1984, 77)

With the support of the military, and lackluster results from the first few months of new austerity measures, the Demirel administration allowed Ozal to develop and implement a radical departure from politically safe programs of the previous five years:

> By January 1980, the authorities realized that they had no choice but to embark on a comprehensive and far-reaching economic programme. Economic policy was completely reoriented with an emphasis on exports,

with a greater reliance on market forces and a turning away from government regulations and controls. The exchange rate was kept flexible after an initial devaluation of 33 percent. Price controls were eliminated and the authorities adopted a flexible interest rate policy (rates charged by banks now range from 60 to 120 percent and average 70–75 percent). (Bogdanowicz-Bindert 1983, 67)

The immediate effects of the reform package were promising. In two years (1980–81) more foreign investment came into the country than in the previous twenty-five years. (Carvounis 1984, 95) Prices on basic commodities increased dramatically: oil product prices rose by 40-100 percent, 100 percent for coal, and large rises for iron, steel and cement, thus making the SEEs more profitable. (*IMF Survey* 1980a, 60–61) Export receipts rose $700 million from $2.2 to $2.9 million in 1980 over 1979, helping to reduce the current account deficit by two-thirds, to $1.2 billion. (*Institutional Investor* 1984, 144) Inflation fell from a high of roughly 130 percent in 1980 to 40 percent in 1981. Overall spending by the government fell from five percent of GNP to one percent of GNP from 1980 to 1981. Consumer goods were once again in plentiful supply and interest rates rose to positive real values. (Carvounis 1984, 90,93, von der Bay 1983, 351)

Within a few months, foreign creditors and the IMF restored relations with Turkey. It is important to note that Turgut Ozal himself had much to do with the enhanced status of Turkey in international markets, as explained in an article written for *Institutional Investor*, the news magazine of international bankers:

[U]ndersecretary for both the Prime Minister and the state planning organization, [Turgut Ozal's] excellent relations with the Fund and his reputation in internal banking circles have, if anything, given the country greater flexibility in its debt rescheduling. (*Institutional Investor* 1984, 144)

The short-term results of the program were not entirely good for all Turks. As prices for basic staples rose to world market prices, the purchasing power of the Turkish working class plummeted. As new foreign investments flowed into the country, radical nationalists took to the streets and orchestrated terrorist attacks to oppose such "imperialism." As government spending was cut, jobs and salaries of government workers were reduced. The DISK took the lead in organizing massive demonstrations and strikes. (von der Bay 1983, 354)

It was at this point that the military, led by General Kenan Evren, put into action its plans for a take-over that had been incubating for over a year. On September 12 the military mobilized, taking quick control of media installations and public buildings, arresting political leaders, including Demirel and Ecevit, and imposing martial law on all of the countries provinces. (von der Bay 1983, 354, Pevsner 1984, 81–82) Ozal was proclaimed Deputy Prime Minister for Economic Affairs and was left to lead to austerity measures put in place in January and confirmed by the IMF in June. The legislative deadlock was resolved and the massive tax reform package was passed by January 1981. The turkish lira was allowed to float, within bounds, export incentives were expanded, and import controls further relaxed. (Lewis & Urata 1983, 20)

The military-dominated regime was consolidated in 1982 with the adoption of a French Fifth Republic-style constitution and the election in November of Evren for a seven-year term as President. Assembly elections were held in late 1983. Although Turgut Ozal had resigned earlier over a policy dispute with the Finance Ministry, Ozal was elected Prime Minister when his "Motherland Party" collected 45 percent. In April 1983, the military began relaxing restrictions on political participation and many of the problems endemic to the pre-1980 period began to reemerge in parliament. As of 1984 prognoses differed concerning the ability of the Ozal administration to cope with the political realities of austerity programs in Turkey.

B.J. Cohen feels that Turkey is not a success since the democratic system was lost and economic success was merely temporary. (Cohen 1981, 219) Remmer points out that in many cases only military governments are capable of implementing IMF austerity packages, given the high sensitivity to public interests experienced by most democratic systems. (Remmer 1986) Körner et al. stress the inevitability of political instability in the context of indebtedness. (Körner 1986, 144–5) This issue goes beyond the question of how the IMF formulates its conditionality.

Overall, it was the Turkish technocrats who orchestrated the massive IMF loan, through a combination of negotiation and compliance, as well as a certain amount of financial daring. The IMF lost the initiative throughout the period under consideration and merely acted as evaluator and/or certifier of Turkish adjustment programs.

The Turkish technocrats under Ozal's leadership were able to speak the language of the Fund, in part perhaps because Ozal himself was a former World Bank official and had significant personal contacts at the two institutions. As mentioned previously, Ozal's credibility was very high in international financial circles. This facilitated the negotiation process.

As will be discussed later, the scale of the 1980 IMF loan goes far beyond any "functionalist" prediction. At this point, the simplest explanation is that bargaining was the dominant decision-making system.

The IMF. The IMF approached the initial negotiations with Turkey with scepticism, given the country's long-standing socialist traditions. As time passed, however, the staff of the Fund became better acquainted with Turkish motives and intentions and became thereby more sensitive to its needs. (de Vries 1985) The Turkish case is a good example of learning on the part of the Fund. It also illustrates how IMF conditionality can threaten political stability in certain countries with serious financial difficulties and a weak tradition of democracy.

The IMF began negotiations with Turkey in late-1977 amid a severe balance of payments crisis. The Fund allowed Turkey certain critical concessions in the early stages of negotiations—it allowed the Demirel administration to devalue its currency by ten rather than twenty percent and allowed the Ecevit administration to retain a multiple system of exchange rates, rather than to unify the system as required by the Articles of Agreement. (*IMF Survey* 1979d, 235) The senior Fund staff also overrode a recommendation to withhold the first disbursement of the 1978 stand-by until August and offered instead to make it available immediately. (McCauley 1979, 148–9)

Turkey's total debt as of April 1978 came to roughly $6.5 billion, with nearly thirty percent tied up in CTLDs and another thirty percent in trade arrears to OECD countries. (McCauley 1979, 146) Thus the IMF loan of SDR 300 million ($370 million), disbursed over a two-year period, was clearly not intended as massive relief but as the catalyst for rescheduling and other assistance to come from OECD countries and private banks. Objectives of the stand-by included reducing the balance of payments deficit from seven percent to four percent in 1978 and bringing inflation down from over 30 percent to 20 percent by April 1979. In addition the government was expected to substantially reduce its overseas obligations. (*IMF Survey* 1979a, 142; von Der Bay 1983, 348) Instruments employed to achieve these ends included: (1) increasing competitiveness of Turkish exports by providing specific incentives to exporters; (2) decreasing government debt by reducing payments to SEEs (possible by allowing an increase in SEE prices), limiting new foreign borrowing and reforming taxation policies; (3) reducing public and private bank credit and increasing savings through massive increases in interest rates; and (4) commitments to "prevent any further increase of arrears of foreign debt." (*IMF Survey* 1979a, 142; von Der Bay 1983, 345)

"In December, 1978, the IMF's monitors [mission] in Turkey reported that the Turks were not complying with the conditions attached to its standby austerity measures, including another official currency devaluation." (Carvounis 1984, 91) Talks between Turkey and the IMF were cut off and OECD countries abandoned plans for a second rescheduling, pending a new IMF agreement. The IMF determined that Turkey's non-compliance was due not only to such obvious external factors as the fresh rise in oil prices and the lack of funds from abroad, which in turn created shortages of imports for industry, but more importantly it was due to weakness on the part of the Ecevit administration, in that it was unwilling to place sufficient limits on internal demand for imports. (*IMF Survey* 1979c, 217)

As mentioned earlier, the Ecevit administration developed a new austerity program to attract additional funding from the IMF in 1979. With the help of a German central bank official, the Fund restored negotiations and developed a package with the government. The efforts of the Ecevit administration were rewarded with an even smaller IMF package of SDR 250 million ($320 million or 125 percent of quota) covering only one year. The terms of the agreement were "essentially the same" as those of the 1978 accord, "but more stringent." (von der Bay 1983, 349) They included the goals of lowering inflation, capping credit expansion and improving Turkey's ability to obtain foreign financing. Instruments to be used included lifting depressed interest rates closer to inflation levels, allowing increased SEE pricing flexibility, and limiting the government's budget deficit. (*IMF Survey* 1979c, 217)

As the 1979 program faltered, the new Demirel developed the "January 24 program." The program was such a "radical break with the country's long-standing tradition of state socialism" that it surpassed even the IMF's expectations. (*Institutional Investor* 1984, 144) As mentioned in an interview with Tom deVries, an IMF official directly involved in the Turkish loan, the government's enthusiasm was greeted at first with some scepticism in IMF circles. (deVries 1985) SEEs were freed from government controls and support and were placed under independent management, a necessary step to deal with the entrenched bureaucratic network found in the SEEs. New export incentives were introduced (e.g., imports used in the production of exports would be duty-free), regulations on foreign direct investment were liberalized and a "Foreign Investment Department" created, new investments were made in transportation, energy and agriculture, and taxation collection was tightened to increase public revenues. (Carvounis 1984, 95; *Institutional Investor* 1984, 144; von der Bay 1983, 351; Lewis & Urata 1983, 19; and Bogdanowicz-Bindert 1983, 351)

After five months of continual application and even strengthening of the Demirel stabilization program, and after protracted negotiations, the International Monetary Fund agreed to its largest single loan to a member to that point. The 1980 Turkish loan was also the first multi-year stand-by arrangement and set the tone for the use of the extended fund facility arrangements in the 1980s. (Carvounis 1984, 91) It offered SDR 1.25 billion ($1.65 billion) in assistance to be disbursed over a three-year period (SDR 417 million each year, the arrangement offered even more than the first rather generous SDR 300 million loan of 1978.). When the stand-by is added to Turkey's outstanding obligations to the Fund in loans already disbursed, the total Turkish borrowing from the Fund to 1980 amounted to over $2.5 billion, or nearly 1,000 percent of quota (the new stand-by alone was equivalent to 625 percent of Turkey's $260 million quota.). (*IMF Survey* 1980b, 177, 187–8)

The stand-by's goals were similar to those of previous agreements: (1) lowering inflation, (2) greater SEEs reliance on market forces, and (3) opening up the Turkish market to foreign investment and trade. These goals would be achieved by perpetuating the programs already put in place by the government: monetary restraint, gradual elimination of deficit financing in the public sector, raising of interest rates, tax reform, and other institutional reforms in the financial system of the country. Turkey showed its earnestness for the program by immediately implementing some of the IMF's new demands—prior to disbursement of the funds: "July, 1980, the rediscount rate of the Central Bank on short-term notes was raised considerably and interest rate ceilings on savings and loans were eliminated." (Lewis & Urata 1983, 19–20) The program was presented in a clearly optimistic manner, the announcement was the lead story in the bi-weekly IMF Survey and the tone uncharacteristically buoyant. (*IMF Survey* 1980b, 177, 187–188)

As the plan was implemented by the new military regime, the IMF continued regular disbursement of its loan. The turnaround for Turkey has been described as a "miracle," a term not usually associated with debt rescheduling. (Pevsner 1984, 109) The improvements were not long-lived for reasons that go beyond the scope of this study. Later IMF packages offered sums comparable to pre-1980 levels and were cancelled prematurely due to non-compliance. Inflation rose to over 40 percent again, real interest rates fell, the current account deficit rose by 80 percent in 1983, and unemployment hit 25 percent. (Pevsner 1984, 110–1)

Overall, during the period 1977 to 1982, the IMF demonstrated a certain amount of creativity by allowing Turkey access to large amounts of the Fund's resources and by recognizing the validity of "homespun" austerity packages. Although the Fund's 1978 and 1979 programs were fairly traditional, they displayed a certain degree of flexibility to Turkish demands and needs. The IMF seems to have displayed a tendency to "reward" Turkish efforts in certain cases (1978 and 1980), although it was quick to rescind its loans when compliance and attitude deteriorated.

Finally, there were personal and idiosyncratic dimensions of the Turkish debt crisis that cannot be ignored. As mentioned by Tom de Vries, IMF official familiar with the Turkish case, as Turkish officials dealt with the Fund, over time personal misunderstandings and scepticism waned (there were fewer "contre-coups," as he put it), which allowed for a more congenial and productive negotiating atmosphere. Also, the experience of Turgut Ozal in the World Bank in the early 1970s gave him not only personal ties to the institutions of the Bank and the Fund, but gave him familiarity with the language and values of the institutions themselves. Also, as mentioned, his former affiliation and reputation enhanced his credibility with international financial institutions and increased their willingness to cooperate. (de Vries 1985)

With regard to the three models, the IMF's behavior seems consistent with the bargaining model in many dimensions. The Fund showed a willingness to compromise and negotiate flexibly over conditionality. Also, the staff of the Fund seem to have changed their attitudes regarding Turkey over time, and these changes in attitude had a significant effect on conditionality, especially in the case of the 1980 loan where the Fund moved beyond traditional lending levels. Finally, the senior leadership of the Fund played a direct and significant role in softening the terms of Turkey borrowing, especially in the early stages of the negotiations.

Secondary Actors

The OECD. The Organization for Economic Cooperation and Development draws together the industrialized nations of the world for purposes of economic planning and analysis. In the case of Turkey, the OECD played the rather unusual role of debt negotiator and rescheduler. This role was in part forced upon it by the myriad of private creditors who sought relief from the Turkish debt overhang. Given the largely overlapping memberships of the OECD and NATO, Turkey benefitted from the political desire of OECD members to strengthen a marginal ally.

The OECD organized a series of reschedulings in conjunction with each of the the IMF loans. Western governments and bankers kept in close contact with each other, the bankers providing a laundry list to Turkey in February 1978 of policies they hoped to see adopted. The OECD countries prepared a rescheduling program with the bankers that included plans for fresh capital. All was in place by the time Turkey's first in a series of stand-by arrangements was announced on April 24, 1978. (Carvounis 1984, 91, von der Bay 1983, 344–5)

The OECD nations' program involved a nine-year rescheduling of $1.5 billion in overdue debt. "The public creditors rescheduled four-fifths of principal and interest due on long-term (over one year) loans for 30 months starting January 1977." (McCauley 1979, 148) At the insistence of the United States, Turkey's short-term debts were also rescheduled. The United States was concerned that there in fact be money available to pay back the long-term loans in which it had participated in a major way. (McCauley 1979, 148) In addition, $2.4 billion in trade arrears were rescheduled by a large number of individual trading companies involved in Turkey. (*Institutional Investor* 1984, 144)

As was mentioned previously, the OECD also intervened to restore warm relations between the Fund and Turkey in 1979 as the Ecevit administration delayed and partially failed to implement conditionality. A German representative of the Deutsche Bank, Walter Leisler-Keip, who "acted as an intermediary on behalf of the West German government and the other OECD countries, was able to bring the Turkish government and the Fund on to speaking terms again." (von der Bay 1983, 349)

In return for the 1979 austerity plans of Ecevit, the OECD promptly offered $900 million in assistance from the governments, especially the U.S. and West Germany, $400 million from private banks and another $400 million in rescheduled debts, completed by a recommendation to the World Bank for $300 million in project loans, bringing the total aid package to more than $1.430 billion. (*IMF Survey* 1979b, 195–196) The OECD made it clear in their announcement of the package that it would go into effect only with "the conclusion of a new stand-by arrangement between the Turkish authorities and the IMF." (*IMF Survey* 1979b, 195–196) This is important, since it illustrates the symbiotic relationship between the Fund and the OECD: by promising a loan, the OECD exerted indirect pressure on the Fund to accept the Ecevit government's letter of intent promptly. On the other hand, the OECD was sending a clear message to Ecevit that he would need to display more flexibility in IMF negotiations.

The next major intervention of the OECD followed the announcement of the June 1980 IMF loan. Following the completion of the negotiations, the OECD countries followed suit with a large-scale rescheduling of Turkish debt, following a pattern by now well in place. three billion dollars of Turkey's debt, of which $2.3 billion was to fall due before July 1983, was rescheduled in July 1980. Marilyn Seiber elaborates:

> Turkey pledged to pay ten percent of that in two percent annual installments between 1980 and 1985 and the remained over the next five years. In addition, $100 million to $800 million [sic.] of the previously rescheduled debt of 1978 and 1979 would be rescheduled again. . . . By July 1980, Turkey had received total aid pledges of $1.65 billion from OECD members, $1.65 billion from the IMF, $100 million from the Common Market, $600 million from the World Bank, and $250 million from Saudi Arabia. (Seiber 1983, 72)

As already mentioned, the results over the short run of the 1980–81 reform efforts were remarkable by any measure. OECD countries offered yet another round of rescheduling and aid in May, 1981, and would later offer a massive aid package amounting to over five billion dollars in 1982.

The role of the OECD was generally positive, in that it facilitated communication and negotiation by serving both as catalyst and mediator. The motives of the OECD members involved a mixture of political and economic motives, in that the OECD was interested in preserving Turkey's creditworthiness and economic stability. Given the fact that the OECD typically argued for accommodation and compromise, it would seem that it was generally more concerned with resolving the immediate crisis and restoring stabiity than bringing about long-term liberalization and adjustment.

Marilyn Seiber stresses the importance of Turkey's role relative to the NATO alliance as the key factor in its ability to extract concessions from the OECD and the IMF:

> In the case of Turkey, when a crisis debt-servicing situation occurred, the OECD countries scrambled to the rescue not only because their commercial banks were heavily loaned-out to Turkey, but because Turkey is an important military interest to the West. Hence, Turkey's bargaining position on the debt issue was enhanced, and the OECD members agreed to most of Turkey's demands for the debt rescheduling. . . [Turkey used] its political chips in the form of its political importance to NATO countries as persuasion. (Seiber 1983, 145)

It would seem that the role of the OECD nations is generally consistent with the political model of decision-making, although it is not clear whether executive board representatives of these nations directly intervened in IMF policy-making. For example, in spite of harsh rhetoric from the Ecevit administration regarding the pending 1978 agreement, the Executive Board approved the letter of intent without change. It is clear that the OECD played a role in fcilitating and encouraging negotiations, but this involved pressure on both parties (Turkey and the IMF).

It would be premature to conclude that the OECD activities shifted IMF policy-making into the political model, although it clearly acted as an actively interested bargaining partner.

Private Creditors. Some, including Fund officials, felt that private creditors were largely to blame for Turkey's debt crisis in 1977 because they made heavy use of the CTLD program in the first place. (Sampson 1981, 328) As Turkey found itself unable to honor its committments through the CTLDs in mid-1977, it found itself with a two billion dollar debt due immediately. (von der Bay 1983, 340) Bankers sought to extricate themselves from what now appeared to be a very hazardous investment by making further lending conditional on IMF and OECD support. (von der Bay 1983, 343) In 1978, for example, bankers pressed their demands on OECD members for specific policy reforms in Turkey. In particular, they demanded a significant devaluation of the lira. (McCauley 1979, 146)

Once the IMF and the OECD became involved, private creditors behaved very cautiously, waiting until a formal letter of intent had been approved and the OECD had committed itself to further aid before rescheduling old Turkish debts. In 1978, for example, after the OECD assembled $1.5 billion, private bankers rescheduled $2.6 billion in Turkish short-term and CTLD debts.

Private banks received strong pressure from both the Turkish government and Western public creditors. In July, the Turkish Minister of Finance demanded softer terms for the 1979 rescheduling of $2.9 billion. "Banks have made and will continue to make profits from developing-country borrowers. . . and must, therefore, play their part in dealing with problems of the world economy." OECD and IMF officials concurred, although less blatantly, in this assessment and resented efforts by banks to pull out of Turkey. (*World Business Weekly* 1980, 50)

Turgut Ozal was well-respected in international financial circles and seems to have facilitated warmer relations with the private banks. The private banks played a direct role in initiating the IMF lending process, since it was their unwillingness to reschedule without an IMF program that led to the 1977 Turkish debt crisis. However, after the IMF and the OECD intervened, private creditors seem to have removed themselves from the day-to-day negotiating process. It is not clear whether bankers were satisfied with Turkey's adjustment programs after 1978, although one can assume that they were impressed with the IMF support and endoresment Turkey received. Overall, the bankers seem to have played a relatively passive role in Turkish negotiations after 1978, implying that neither the political nor the bargaining models would entirely explain their behavior. By implication, the absence of continual private bank involvement implies the Fund was left to operate on its functionalist logic.

Turkish Worker Organizations and Extremist Groups. Turkish workers, many of whom were dependent on the government expenditures, were well-organized and highly mobilized during the period under consideration. Many wide-spread strikes broke out as various austerity programs were proposed and implemented from 1977 to 1982. DISK, the left-wing Turkish umbrella union organization, "took the lead in opposing the attempts of the 'fascist Demirel regime' to impose austerity" which resulted in a dramatic decline in real Turkish wages. (Pevsner 1984, 79) Increased strike activity in January to August 1980 "resulted in the loss of 7.7 million workdays, compared to only 1.1 million workdays in all of 1979." (Lewis & Urata 1983, 20) In February, clashes between strikers and government troops involved more than 10,000 individuals. In 1980, as real wages for workers declined as a result of the January 24 austerity measures, more strikes broke out. Nearly eight million workdays were lost in the first three quarters of 1980, more than the total number of workdays lost in strikes during the eight preceding years. (von der Bay 1983, 354)

Throughout the period of democratic rule in the 1980s, Turkey suffered from wide-spread political instability. Beyond the activities of labor unions, terrorist groups committed an ever-increasing number of attacks on political targets. For example, during the Ecevit administration, 2,500 were killed in terrorist attacks. (Pevsner 1984, 73; Carvounis 1984, 96; von der Bay 1983, 359) During the Demirel austerity program, terrorist incidents increased to as many as 1,150 in a single month. (Pevsner 1984, 87)

The military coup came as a relief to most Turks, who had grown weary of extremist violence. As was expected, the military government quickly restored a semblance of calm in the urban areas, bringing the number of monthly terrorist incidents from 1,150 to 358 per month within a short time. Thousands of extremists were "rounded up," regardless of their political motives. (Pevsner 1984, 87)

In point of fact, then, the terrorist and opposition groups in Turkey increased the leverage of technocratic elements in Turkey's government. As the violence limited the flexibility of the democratic governments in dealing with the need for economic adjustment, the military option became more and more desirable for many Turks both in and out of government. This in turn played into the hand of international capital. The implications of this process for the three models of IMF decision-making is important: there exist absolute limits of negotiating flexibility for many debtor nations which increase the likelihood of IMF dominance over the long run.

Conclusion

Turkey received massive assistance from the Fund, relative to its lending history. This was achieved after several more stricter and smaller loans were agreed upon, but not implemented. The willingness of the Ozal-dominated regime to independently adopt and implement a very strict set of programs seems to have been the key to Turkey's eventual success in reaching agreement with the fund for a generous and lenient program. This program's implementation came, however, at the cost of Turkish democracy.

The bargaining model offers some interesting explanations of the Turkish case the other two models would not provide. For example, it was pointed out that Turgot Ozal, the spear-head of the adjustment program, was a former World Bank official and was well-known by and well-acquainted with Fund staff. In addition, the period of interaction between Turkish officials and Fund staff was sufficient to eliminate some of the suspicion and misunderstanding that existed in the early years. This easier interaction of 1980 undoubtedly assisted in the successful conclusion of negotiations. Conversely, the reluctance on the part of the government to implement certain provisions of the IMF package for political reasons was a serious impediment to successful negotiations prior to Ozal's arrival on the scene. The government was divided, society was polarized, and political institutions and traditions did not encourage peaceful resolution of social conflicts. Although internal opposition is sometimes used to advantage by some states to extract concessions from the Fund, the suspicion and mistrust of the early days were too great to be softened by pleas for clemency. Turkey had too long of a history to ignore.

However, much of the IMF's approach can also be explained in terms of simple functionalism. The staff had observed Turkey's historical experience and its present problems and, in rather strict application of its economic models, offered a program which, though unrealistic, was certainly correct. The second of its two "strict" programs was slightly tougher, but not by very much, consistent with the slight deterioration of Turkey's economy during the interim. The third, generous program was offered only after the administration had proved itself willing and able to carry out serious reform. The economy had already showed significant progress, and it was not in need of such dramatic adjustment: hence the more lenient package. The progression follows sound economic logic and common sense. Personalities, tactics and political will had nothing to do with the content of the packages.

Although this interpretation may be consistent with the results of the plans, it does not account for the day-to-day process of negotiation. The staff was not unanimous in its appraisal of Turkish performance, and disagreements emerged in the case of the first program. Also, if the Fund had applied strict economic criteria to its conditionality, the first assistance package would have been "cancelled" prior to its initiation, since Turkey had fallen out of compliance before the program had been reviewed by the executive board. It seems significant to recall the role of opposition elements as well, even though the results are the same, since it was ultimately the silencing of these forces that made implementation of the program possible.

The political model also offers some interesting perspectives, since the NATO element was reported to be a significant factor in OECD policy-making. Because the private banks played a relatively minor role in debt restructuring, this political factor may have indeed have a significant effect overall. The specific approach of the OECD creditors was, in a manner similar to the Americans in the case of Great Britain, conditional on successful completion of an IMF package. This, as in the case of Great Britain, gave the Fund a great deal of autonomy in its policy-making. However, it may be more correct to assign the political influences to the decisions of the OECD, but not necessarily to those of the IMF. Unfortunately, information is not available to draw a definitive conclusion.

Also, the political model does not account satisfactorily for the dramatic change of IMF policy, since the change did not coincide with changes in Turkish foreign policy or alliance structure. The possibility of withdrawal from NATO was alluded to throughout the negotiations. If this was the principal, or even a major cause, for the leniency of the 1980 program, it is difficult to explain the strictness of the preceding packages.

Although the bargaining and functionalist models account almost equally for the policy outcomes, the bargaining model accounts better for the day-to-day process of negotiation.

Bibliography

Aronson, Jonathan. 1977. *Money and Power: Banks and the World Monetary System.* Beverly Hills: Sage Library of Social Research #66.

Bogdanowicz-Bindert, Christine. 1983. "Portugal, Turkey and Peru: Three Successful Stabilization Programmes Under the Auspices of the IMF." *World Development* 11 (January): 65–70.

Carvounis, Chris C. 1984. *The Debt Dilemma of Developing Nations.* Westport, CN: Quorum Books.

Cohen, Benjamin J. 1981. *Banks and Balance of Payments: Private Lending in the International Adjustment Process.* Mountclair, N.J.: Allan Held, Osmun.

de Vries, Thomas. 1985. Interview with the author. Embassy of the Netherlands, Washington, D.C. June 19.

Dodd, D. H. 1983. *The Crisis of Turkish Democracy.* Northgate, UK: The Eothen Press.

International Monetary Fund. 1978. *International Financial Statistics.* 31 (October): 374.

IMF Survey. 1979a. May 4: 142.

———. 1979b. June 18: 195–196.

———. 1979c. July 23: 217.

———. 1979d. August 6: 235.

———. 1980a. February 18: 60–61.

———. 1980b. June 25: 177, 187–188.

———. 1982. August 2: 229.

Institutional Investor. 1984. September: 136–150.

Journal of Commerce. 1977. September 7: 11.

Körner, Peter, Mass, Gero, Seibold, Thomas, and Textlaff, Rainer. 1986. *The IMF and the Debt Crisis.* London: Zed Books.

Lewis, Jeffrey D., and Urata, Shujiro. 1983. "Turkey: Recent Economic Performance and Medium-term Prospects, 1978–1990," *World Bank Staff Working Papers* #602.

MacKenzie, Kenneth. 1981. *Turkey Under the Generals.* London: Conflict Studies.

McCauley, Robert. 1979. "A Compendium of IMF Troubles: Turkey, Portugal, Peru, Egypt," in Franko, Lawrence and Seiber, Marilyn, eds. *Developing Country Debt.* New York: Pergamon Press.

Middle Eastern Economic Digest. 1978. August 11: 25.

Pevsner, Lucille. 1984. *Turkey's Political Crisis: Background, Perspectives, Prospects.* New York: Praeger.

Remmer, Karen. 1986. "The Politics of 'Economic Stabilization: IMF Standby Programs in Latin America, 1954–1984." *Comparative Politics* 19 (October): 1–24.

Sampson, Anthony. 1981. *The Money Lenders: Bankers and a World of Turmoil,* New York: Viking Press, NY 1981.

Seiber, Marilyn. 1983. *International Borrowing by Developing Countries.* New York: Pergamon Press.

von der Bay, Helmut. 1983. "*Experience with the Rescheduling of International Debt.*" in Fair, Donald, ed. *International Lending in a Fragile World Economy.* The Hague: Martinus Nijhoff: 338–360.

Williamson, John. 1982. "The Lending Policies of the International Monetary Fund." *Policy Analyses in International Economics.* 1 August.

World Business Weekly. 1980. July 7: 50.

9

The Case of
Argentina: 1982–1987

The experiences of Argentina during the mid-1980s illustrates how a nation can use its excessive indebtedness to advantage in certain negotiating situations. It also illustrates the capacity of the managing director of the Fund to circumvent the executive board through direct intervention in the negotiating process. Finally, Argentina's experience also shows the vulnerability to internal pressures that is experienced by a heavily indebted government. Overall, the Argentina case provides strong support for the need for a bargaining model of IMF decision-making.

Background

In the mid-1970s, after several decades of import-substitution industrialization, a succession of authoritarian regimes attempted to liberalize the Argentine economy by opening it to foreign competition. This strategy was combined with almost limitless foreign borrowing to finance Argentine industry (much of it heavily subsidized). The hoped-for revitalization was fitful, however, and the early 1980s saw Argentina strapped by an insurmountable foreign debt and a stagnating economy, both of which were accompanied by political and social instability.

As described by Carvounis, Argentina in the mid-1970s suffered from six "chronic ailments":

(1) Excessive dependence on unreliable international commodity markets, (2) similarly excessive reliance on foreign capital, (3) ineffective government interventionism in domestic markets, (4) antiquated industry and technological stagnation in agriculture, (5) a highly-mobilized labor movement, and (6) a bloated public sector, featuring high levels of deficit spending. (Carvounis 1984, 139–140)

The military government of General Jorge Videla was quick to announce a series of drastic austerity measure to be administered, in classic bureaucratic-authoritarian style (O'Donnell 1985), by the "super-minister" of economic policy, José Martinez de Hoz. (Pion-Berlin 1985, 57)

Central among the minister's policies was the "proceso," which consisted of a harsh program of economic reform. The economic goals of the government included: (1) lowering inflation through wage restrains and fiscal austerity, (2) reducing money supply growth by 50 percent through interest rate liberalization, (3) stimulating and rationalizing industry through privatization and trade liberalization. (Pion-Berlin 1985, 58–9, Carvounis 1984, 140) A particularly unusual dimension of the program was the "tablita," a program of maintaining a slightly overvalued but declining currency in order to stimulate imports and eventually bring domestic prices to international levels. (Pion-Berlin 1985, 59)

From 1975 to 1978, the effects of proceso were promising. They included: a decline in the inflation rate, an increase in foreign currency reserves, a growth of the GNP, and a dramatic improvement of the balance of payments current account. (Carvounis 1985, 140, Marshall et al. 1983, 277, 304) However, this growth came at the expense of Argentina's privately-owned industry which could not compete with the foreign manufacturers. "One economist calculates that the dismantling of industrial plant amounted to 30 percent of fixed assets in that sector between 1976 and 1981." (Stallings 1983, 32) Inflation was reduced in large measure because of a government-imposed 40 percent reduction of wages in 1976. (Marshall et al. 1983, 304) As the decade came to a close, the military government began losing its support and became progressively more isolated.

An unusual aspect of the economic program was the guarantee extended in 1977 by the government covering ninety percent of all deposits in the banking system. (World Bank 1985a, 207) This guarantee would eventually come back to haunt the regime. As the government borrowed heavily during the late-1970s, Argentina's total foreign debt doubled in 1974–78 from $4.9 to $8.9 billion and coubled again from 1978 to 1982 to more than $18 billion (see Table 9.1 and Figure 9.1).

In March 1980, four of Argentina's largest banks failed almost simultaneously under the pressure of over-extension and an inability to collect on domestic loans to private industry. The government liquidated the largest bank and, for a time, attempted to prop up the others. Capital flight increased dramatically and shook the economic policymakers in the government deeply, precipitating a major review of the proceso. (Pion-Berlin 1985, 60)

TABLE 9.1 Argentina's Foreign Debt, 1974-1983 ($US million)

	1974	1976	1978	1980	1981	1982	1983
TOTAL FOREIGN DEBT	4936	6541	8963	12350	14426	18303	26449
Public Official Debt	1777	2262	2889	3009	3427	3653	3458
bilateral	559	637	902	1087	1229	1321	1413
multilateral	528	552	750	824	699	687	600
Private Debt	2161	3239	5095	8285	8665	13870	22579
TOTAL DEBT SERVICE	729	868	2118	1990	2115	2347	2343
Public Official Debt	136	191	223	346	329	358	318
Private Debt	656	677	1895	1625	1825	1989	2025
DEBT SERVICE/EXPORTS	16.80%	18.50%	27%	17.80%	18.20%	24.10%	24.00%

Source: World Bank 1983b.

FIGURE 9.1 Argentina's Foreign Debt, 1974-1983

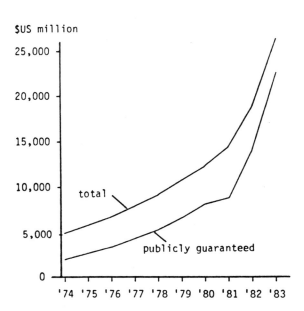

Source: World Bank 1985b.

A new Minister of the Economy, Lorenzo Sigaut, adopted a program that stradled the dual objectives of economic recovery and balance of payments adjustment. This required manipulation of policy mechanisms with contradictory effects with no clear solution in sight. (Carvounis 1984, 142) Hardliners in the junta, who came to power with Galtieri in December 1982, sought a more consistent liberalization program and appointed Roberto Alemann to replace Sigaut.

Alemann's efforts to control both the foreign debt and inflation failed. A rescheduling in 1980 left the country with more debt to be paid at a higher, floating interest rate. In spite of wage freezes, inflation reached 165 percent in 1982 and 344 percent in 1983. Argentina also began to experience massive capital flight, in spite of government guarantees. (World Bank, 1985b, 3, 222)

The government's economic policy reversed itself in mid 1982 with the departure of Galtieri after the Falklands War. Dagnino Pastore, the new Minister of the Economy, returned to a more populist economic strategy. His goals were "boosting exports and encouraging domestic consumption." (DelaMaide 1984, 114) The government stalled on payment of its arrears and relations with British banks remained strained after the war. In the words of Corradi: "The entire financial system had the solidity of a house of cards, eventually requiring the massive intervention of the very same state that, according to official doctrine, was to stay out of business." (1985, 132) Pastore was succeeded by Jorge Wehbe who chose compromise rather than confrontation, both regarding foreign investors as well as in choosing between austerity and expansion. It was Wehbe who first undertook serious negotiations for a large-scale adjustment loan from the IMF in 1982.

Argentina's Experience with the IMF

After protracted negotiations the IMF and Argentina agreed to its first major loan in December 1982. The IMF agreed to provide $1.6 billion over a fifteen-month period (the amount of time remaining to the lame-duck military government), along with $550 million from its Compensatory Financing Facilities. (Stallings 1983, 35) The conditions of the agreement included an Argentine pledge to reduce the public sector deficit by 43 percent (from 14 percent of GNP in 1982 to 8 percent in 1983) and keep inflation to 150 percent (down from roughly 500 percent). (*IMF Survey* 1983, 1) The IMF agreement opened the way for a $1.1 billion private bridge loan to allow Argentina to catch up on arrears, as well as $1.5 billion in fresh loans. (*Wall Street Journal* 1982b, 34)

In November 1983, Argentina carried out a massive, unilateral debt rescheduling by converting $5.5 billion in private debt into public bonds. As explained by DelaMaide:

> The decision in late November to 'nationalize' the $5.5b. debt of Argentina's private sector did not help any. It amounted to a unilateral rescheduling of the debt, contracted a year and a half earlier by private enterprises with exchange rate guarantees from the Argentine government. Subsequent devaluations of the peso had made the dollar debt prohibitively expensive for the government as guarantor. It didn't have any extra dollars, and $3.2b. of the debts were falling due in the next few months. So it decided to issue government bonds to the creditors of the private companies, who technically owed the money. The five-year bonds were to be redeemed in four installments beginning in 1986. Interest was set at 1 point over Libor. The only alternative open to creditors, short of declaring default, was to write off the debt. (1984, 116)

The military failed to keep inflation below 400 percent, far short of the 150 percent IMF objective. In addition, the government fell further in arrears on its foreign debt, waiting until the the deadline at the end of each quarter to draw sparingly from consistently high foreign currency reserves. (*Wall Street Journal* 1983a, 37)

With the arrival of democratically-elected Raúl Alfonsín at the end of 1983, Argentina's government took a more intransigent approach to IMF negotiations. Pinelo calls new Minister of the Economy Bernardo Grinspun's strategy economic "brinkmanship." (1985, 19) As the March 30, 1984 deadline for interest payments on private foreign debt approached, Grinspun made it clear that Argentina would not be able to pay (in spite of its adequate reserve position). (Watkins 1985, 43) Private U.S. bankers and even several Latin American governments provided short-term lending on condition that the government undertake negotiations with the IMF within 30 days. (Pinelo 1985, 20)

Argentina initiated negotiations with the IMF in the spring of 1984 and quickly reached an impasse. To break the deadlock, Argentina composed its own "letter of intent" and forwarded it to the executive board for approval. The action was highly unorthodox and the proposal was greeted with contempt since it lacked the managing director's approval. (Kafka 1985) By the time the details were sorted out, however, yet another arrears deadline had arrived (June 30, 1984), requiring yet another round of intense negotiations in order to prevent bankers from recording a loss for the quarter. Bankers provided $125 and rescheduled the deadline for Argentina's interest payments.

An agreement was finally reached between Argentina and the Fund for $1.66 billion over fifteen months with the following conditions: (1) reduction of inflation to 300 percent from current levels of 1,200 percent, (2) gradual elimination of price controls, (3) reduction of the public deficit from 8.1 percent of GDP to 5.4 percent, and (4) expanding agricultural exports. In response to the agreement, private bankers renegotiated the debt and provided $4.2 billion in fresh loans. Within three months, however, the program was cancelled due to non-compliance and new negotiations were initiated.

Throughout this period, Argentina's domestic economic condition continued to deteriorate. Inflation remained at roughly 1,000 percent throughout 1984, the country's debt-service ratio neared 50 percent, and the aggregate domestic economy began to contract. (Watkins 1985, 39) In the context of these persistent and grave problems, the Alfonsín administration developed and implemented a severe austerity/liberalization program without IMF advice (although negotiations with the Fund were being carried out in parallel channels). The so-called "Plan Austral" was announced in June 1985 and involved freezing wages for three months, following which wage hikes would be indexed to 90 percent the inflation rate, elimination of the public sector deficit by 1986, and a change in the Argentine currency (from the peso to the austral) coinciding with a devaluation. (Pinelo 1985, 25)

TABLE 9.2 Exchange Rate of Peso/Austral, 1985 (relative to $US)

	Official Rate	Parallel Rate
Jan 18	201	240
Feb 15	242	317
Mar 15	306	402
Apr 19	396	527
May 17	525	619
Jun 13	789	920
Jun 21*	0.8	0.82
Jul 19	0.8	0.94
Aug 16	0.8	0.92
Sep 09	0.8	0.96

* Currency reform
Source: Data for this table are taken from International
Currency Review, published by World Reports Ltd.,
108 Horseferry Rd., London SW1P 2EF, England:
Volume 17 #2 (October 1985), p. 47.

In the wake of the announcement and implementation of the Plan Austral, the IMF extended the deadline on an already expanded 1984 agreement (now worth $1.8 billion) and began negotiations on a new $1.4 billion package that was approved in January 1986. The program's objectives were not significantly different from those outlined in the Plan itself.

The Plan had immediate, positive effects (see Table 9.2 and Figure 9.2), although they did not persist over the medium term. By late-1987 Argentina's negotiating position had stiffened as evidenced by its threat to cease payments of its arrears. The IMF declared Argentina out of compliance with the 1986 program and withheld disbursement of the final $750 million installment. As Peronist pressure mounted throughout the period 1986–1989, the Radical government was put on the defensive and compelled to make concessions to labor and consumer groups. Ironically, when the Peronist victory finally came in mid-1989, the new president immediately announced austerity measures comparable to the Plan Austral.

Analysis of the Players

As with other case studies, the decision-making process in Argentina's case is more clear if one breaks down the players into major groups. In this case, the technocrats and the populists represent major decision-making groups within the Argentine government, while the the managing

FIGURE 9.2 Argentina's Monthly Inflation Rate, 1985-1986

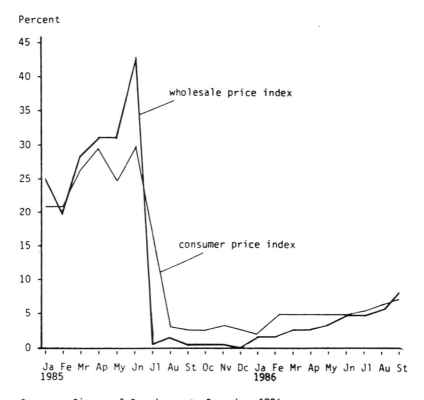

Source: Finance & Development, December 1986.

director, the executive board, the staff and even certain outside creditors
play important parts in the Fund's decision-making.

Primary Actors

Argentine Technocrats. In his significant work on bureaucratic authoritarianism, Guillermo O'Donnell discusses the role of technocrats in
the military governments of several Latin American nations during the
1970s. (1973) However, what is lacking in his original study is the
observation that these technocrats did not simply vanish with the arrival
of democratically-elected governments in the 1980s. Instead, they persisted, sometimes permeating entire ministries with a technocratic culture
of their own. This was the case, to a certain degree, in Argentina, where

many of the technocrats the military government had relied upon during the late-1970s remained in their posts after the 1983 transfer of power to the Alfonsín administration.

In general, the staff of the Ministry of the Economy were the most "technocratic" elements of the economic policy-making bodies in the early-1980s in Argentina. When negotiations were underway in 1982, the IMF team found a relatively sympathetic ear in the economy ministry, so much so that a former junta member called for the immediate dismissal of all civil servants who received their training in the United States, charging that they served as "Trojan horses" to the western creditors and negotiators. (DelaMaide 1984, 115) Once the agreement was reached, however, the influence of these elements of the bureaucracy was reduced, as evidenced by junta decisions to violate the terms of the IMF loan almost immediately. (DelaMaide 1984, 116)

By the end of the military government's rule, many conservative economists criticized its poor treatment of private capital. The eminent Argentine economist who spear-headed ECLA (UN Economic Commission for Latin America), Raúl Prébisch, now a member of the Radical Party opposition, pointed out that "the policy followed here has suffocated enterprise instead of promoting it." (Carvounis 1984, 148) Aldo Ferrer, another prominent economic advisor to the Radical Party, also criticized the military government's wastefulness. (Ferrer 1985, 32)

In spite of the criticisms of the military government's policies, the incoming Radical Party government adopted many of the same strategies and tactics with regard to negotiations with the IMF and implementation of austerity measures. As will be seen later, policy-making during this period was dominated by Bernardo Grinspun, a populist-oriented economist.

By 1985, however, economic conditions in Argentina had deteriorated to a crisis point and the Alfonsín administration made a dramatic break with populist policies. The most important indication of change in the government's attitude came early in 1985 with the swapping of posts by Grinspun and Planning minister Juan Sourouille. Sourouille took over the economic portfolio in February, with the enthusiastic support of Western financiers: "what Sourouille offers is order and coherence in monetary, fiscal and wage policies. . .he isn't a Radical Party hack." (*Wall Street Journal* 1985c, 35) Grinspun, along with departing Central Bank President Enrique Garcia Vazquez, were not mourned by IMF staff, having been described as "abrasive," "not a very strong economic team," and on "shouting terms" with IMF officials. (*Latin America Weekly Report* 1985a, 1)

Over the next two months, Argentina adopted an approach not unlike that of Turkey and India: the government attempted to present a program which was more drastic and austere than even the IMF had been able to construct and propose. The tactic is based on sound logic, even though it may appear at first a bit foolhardy. First, in the case of Argentina in 1985, a drastic plan was clearly needed, given the economic crisis at the time. But more important, for the government to take the initiative, rather than to simply sign on to an IMF program would defuse the accusation of being "coerced" into the program by outsiders. For a country as nationalistic as Argentina, this was a crucial element in a successful adjustment program. Ultimately, there was little to lose from such a tactic. If the program worked, the government would receive the praises of both foreign and domestic observers, translating into solidified support internally and fresh capital from abroad. If it failed, a more tentative program would have undoubtedly failed as well, and the government could not be faulted for failure of nerve. The crucial element in the choice of such a strategy, however, is to wait until the economic situation has deteriorated to such as extent that the costs to the population of implementing an austerity program are lower than the costs of doing nothing. All of these considerations seem to have played into the Argentine decision. (*Wall Street Journal* 1985c, 35)

As early as late-April, while Sourouille and his team of American-educated economists was studying the historical experience of such debtors as Germany, Israel and Bolivia as preparation for developing a plan for Argentina, President Alfonsín announced cuts of twelve percent in 1985 public expenditures and a forced savings plan targeted at the wealthy. (*Wall Street Journal* 1985b, 36) Sourouille announced plans to tighten hard currency capital flight. (*New York Times* 1985a, I:34) In mid-May all dollar-denominated and other foreign currency-denominated accounts in Argentina were declared frozen for 120 days. (*New York Times* 1985c, I:1) This action closely followed the failure of Argentina's third-largest bank, and was welcomed by domestic bankers. (*New York Times* 1985b, IV:10)

The degree to which Grinspun was excluded from policy-making circles is evidenced by his ignorance of the "Plan Austral". It was his threat to expose the plan to the press that prompted Alfonsin's decision to go public. (*International Currency Review* 1985, 45–6)

On June 14, 1985, Raúl Alfonsín appeared on national television to announce his "plan austral," or "war economy." (*New York Times* 1985d, I:1) The plan was described as "audacious," "courageous," "more IMF than the IMF" and the most radical program in Argentina's history. (*International Currency Review* 1985, 41) The plan provided for a bold attack on inflation by freezing wages and prices for three months, following which wage increases would be limited to 90 percent of inflation (equivalent to a 10 percent real wage cut) (Pinelo 1985, 25), and a reduction of money supply growth to zero. (*International Currency Review* 1985, 41) In addition, the public sector deficit was targeted for elimination by 1986 after reduction to four percent of GDP in 1985 from its 13.5 percent level. This would be achieved through higher taxes and utility charges and reductions in military and capital expenditures. Finally, as a more symbolic than substantive measure, the currency would be changed from the peso to the austral, at a value of 1,000 old pesos. The new currency's official rate of exchange was 1 austral=$1.25—a slight devaluation. (*New York Times* 1985e, I:4) Banks were closed for three days to adjust their records, as well as to prevent a run on the banks in case the plan backfired. Unfortunately, the change in currency did little to affect currency speculation on the active parallel exchange market.

In economic terms, the program was successful in the short-term. Inflation plummeted to a two percent annual rate by November, although it appears that inflationary expectations were not yet broken. (*Latin America Weekly Report* 1985c, 1, *International Currency Review* 1985, 46) By September, frozen assets in foreign bank accounts were released. Argentine exports were also improving, producing a $4 billion trade surplus in 1985, although European dumping of beef and grain on the international market pitted Alfonsín against the EEC. (*Latin American Weekly Report* 1985b, 4)

The program also gave Alfonsín the initiative with the IMF, in that there was nothing the IMF could add to its terms when granting a new loan in January 1986. As was mentioned, this seizure of the initiative was comparable to what both India and Turkey had done before. More will be said later about the role of the Fund.

In terms of the three decision-making models proposed earlier, the behavior of the technocrats in the Argentine government during the period 1982–1987 is intriguing. Normally in a Third World debtor nation, one would expect the technocrats to play the part of advocate for the IMF's position—a belief based on their Western training and value orientation. However, in the case of Argentina, the technocrats seem to have been made to play a more nationalistic part by increasing the government's leverage with the Fund. This of course discounts the argument that the government was itself manipulated by the technocrats. The principal reason for rejecting this reasoning is the fact that Alfonsín controlled the appointment process and seems to have controlled the decision-making process itself—see the appointment of Sourrouille and exclusion of Grinspun as evidence. The implications of this development are interesting, not only because it tends to strengthen the bargaining model, but also it indicates that the existence of a techncratic class does not necessarily undermine democracy and civilian government.

Argentine Populists. Just as there were technocratic elements and philosophies that persisted after the fall of Argentina's military government, there were also populists elements that existed in both the democratic regime and its military precursor. Especially during the closing years of the military government, the regime became extremely concerned about questions of legitimacy and, by implication, of social welfare and nationalism. In the weeks preceding the 1983 election, the military had even attempted a electoral alliance with Peronist and worker organizations. These populist elements, while small in the military government, were far more dominant in the early years of the Radical Party administration and heavily influenced economic policy and negotiating strategy with IMF.

The military, by the end of 1983, was most preoccupied with making the transition to democracy as painless as possible for themselves. For example, the junta passed an "Amnesty Law" which would have impeded prosecution of military leaders after the transfer of power. (Viola & Mainwaring 1985, 208) There were those in the junta—especially the air force officers—who argued that the debt negotiations should be suspended, or at least stalled, and the debt crisis left to the civilians. (*Wall Street Journal* 1983b, 33) Others in the military hoped to stay within advising distance of the civilians by negotiating with the front-running Peronist candidates. This strategy backfired, in that it discredited the Peronists and helped to bring about their electoral defeat in October.

The military prided itself on the concessional loan it negotiated with the IMF prior to elections. As described by Economy Minister Jorge Wehbe, the new stand-by would allow the constitutional government "to act free of problems and to be acle to meet all the committments entered into, without this meaning any interference in the future administration. . ." (*Economic Information on Argentina* 1984, 4) However, by failing to comply with the terms of the agreement, the military did little more than prepare the way for yet another round of difficult negotiations.

Alfonsín's administration, led on the economic front by Bernardo Grinspun, adopted a confrontational strategy with the IMF described by one as "brinkmanship." (Pinelo 1985, 19) This strategy can be explained by several factors. First, as a democratic regime, the new administration was vulnerable to electoral defeat and thus had to take into account the strong public opposition to IMF conditionality. It would be necessary to at least appear to resist terms to prevent the public feeling that the government had "sold out." In addition, conflicting policies of deflation and public service expansion were necessary to forestall unrest, but, in turn placed the government at odds with the IMF and economic logic. (Rouett 1985, 217) Second, the administration was constrained by a newly activated and self-assured representative branch within the government. The Senate budget committee, in particular, would prove a worthy rival. (Viola & Mainwaring 1985, 210) A third reason was that the government felt it had less to lose than the bankers, since Argentina, perhaps more so than any of the other major debtors, could survive a default and the resulting ostracism by the financial community. This was acknowledged in a Brookings Institution study by Mattione and Enders in 1984 in which the authors recommended debt repudiation. The government felt that it could extract concessions by at least carrying on the appearance of genuine, if tough negotiations, a view that is borne out by events. (Watkins 1985, 44, Milivojevic 1985, 118) Finally, as a prospective leader of the Third World's non-aligned movement, and as a prominent member of the "Quito Declaration" group that urged subordinating debt repayment to development, (Watkins 1985, 41) a highly-publicized confrontation with the West would not fail to score points with its Third World audience. In sum, Argentina had much to gain and little to lose with its strategy—and had much more to lose with a more pliant approach, since it would lose political support both domestically and internationally, even if it managed to solve some of its financial problems. Ultimately, Argentina's attitude was due more to political will and expediency than to economic circumstances. (Milivojevic 1985, 117–8)

Alfonsín spoke frequently in public about the fact that Argentina, "with its own beef, grain, industry and energy sources. . . could go it alone." (Watkins 1985, 43) In an important speech, he lamented:

> It is as if the [financial] centers have gone mad, but we will not pay usury. . . It would seem as if the developing countries were being attacked with a neutron bomb in reverse, which would leave men, women and other creatures alive, while destroying the nation's productive apparatus. This madness must be ended once and for all. (Monteón 1987, 21)

As the situation with foreign creditors and deteriorated, the administration had less room to maneuver. On the one hand a militant Peronist union movement organized strikes, (two million walked out in June) that cost the Labor minister his job (*New York Times* 1984c, I:5) declaring that "we refuse to pay the foreign debt out of the workers' pockets." (*Wall Street Journal* 1984a, 32) On the other hand, a bolder cabinet began insisting on results. Alfonsín's senior advisor, former finance minister Aldo Ferrer, put the problem this way: "The question now before Latin America's debtors is how much of their domestic resources should be appropriated to meet their foreign commitments," pointing out that Argentina would be better off to repudiate the debt entirely, or at least limit repayment to 15 percent of export earnings. (Watkins 1985, 41) It was in these circumstances that Grinspun composed the "letter of intent" that was forwarded to the executive board without prior managing director approval.

Argentina, by submitting directly to the board a letter of intent that did not have the approval of the managing director, could not have expected to achieve more than making a public case for itself (Confidential Executive Director interview). Grinspun denied that he was leaving the technical economic realm, claiming instead to be presenting a viable and realistic economic program. (*Wall Street Journal* 1984b, 38) It is worth noting that, although it went nowhere in the Board, it was a "hit" at home. (*New York Times* 1984d, IV:1) In addition, the presentation of the letter stalled rescheduling the arrears due on June 30 to the point that arrangements would have to be worked out under crisis conditions— always an advantage to the borrower. (*Wall Street Journal* 1984b, 38)

After another month of rancorous debate with the IMF mission over the proposed letter of intent, Grinspun himself took over the Argentine delegation and adopted a slightly more conciliatory approach than in the past. (*Wall Street Journal* 1984e, 30) While giving in on the issues of inflation and public expenditures, the government reduced its arrears by making several overdue payments—of $300 million to Latin lenders, and of $125 million to bankers (Note that the later was about to be collected from Argentine deposits, anyway.). (*Wall Street Journal* 1984f, 31) The rather inept head of revenue-collection in the Argentine cabinet was removed on August 26—a sign that revenues, crucial to an IMF agreement, would be more plentiful. (*Wall Street Journal* 1984g, 35)

> [W]hen push came to shove, precisely because it had been so ornery, Argentina walked away from the bargaining table with a better deal than Mexico which was given more time to pay, but not more money with which to pay. . . . Argentina was not paying the banks on time and there was very little the banks could do about it. When they signed the agreement with Argentina, for example, that country was already more than $1b. behind on its required interest payments and $10 b. behind on its principal payments. . .[to avoid losing earnings] bankers showed that they are willing to go to almost any lengths to maintain the fiction that everything is for the best in the best of all possible worlds. (Watkins 1985, 44)

However, by the beginning of 1985 economic realities had begun to catch up with the Argentines. With inflation increasing its headlong pace into financial no-man's-land, a debt-service ratio of over 50 percent for the foreseeable future, (Watkins 1985, 39) and with economic growth dipping into the negative with attendant increases in unemployment and the public debt, it was clear that confrontation and defiance, while useful ploys to reduce political opposition at home, would ultimately not resolve the very real economic crisis. It was at this point that Alfonsín chose to make use of the country's corps of technocrats to develop an effective austerity plan that would bring about a dramatic and rapid reversal of the country's situation. Grinspun was excluded from decision-making circles and Sourrouille was elevated to Minister of the Economy.

The Plan Austral, for all its belt-tightening, was well-received by the Argentine public. Early polls indicated 80 percent approval for the plan. Attempts by the labor unions to mount general protest strikes failed dismally. (*International Currency Review* 1985, 42) Congressional elections in November brought an even larger majority to the Radical party while old-line Peronists were nearly eliminated from national politics. (*Latin America Weekly Report* 1985b, 5) An impressed Peronist candidate stated that "not since Juan Perón do the Argentine people seem willing to put their trust in one politician." (*Washington Post* 1985, M-1) In the international community, the plan allowed for a quick disbursement of $473 million in connection with a fresh standby arrangement and private banks agreed to lend $483 million to allow repayment of arrears. (*New York Times* 1985f, IV:26) Ultimately, a large rescheduling took place on August 27 with roughly four billion dollars in fresh funds. (*New York Times* 1985g, IV:9) By the end of November, Argentina would be current on its interest payments for the first time in three years (since the beginning of the debt crisis).

During 1986 and 1987, the populist elements both within and outside of the Alfonsín administration began to reemerge as the Plan Austral began to falter. With economic growth slowing and inflation accelerating, public support with the program began to wane in mid-1986. Sourrouille made the rather insensitive remark that massive public demonstration against double-digit monthly inflation rates in mid-1986 were rather unwarranted, considering inflation had been twice those levels one year before. The austerity and budget cuts of the Plan were no longer politically sustainable by late-1986 and the Peronist Minister of Labor Carlos Adelerte began to deliberately expand government programs for the working class in spaite of the fiscal deficit. Elections in November 1986 brought the Peronists a near-majority of 40 percent of the seats in the Chamber of Deputies.

The government, attempting to simultaneously preserve a progrssively more elusive popular support and retain access to foreign sources of credit, concluded negotiations with the IMF in late-1986 with mixed results. Although the government obtained access to $1.4 billion, one of the preconditions for disbursement was an agreement between Argentina and the banks regarding its sizeable arrears—an agreement which was five months in the negotiating. Even with the agreement, nationalist/populist elements in the administration pressed for continued withholding of interest payments and a continual increase in the public sector deficit in the interests of keeping resources at home. The failure of the administration to abide by the IMF package resulted in the cancellation of the loan in late-1987. Much like the experience of Turkey, without a significant improvement in the growth of the Argentine economy and a reduction of its foreign debt, the government felt compelled, for the sake of political survival, to abandon its austerity measures and allow the economy to inflate again.

To what extent does the behavior of populist elements in the Argentine polity inform our models of decision-making? Again, the government, when dominated by nationalistic elements, adopted a very independent posture, often leading to confrontation. However, as the domestic political demands and the international economic necessities increased, the government found itself more and more a passive player strugling for survival. The developments in the period 1983–84 and 1986–87 illustrate the fact that in some cases the more confrontational and nationalistic a debtor nation's policies are, the worse the medium-term economic and political outcomes. This said, it should be repeated that the Alfonsín administration was successful in gaining significant concessions for a time from the IMF and private creditors by using a confrontational approach. There were, however, economic realities that were simply not remedied by easy terms with foreign capital.

IMF Executives. In 1982, with the eruption of the Debt Crisis, the Managing Director made a determination to deal with the major debtors on a "case-by-case" basis. This language implied that domestic social and political circumstances would be taken more explicitly into account during negotiations. This, incidentally, implied in turn that the role of the Exchange and Trade Relations department would be diminished, since its usual role was to promote uniformity across various country programs. (Confidential interviews with Fund staff) We will see that Argentina's treatment was in fact relatively lenient, indicating that the Managing Director's wishes were observed. To illustrate this, when the Fund negotiated with Argentina's military government in 1982, the time period for the agreement was deliberately limited to the rather unusual time period of fifteen months, which coincided with the arrival of the upcoming democratic government.

The IMF traditionally avoids publicizing its negotiations and is in particular reluctant to inform the press of specific developments, except as it relates to pulling other actors into the process. In the case of Argentina, however, in order to counteract the significant public relations efforts of the government, Fund leaders began making their tactics and strategy public knowledge. In a rare comment about on-going negotiations, Managing Director DeLarosière told reporters that the IMF would resist new lending to Argentina unless the inflation rate is reduced from its 560 percent level and public spending is reined in. (*New York Times* 1984g, IV:1) Note that this comment clearly demonstrated the significant influence the Managing Director held in the day-to-day negotiations.

An important test of the limits of the IMF leadership's flexibility came when Grinspun submitted a home-made letter of intent. As discussed previously, such a move threatened the institution's very raison d'être.

Argentina, by submitting directly to the Board a letter of intent that did not have the approval of the Managing Director, could not have expected to achieve more than making a public case for itself. (Confidential interview with an Executive Director) Grinspun denied that the proposal was merely rhetoric, arguing that it represented a viable and realistic economic program. (*Wall Street Journal* 1984b, 38)

The plan called for a raise in real wages of six to eight percent (too high for the IMF), lowering private bank interest rates (this would have increased the money supply beyond Fund-imposed limits), and limiting debt repayments to levels that will not require excessive reduction of imports. Although default was not the issue, the "letter of intent" clearly placed payment of the foreign debt behind national growth in Argentina's national priorities. (*Wall Street Journal* 1984b, 38) A "technical mission" was dispatched by Argentina to IMF headquarters to lobby for the proposal. (*New York Times* 1984e, IV:16)

As will be recalled, IMF missions begin their negotiations with member countries only after they have been briefed and a plan of action detailed by senior Fund staff. In many cases, the IMF mission is not permitted to deviate from the initial negotating terms. The letter of intent represents the results of the mission's best efforts to persuade the member country to accept Fund advice (not always successfully, as we have seen elsewhere). The letter of intent is forwarded to the board for approval only after it has been accepted by the managing director. There are thus at least two junctures during which the senior Fund staff attempt to shape the content of the letter of intent. This procedure is consistent with the IMF staff's technocratic orientation and mandate. Since letters of intent are the result of negotiations. To allow nations to submit their own letters of intent without prior IMF approval would make the Fund staff unneccessary and superfluous. Furthermore, it would imply that the Fund staff's sophisticated economic expertise and the monetarist model were merely academic experiments and carried no genuine intellectual superiority over other policy programs. Both of these implications alter the operation of the Fund in such fundamental ways as to be unacceptable to the staff. Furthermore, the executive board's function would be dramatically altered by the circumvention of the staff as advocated by the Grinspun tactic. Most importantly, the Board would suddenly be thrust into the position of making complete reviews of country programs and passing judgement of their validity. One might remark that this is already the proper function of the Board. However, as was seen in chapter two, the Board has developed customs and procedures to avoid making publicized choices. Through the custom of non-voting, for example, individual executive directors avoid the problem of taking publicized positions for which they will be held responsible in the future. Such a process has been found to serve the long-term interests of both the creditor and debtor nations. (Eckhaus 1986) This also shows that the Board avoids an explicitly politicized decision-making process when possible. The implications of Argentina's action for both the staff and the executive board make it clear why neither group took the action seriously.

The Executive Board played a relatively passive role throughout the IMF's negotiations with Argentina. The final approval for the 1982 loan with the military government in January 24, was granted without protest. (*IMF Survey* 1983, 1) Note the comments (paraphrased) made by an Executive Director after the announcement of the Plan Austral in the context of on-going IMF negotiations:

> First, on 28 December [1984], we approve a Stand-by Arrangement for the equivalent of $1.5 billion. We subsequently learned, *through the press,* that some of the conditions had already been broken—even while we were considering the staff report. Next, less than three months later, we are informed that the arrangement has been suspended due to non-compliance. Then, the staff returns from Buenos Aires with a deal, perhaps marginally better than the last one, which collapsed so quickly, after what we were told had been a difficult set of negotiations. Almost immediately thereafter, we learn, *again through the press,* that the Argentine authorities have themselves, spontaneously, without any pressure from this or any other institution, enacted a series of measures which make the programme agreed with our staff look like a pale imitation of what a stabilisation plan ought to resemble. Finally, we receive yet another report telling us that the staff fully endorses the government's plan, and asks us to accept it as a basis for the stand-by. I do not think I am the only one here present who justifiably feels confused over this sorry string of episodes. [These events] call into question the once high prestige of IMF staff in the Latin American region. (*International Currency Review* 1985, 44)

In general, the direct part played by the Managing Director in IMF negotiations and the relatively passive role played by the executive board support the assumptions of the bargaining model of IMF decision-making. However, resistance to the unorthodox tactics of Grinspun demonstrate that there are clear limits to the IMF's flexibility, and illustrate the technocratic elements in IMF decision-making. Overall, both the first and second models are supported, although there is little evidence in Argentina case for political manipulation of the process.

Secondary Actors

IMF Staff. In July, 1982, after some foot-dragging by Bignone, an IMF mission arrived in Buenos Aires to consider the possibility of a standby arrangement. Its initial reaction was pessimistic. (*Wall Street Journal* 1982a, 31) The mission itself was in a rather difficult position. As was mentioned earlier, the IMF leadership had reserved itself the right to supercede the staff's advice if, based on "case-by-case" considerations, it was felt that domestic political and social conditions demanded it.

They did in fact offer a list of fairly reasonable policy objectives, including (1) reduction of the annual inflation rate from roughly 500 percent to 150 percent, (2) initiation of a program of monthly IMF visits to monitor compliance, rather than the typical quarterly schedule, and (3) 15 month time period for the stand-by in anticipation of the transfer of power to a new civilian government in early 1984. (DelaMaide 1984, 115; Carvounis 1984, 146)

With the arrival of the new government, the staff confronted a very mistrusting Argentine negotiating team. The feelings became mutual as the IMF became exasperated with Argentina's confrontational rhetoric. As put by one Argentine official, "They [IMF representatives] just aren't serious about us." Even when, on one occasion, the Fund team complained about the Argentines' inability to present tough policy proposals, they showed little interest in a new proposal to cut the budget deficit from 10.1 percent of GDP to 9.1 percent. "I don't think they were trying to play tricks, they just didn't know [how to deal with Argentina's crisis]." (*Wall Street Journal* 1984d, 2) It was partly this mutual distrust that led the Argentine government to circumvent the normal procedures and draft its own letter of intent. (*Wall Street Journal* 1984b, 38)

By the time he left the Economy Ministry, the IMF mission had developed a profound dislike for Grinspun, as well as departing Central Bank President Enrique Garcia Vazquez. They were described as "not a very strong economic team" and "abrasive." It was also conceded that the two groups were on "shouting terms" with each other. (*Latin America Weekly Report* 1985a, 1) It appears, in retrospect, that there may have been as many cultural as substantive obstacles to the negotiations, since the two teams were speaking a very different language—one of autonomy, the other of stability. The negotiations quickly degenerated into arguments of principle rather than attempts at compromise. In Zartman's words, they had not succeded in developing a formula for negotiation, let alone a final set of acceptable terms. (Zartman 1979)

The Argentine economic policy-making organs, under the new leadership of Sourrouille, did not negotiate with any better faith, in the sense that there was no clear intention to abide by the terms of the IMF agreement of 1984. The Argentine's seem to have manipulated the IMF mission to promise assistance in order to get a reprieve from impatient private creditors who insisted on such agreements prior to rescheduling arrears. In particular, the situation in the first half of 1985 was particularly urgent, since American bankers threatened to downgrade Argentina's credit risk to "substandard"—a term reserved for such "basket cases" as Sudan and Zaire. (Pinelo 1985, 24) The plan agreed to with the IMF in mid-1985 was soon made irrelevant by the Plan Austral, however, it is most interesting to note that the terms finally agreed to with the IMF were much less stringent than those developed autonomously by the Argentine government itself. This fact led some Executive Directors to question the utility of the negotiations.

It is difficult, in the case of Argentina's negotiations, to say that the IMF staff was playing any of its traditional roles. The technical expertise provided by the Fund mission was either ignored or superceded by purely national programs. The persuasiveness of the Fund mission was mitigated by the heavy involvement of the Managing Director, the ability of the Argentine negotiators to manipulate the mission to its own ends, and the fear of the Argentine government to appear to be "caving in" the Fund pressure. It was this perversion of the mission's role, among other things, that resulted in its frustration. Its actions are clearly not consistent with the expectations of the functionalist model. It would seem that the bargaining model explains the missions role best, since it was the Managing Director and the Argentine officials who dominated decision-making overall. As will be seen below, the indirect role of private creditors is significant as a backdrop for the action, although the action of major creditor nations within the Fund apparatus does not seem significant as predicted by the political model.

Private Creditors. American bankers were most active in the Argentine debt situation because of American banking rules requiring an accounting of the status of outstanding loans each quarter. As already mentioned, from 1982 to mid-1985 each quarter brought with it a rescheduling crisis. These reschedulings were not always conditioned on prior approval of an IMF program, as was more traditionally the case with other debtors. Furthermore, the Argentine government was not unable to pay much of its arrears in any given quarter. Rather, the Argentine government manipulated private creditors for their own ends by playing what has been called a game of financial "chicken." (DelaMaide 1984, 116)

When the debt crisis erupted in 1982, international bankers, under the direction of Lloyds of London, agreed to reschedule Argentina's debt if the country could reach agreement with the Fund on an adjustment program. (Carvounis 1984, 146) The 1982 rescheduling program ultimately provided $2.6 billion in fresh loans. (Stallings 1983, 35) In late 1983 bankers, anticipating yet another failure to pay its arrears in December, released a $500 million installment of the $2.5 billion loan. (Watkins 1985, 39) This fell far short of the debt moratorium Argentina requested (and threatened).

At the end of March, 1984, with American banks' profits on the line, a last-minute plan was arranged. The suspense could not have been more dramatic, with Lloyds Bank of London holding out on agreeing to the package until 6 p.m. on Friday, March 30th. (*New York Times* 1984a, IV:1) With $2.5 billion in interest due, Argentina could have paid much of it by dipping into its reserves. (Watkins 1985, 43) However, an unusual loan arranged by Mexico, Brazil, Venezuela and Colombia provided $300 million immediately, and $100 million to be provided by private banks at only 1/8th of a percent over Libor, allowed the banks and Argentina to continue business as usual for another three months. (Pinelo 1985, 20) The United States provided little assistance, except to offer money to allow Argentina to repay the Latin loan which was guaranteed by Argentine peso deposits in the New York Reserve Bank. Argentina, in return, promised to complete negotiations with the IMF in 30 days. Alfonsín was praised for having played his cards right and obtaining a very lenient program. (Pinelo 1985, 20)

Part of the reason for Argentina's success, in addition to its "orneriness" mentioned earlier, was this latent threat of a moratorium, made more forceful by the potential of a debtor cartel:

> While the debtor countries vigourously denied any intention of forming a Debtor's Club, the banks became concerned about the growing solidarity among the borrowers and its potential for the formation of such a cartel. They therefore attempted to neutralize the new movement and offered Mexico and Brazil. . . significantly better terms. . . . Later, other debtors received roughly similar treatment. . . . [T]he more powerful borrowers could probably [continue to] reduce transfers to the banks if they were disposed to exercise their bargaining power, by hinting that the alternative to the granting of new loans could be default. (Devlin 1985, 43, 48)

Threats of default were more muted in mid-1984 when private bankers threatened to cut Argentina off from further lending. (Pinelo 1985, 20) Argentina consented to pay off $225 million of its arrears. An Argentine delegation was dispatched to the annual meeting of the IMF/World Bank in mid-1984 in order to influence European bankers and other international financiers, but to no avail. (*Wall Street Journal* 1984h, 1) The Argentines finally succumbed to international pressure and the need for fresh capital by agreeing to an IMF package in early September. (*Wall Street Journal* 1984i, 35) The mid-1984 period was one of fairly high concensus among the financial elite—something which had not previously been the case.

By late-1984, private American banks began quietly writing down their Argentine loans to stretch their losses, all the while balking at rescheduling requests. (Pinelo 1985, 20) Western protests were recorded in the Wall Street Journal's editorial pages. (*Wall Street Journal* 1984c, 35) Tensions mounted over Argentina's arrears. Banks threatened to cut Argentina off entirely from any new funds. Finally, the United States provided $125 million in short term secured loans. (*New York Times* 1984f, I:1) A banker, conveying the exhaustion and frustration felt by negotiators, told a newsman that "you'll write the same story on September 30th." (*New York Times* 1984f, I:1)

Although sceptical at first, private bankers began another round of debt rescheduling, allowing the deadline for the third quarter of 1984 to pass without the usual crisis atmosphere. This was due in part to the fact that a few American bankers had privately acknowledged the "non-accrual" nature of their Latin loans, and $750 million in arrears was simply not being called in. The new rescheduling involved most of Argentina's debt, but focused on the now one billion dollars in arrears and interest due by year-end. Argentina requested $5.5 billion in fresh loans as a bargaining posture, the banks favoring a figure closer to $2.5 billion. (*Wall Street Journal* 1984j, 34) Quickly the figure of $4.5 billion emerged as an acceptable compromise. Finally, and with less argument than expected, private banks with the support of the United States, extended $4.2 billion in fresh loans while rescheduling $13 billion of its debt. These actions were contingent upon Argentina paying $750 million of its one billion dollars due by year end, as well as keeping its policies within the limits prescribed in the IMF package. (*Wall Street Journal* 1984k, 3)

Bankers were naturally pleased with the Plan Austral in 1985 and praised the Sourrouille team. However, the honeymoon lasted merely one year. By mid-1986, the Argentine government had begun adopting a more confrontational approach again, delaying payments on interest and openly threatening a debt moratorium. Bank of Boston publicly reclassified its Argentine debt as "non-accrual" as did most major American banks during 1987. For the first time, some began to speak seriously about debt forgiveness, although it would not be until 1989 and the "Brady plan" before such talk had the support of the United States government.

Overall, the international bankers had leverage with Argentina roughly proportional to the IMF itself. Bankers were more concerned about quarterly reports than long-term solutions. Argentina showed far more resolve during the period than did the bankers.

In terms of the models, it appears that only when Argentina began to threaten the legitimacy of the IMF itself with its home-made letter of intent that international bankers began to coordinate their strategy. This is hardly what the political model would anticipate and far more consistent with the bargaining model.

Conclusion

How does the study of Argentina's experience with the IMF inform our comparison of the three decision-making models presented at the outset? As has been pointed out at different junctures in the chapter, there is some evidence to support each of the models, although the thrust of the case tends to support the pluralist model.

The functionalist model predicted a passive Argentine government and IMF administration with an active staff. It is clear that the functionalist model does not apply in the Argentine case. To begin, the Argentine government was consistently very active in pressing its views and demands on both public and private creditors throughout the period. The military governments, the "populist" period of Alfonsín's administration and the Sourrouille period that followed each articulated a coherent plan of economic development and did all they could to implement it unilaterally. The famous home-made letter of intent illustrates the degree to which the populist elements of the democratic government attempted to manipulate the international system to their own ends. Likewise, the military government manipulated the IMF officials in order to postpone adjustment.

It is perhaps more debatable whether the austerity program developed by the Sourrouille team was a case of Argentine assertion, but I will maintain that it was on the grounds that (1) it was the result of internal analysis and deliberation withing the Argentine government and (2) its substance was significantly different from that proposed by the IMF at the time. It would have been a simple thing to simply allow the IMF team to develop a program, but for reasons of political survival and nationalism, the Sourrouille team made a deliberate effort to take the initiative away from the international creditors and the IMF itself.

As was also pointed out, the IMF staff seems to have been either ineffective or irrelevant during this period. At no time was the IMF staff dominant, although there were most influential during the military government negotiations. Even this "influence" was more illusion than reality since the Argentine military had no intention of actually living up to the terms of the agreement.

Conversely, it is clear that the Managing Director took a very personal interest in the Argentine negotiations, even resorting to publicizing his negotiating position at one juncture. As was the case in the British negotiations as well as negotiations with Mexico and Brazil, the Managing Director himself undercut much of the IMF team's authority.

It was perhaps only whan the Managing Director and the executive board rejected the Grinspun letter of intent that the process followed the functionalist model. At that moment, the IMF leadership sustained the IMF's legal procedures for conducting negotiations. In that sense, the action affirmed the importance of the form of negotiations over substance.

The political model is somewhat more useful in this case, in that it correctly predicts the attempt by private creditors to force liberalization on the Argentine economy. Their failure to do so was not so much because of their unwillingness but rather their inability to counteract the power of the Argentine policy-makers. Likewise, the executive board of the Fund seems to have at least desired a more liberal economy in Argentina, but was unable to take the iniative. But the mere existence of desire and intention reveals little about the actual workings of the decision-making process.

To fully understand the Argentine dynamics, one must utilize the concepts and assumptions of the bargaining model. This model accounts for the failure on the part of the IMF and the private creditors to exert significant influence on Argentine policy, as well as the heavy involvement by the Argentine government and the IMF leadership. Likewise, the shifting balance of power within the Argentine economic policy-making circles is more easily understood in terms of pluralist decision-making and influence-seeking. The fact that the populist elements in the democratic government reemerged in 1986–87 only to recede again in 1989 shows that influence is based on relatively ephemeral forces that are not identified in the more essential functionalist and political models.

Bibliography

Carvounis, Chris C. 1984. *The Debt Dilemma of Developing Nations: Issues and Cases.* Westport, CN: Quorum Books.

Corradi, Juan. 1985. *The Fitful Republic: Economy, Society and Politics in Argentina.* Boulder, CO: Westview.

DelaMaide, Darrell. 1984. *Debt Shock: The Full Story of the World Credit Crisis.* New York: Doubleday & Co.

Devlin, Robert. 1985. "External Debt and Crisis: The Decline of the Orthodox Strategy." *CEPAL Review* 27 (December): 35–52.

Eckhaus, Richard. 1986. "How the IMF Lives with its Conditionality." *Policy Sciences* 19 (October): 237–252.

Economic Information on Argentina. 1984. 126 (January–February): 1–4.

Eskridge, William N., Jr. 1985a. "Santa Clause and Sigmund Freud: Structural Contexts of the International Debt Problem." in Eskridge, William. *A Dance Along the Precipice.* Lexington, MA: Lexington Books: 27–102.

———. ed. 1985b. *A Dance along the Precipice: The Political and Economic Dimensions of the International Debt Problem.* Lexington, MA: Lexington Books.

Ferrer, Aldo. 1985. *Living Within Our Means: An Examination of the Argentine Economic Crisis.* Boulder, CO: Westview.

Heymann, D. 1986. "Inflation and Stabilization Policies." *CEPAL Review* 28 (April): 67–97.

IMF Survey. 1983. February 7: 1.

Inter-American Development Bank. 1984. *External Debt and Economic Development in Latin America.* Washington, D.C.: IADB.

International Currency Review. 17 (December): 40–48.

Kafka, Alexandre. 1985. Interview with the author. IMF Headquarters, Washington, D.C. July 25.

Kubarych, Roger M. 1985. "The Financial Vulnerability of the LDCs: Six Factors." in Eskridge, William. *A Dance Along the Precipice.* Lexington, MA: Lexington Books: 3–16.

Latin America Weekly Review. 1985a. March 31: 1.

———. 1985b. September 20: 4.

———. 1985c. November 8: 1.

Marshall, S. Jonathan, Mardones S., Jose Luis, and Marshall S., Isabel. 1983. "IMF Conditionality: The Experiences of Argentina, Brazil, and Chile," in Williamson, John, ed. *IMF Conditionality.* Washington, D.C.: Institute for International Economics: 275–321.

Mattione, Richard and Enders, Thomas. 1984. *Latin America: The Crisis of Debt and Growth.* Washington, D.C.: Brookings Institution.

Milivojevic, Marko. 1985. *The Debt Rescheduling Process.* New York: St. Martin's Press.

Monteón, Miguel. 1987. "Can Argentina's Democracy Survive Economic Disaster?" in Waisman, C. and Peralta-Ramos, M. eds. *From Military Rule to Liberal Democracy in Argentina.* Boulder, CO: Westview: 21–38.

New York Times. 1984a. April 1: IV:1.

———. 1984b. April 4: IV:1.

———. 1984c. April 25: I:5.

———. 1984d. June 11: IV:1

———. 1984e. June 19: IV:16.

———. 1984f. June 30: I:1.

———. 1984g. July 6: IV:1.

———. 1985a. March 30: I:34.

———. 1985b. May 13: IV:10.

———. 1985c. May 19: I:1.

———. 1985d. June 15: I:1.

———. 1985e. June 16: I:4.

———. 1985f. June 19: IV:26.

———. 1985g. August 28: IV:9.

O'Donnell, Guillermo. 1973. *Modernization and Bureaucratic Authoritarianism: Studies in South American Politics.* Berkeley, CA: Institute of International Studies.

———. 1985. "Why Don't Our Governments Do the Obvious?" *CEPAL Review* 27 (December): 27–33.

Pinelo, Adalberto J. 1985. "Political Implications of International Monetary Fund Conditionality for Latin America." Paper Presented at the American Political Science Association Annual Meetings, New Orleans, LA. September.

Pion-Berlin, David. 1985. "The Fall of Military Rule in Argentina: 1976–1983." *Journal of Interamerican Studies and World Affairs* 27 (Summer): 55–76.

Rouett, Riordan. 1983. "The Return of Democracy? Brazil and the Southern Cone." *SAIS Review* 3 (Summer–Fall): 59–70.

———. 1985. "The Foreign Debt Crisis and the Process of Redemocratization in Latin America." in Eskridge, William. *A Dance Along the Precipice.* Lexington, MA: Lexington Books: 207–229.

Shirano, Louis G. 1985. "A Banker's View." in Eskridge, William. *A Dance Along the Precipice.* Lexington, MA: Lexington Books: 17–26.

Snowden, P. Nicolas. 1985. *Emerging Risk in International Banking: Origins of Financial Vulnerability in the 1980s.* Boston: Allen & Unwin.

Stallings, Barbara. 1983. "Latin American Debt: What Kind of Crisis?" *SAIS Review* 3 (Summer–Fall): 27–40.

Viola, Eduardo and Mainwaring, Scott. 1985. "Transitions to Democracy: Brazil and Argentina in the 1980s." *Journal of International Affairs* 38 (Winter): 193–219.

Wall Street Journal. 1982a. July 30: 31.

———. 1982b. December 13: 34.

———. 1983a. September 19: 37.

———. 1983b. October 10: 33.

———. 1984a. June 8: 32.

———. 1984b. June 12: 38.

———. 1984c. June 15: 35.

———. 1984d. June 18: 2.

———. 1984e. August 10: 30.

———. 1984f. August 13: 30.

———. 1984g. August 27: 17.

———. 1984h. August 31: 1.

———. 1984i. September 10: 35.

———. 1984j. October 22: 34.

———. 1984k. December 3: 3.

Washington Post. 1985. September 1: M-1.

Watkins, Alfred J. 1985. "Going for Broke?" *NACLA Report on the Americas* 19 (March/April): 34–44.

World Bank. 1985a. *Argentina: Economic Memorandum.* Washington, D.C.: IBRD.
_____. 1985b. *World Debt Tables.* Washington, D.C.: IBRD.
Wynia, G. 1986. *Argentina: Illusions and Realities.* New York: Homes & Meier.
Zartman, I. William and Berman, Maureen. 1979. *The Practical Negotiator.* New Haven, CN: Yale University Press.

10

Conclusion

In the beginning of this study we reviewed three "ideal-type" models of IMF decision-making. Each of these models provided us with predictions regarding internal processes as well as policy outcomes of IMF lending policy. In order to determine the utility of these models, we reviewed the findings of over thirty interviews with Fund staff and noted that while the functionalist approach offered much at one level, the bargaining model provided the observer with the concepts that made understanding more complete, although less automatic. It was decided that, although it might apply to programmatic decision-making of the Fund's Board of Governor's and Interim Committee, the political model did not provide much in the way of explanation and prediction of day-by-day internal decision-making processes.

We then took our models to the next step of analysis: how well do they explain policy outcomes of IMF decision-making? It is impossible to know definitively the process and results of IMF lending negotiations, since these are highly confidential. However, in much the same way one can often discover the inner psychological state of an artist by a painting, the decision-making involved in any area might be inferred from the policy results, especially when there is an opportunity to observe at least part of the process itself. This is what we have tried to do with our seven national case-studies. While we cannot psychoanalyze the artist, we do have the comments of eye-witnesses to the policy process in the form of newspaper and government accounts of the negotiations involved in preparing for Fund assistance.

Summary of the Findings

In five of the seven cases—Jamaica, India, Argentina, Turkey and the U.K.—the bargaining model proved most useful in explaining both processes and outcomes of IMF negotiations. In one case—Zaire—the political model was adequate and in one case–Sudan—the functionalist model was most useful. Based on this simple observation, it seems that it would be more useful to begin analyzing IMF lending from a bargaining perspective before moving into the other two models.

In the way of broader generalizations, we have been able to identify several dimensions of IMF lending that are somewhat counter-intuitive, at least from the "first principles" models—functionalist and political. (Ascher 1985, 15) First, it is clear that in the majority of cases, the government of the member country is far more actively involved in shaping the content of IMF packages than one would expect. In some cases, the member country essentially wrote its own letter of intent (Turkey, Argentina, India), while in other cases the government had a minimal position which the Fund was forced to deal with (U.K., Argentina, Jamaica, Zaire). The relative autonomy of debtor nations contradicts the radical interpretation of the IMF lending process as a haven of neo-imperialist exploitation. For example, in a rather sophisticated model assembled by Körner et al., the government is assumed to be a passive element in the negotiations. (1986, 144–45)

Why are governments more assertive than previously assumed? First, it would seem that some theories of debt negotiation have suffered from ethnocentrism, in that both radical structuralists and realists have assumed that a large and powerful Western institution, buttressed by the capital centers of the world would be able to force the hand of whatever developing nation it encountered—for good or bad. Instead, we find that a more sophisticated and symbiotic relationship exists. This new perspective is far more consistent with current literature on North-South relations which emphasizes the dialectical, symbiotic interplay of global and domestic forces in shaping relations of assymetrical interdependence. (Zartman 1987) This is also consistent with the Latin American variation of *dependencía* as articulated by Furtado, Dos Santos and Cardoso (Furtado 1970; Dos Santos 1970; Cardoso & Faletto 1979).

Clearly, national governments, whether authoritarian or democratic, are also far more sensitive to domestic pressures than many analysts realize. In most cases, national governments asserted themselves in negotiations with the Fund in order to win favor with domestic audiences. We saw this to be the case especially in Argentina, the United Kingdom, India, Zaire and Jamaica. However, even more intriguing, the very real need to insure civil tranquility limited the flexibility of some governments, thus pushing them at times into a more obstinant negotiating position. Put more bluntly, no governments are willing to commit political suicide in order to comply with IMF conditionality (with the possible exception of Sudan). As third world opposition movements continue to improve their capacity to articulate and press the demands of certain consumer and labor groups, the tendency for tougher bargaining on the part of debtor nations increases—a trend that is easily observable in Latin America today.

Finally, it seems that IMF flexibility has been underestimated. We found that there exist channels within the Fund itself whereby the interests of the debtor nations can be articulated and defended. These channels become more significant and are amplified as the managing director becomes more directly involved in debt negotiations. The executive board has proved receptive to many dramatic innovations, such as large scale of loans to Argentina, India, Turkey and the United Kingdom, significant concessions on conditionality, as in the case of Jamaica and Turkey, and the general trend toward coordinated rescheduling in which the Fund requires private banks to extend fresh loans to nations that have signed a letter of intent. The board has rarely initiated innovative programs, at least so far as our cases are concerned, but has even more rarely stood in the way of the Fund's evolution.

Since the relative influence of the Fund staff is a central issue in differentiating the functionalist and bargaining models, it is important to comment on why in some cases the staff had more influence than at other times. Since the missions the Fund sends to member nations prior to drafting a letter of intent are empowered to articulate positions taken by the Fund management, one could alternatively say that in these instances the IMF's traditional *channels* are sufficient to achieve its objectives. These channels, as discussed earlier, include a significant role for the Exchange and Trade Relations Department. Where the IMF leadership intervenes directly in a negotiation, it is primarily ETR that loses influence. And so the question should be asked differently—why does the IMF leadership circumvent ETR at times?

In those cases—Argentina, Great Britain, Turkey, Jamaica, Zaire and India—where the managing director took a direct part in negotiations, it seems that the situation was especially critical to either the viability of the broader international system or the viability and/or legitimacy of the Fund itself. In the case of Argentina and the United Kingdom, failure to resolve their financial difficulties would have resulted in greater instability and major short-term losses for the international financial system. This also may explain why in the cases of negotiations with Peru, Mexico and Brazil, not discussed in this study but no doubt familiar to may readers, the managing director intervened directly.

In the cases of India, Zaire, Jamaica and Turkey, the managing director's intervention was increased because of the significance of the situation for the IMF's role (the same can be said for the U.K. intervention as well). Because Turkey and India had each drafted a significant austerity package, the managing director was motivated to insure that these nations were "rewarded" for their actions. In the case of India, this would only occur if significant opposition from the United States were overcome with high-level diplomacy. The same can be said for Jamaica, since some opposition to aid to Manley existed in the board. In the case of Zaire, the scale of the intervention and the manpower involved required hands-on involvement at the highest levels of the international bureaucracy.

It is perhaps more significant to note that in cases of "business as usual," where no overriding principle or fundamental international structure is being challenged (Sudan), the managing director merely allows the regular channels to carry out their previously assigned tasks. Note that the significance of negotiations with a particular nation may vary over time. Until 1987, the debt situation in Africa was considered a low priority, not worthy of high-level intervention. However, as the debt ratio of these nations swelled to unprecedented levels, the managing director chose to intervene directly and create special lending facilities for African debtors in the early-1980s. As the debt crisis world-wide deepens, and situations that had previously been labeled "crises" only for rhetorical flourish develop into full-blown and urgent policy problems, it is likely that the managing director will feel compelled to become more and more heavily involved in more and more situations, rather than leaving things to the ordinary channels. The implications of this trend for the structure and functioning of the Fund are far-reaching. It is possible that an entirely new *de facto* IMF structure will emerge alongside the de-jure arrangements in existence since the 1950s—one in which the line staff are relegated to purely supportive roles while the senior staff exert greater control over more and more policy decisions. Perhaps, in the long run, this will lead to a weakening of staff morale and a degeneration of its competency as talented individuals seek professional opportunities elsewhere.

An important set of observations can be made regarding the question of whether the debtor nations have genuinely affected the Fund's treatment of their case. The following can be said: (1) Those nations that anticipated economic difficulties and approached the Fund early with a program already in place were able to achieve a negotiated outcome more proximate to their stated national objectives (India and Turkey are the best examples). (2) Those nations that were candid with the Fund were often rewarded for their cooperation, as opposed to those that deliberately manipulated the institution and deceived it (Argentina in 1983–85, Zaire). (3) Nations with a more complex internal decision-making process tended to increase their leverage because there existed more obstacles to approval of IMF terms. These observations, although apparently contradictory, indicate that although nations seem to enhance their ability to control negotiation outcomes if they behave as "honest" and "eager" bargainers, it also pays to delay final acceptance of terms through complex internal decision-making processes. These conclusions are generally consistent with observations made regarding other bargaining situations at other levels. (Raiffa 1982)

Finally, another observation that should be made from these case studies is the great significance of the role of private creditors in the debt negotiations. Just as the degree of civil unrest creates limits of flexibility for national governments, the degree of impatience of private creditors and their total bargaining leverage creates negotiating limits. To a large degree, both the national government and the IMF itself are caught between these opposing forces. It is important to recognize, however, that the behavior of private creditors is far less consistent than the functionalist or political models would predict. In the cases of Sudan, Zaire, the United Kingdom and Jamaica, the private creditors clearly pressured the national governments into major reform, pending the threat of financial isolation. However, in the cases of Argentina, Turkey and India, the pressure that creditors exerted was sporadic and often very small. India went to the Fund with almost no foreign debt, and therefore creditors had very little leverage. Bankers' concern that India was underborrowed was understood, but did not influence the IMF's decision-making. Argentina was able to virtually ignore appeals for adjustment made by private creditors for several years, largely because its debt was so large that a unilateral moratorium would have devastated many banks. Given the very wide array of situations that currently exist in third world debt, it is more useful to analyze each negotiation individually to identify the unique constellation of interests and bargaining assets.

Critics might argue that this study is too restricted in space and time, that a more rigorous test of the models should have covered several decades and many more cases. I selected these seven cases that differed markedly in terms of their levels of economic development, the nature of their economic problems, their type of political system, their degree of involvement with the Fund, and the results of their experience—all factors that seem to have an impact on bargaining behavior. One should choose different case studies, or perhaps carry out a more large-scale study, to determine whether this criticism is valid—the author urges further research in the area of case studies of debt negotiation. It appears that the consistency of the bargaining model's explanatory power across cases bodes well for a more rigorous trial.

While an addition of more case studies is *prima facia* an appropriate methodological improvement, the expansion of the temporal scope of the study will produce questionable results. The IMF has experienced a major increase in activity and a change in roles over the past fifteen years that make long-term historical study largely misleading. In fact, it is tempting to focus only on the post-1982 period, given the dramatic surge of IMF activity and the prevalence of debt-rescheduling during that time. Furthermore, changes in the global security system and the United States in general appear to be leading to new decision-making patterns in the IMF's Board of Governors since the late-1980s which may eventually alter the behavior of the Fund itself in years to come. If this proves to be the case, then the study you have just read will be simply a historical analysis of IMF behavior during a very active period. At any rate, the time period is very significant and should not be expanded in the interest of greater comprehensiveness.

A more serious criticism of the bargaining model is the objection that the model should not be compared with the functionalist and political perspectives on the grounds that the models address different sets of problems. It might be argued that the functionalist model attempts primarily to explain long-term trends in decision-making, while the political model explains those few cases which cannot be explained in functionalist/economic terms. In this sense, political factors play a residual role. The bargaining model, finally, addresses ordinary day-to-day interactions at the micro-level. Further research is encouraged to attempt an all-inclusive theory of international organization decision-making which would account for long-term "programmatic" decision-making as well as day-to-day administrative decisions (See Assetto 1989).

Implications of the Study

As is evident, the study has attempted to develop a more useful image of how the IMF arrives at its lending terms. In so doing, it has also attempted to call into question more traditional interpretations that have been presented in the past. For this reason, the most significant implication of this study is that any analysis of IMF policy-making should assume that bargaining is taking place, and dismiss this interpretation only if contrary evidence is found. Admittedly, this approach is not necessarily the most parsimonious, but the costs of adopting a less elegant model are outweighed by the greatly improved odds of achieving a full understanding of the situation.

Will the assumption of the bargaining model change one's assessment of the general problem of third world debt? Not necessarily. The bargaining model eliminates some of the tendency for prejudgement and emphasis on extremes that hampers the utility of radical models, but this model does not address the view that the *results* of IMF lending and adjustment are deleterious to large numbers of the Third World's inhabitants. The bargaining model simply offers to the analyst to a wider array of causal factors. There is no automatic villain in this model. What is often neglected in contemporary studies of IMF negotiations is the IMF's flexibility, as well as the motivations of the borrowing nation's governing elite.

The bargaining model also helps to identify possible approaches to resolving the debt problems of many countries. Since bargaining tactics seem to matter, it is possible that the development of greater bargaining skills could significantly affect the outcomes of IMF negotiations for particular countries. If timing is as important as the cases in this study seem to imply, it might behoove a debtor to improve its tactics along the temporal dimension. For example, it is advisable for a nation that anticipates significant balance of payments shortfalls in the coming year to immediately draw up an adjustment program and seek the IMF's assistance early on. Also, if the nature of one's international contacts is important, a concerted diplmomatic and social effort might be undertaken with little cost. Conversely, private creditors might seek to "divide and rule" to disrupt these relationships in order to prevent the coordination of negotiations by debtors. (O'Donnell 1986) The IMF, likewise, could approach the negotiations as a bargaining situation and deliberately demand tougher conditions than it feels are realistic or necessary in order to allow itself room to make concessions and still come out with it considers a strong program. Finally, when such global action programs as the Brady Plan are developed, the bargaining leverage of each actor should be taken explicitly into account, so that the result will be a genuine compromise based on interests and assets, rather than on some grand and unrealistic set of principles. Such an approach will likely yield more direct fruit.

Bibliography

Ascher, William. 1985. "A Preface to Exploring the Fund and the Bank." Paper Presented at the Annual Meetings of the International Studies Association, Washington, D.C., April.

Assetto, Valerie. 1990. "Member Influence on Organizational Change in the International Monetary Fund." Paper Presented at the Annual Meetings of the International Studies Association, Washington, D.C., April.

Cardoso, Fernando Enrique and Faletto, Enzo. 1979. *Dependency and Development in Latin America.* Berkeley, CA: University of California Press.

Dos Santos, Theotonio. 1970. "The Structure of Dependency." *American Economic Review* 40 (May): 231–236.

Furtado, Celso. 1970. *Economic Development of Latin America: A Survey from Colonial Times to the Cuban Revolution.* Cambridge: Cambridge University Press.

Körner, Peter et al. 1986. *The IMF and the Debt Crisis: A Guide to the Third World's Dilemmas.* London: Zed Publishers.

O'Donnell, Guillermo. 1985. "Why Don't Our Governments Do the Obvious?" *CEPAL Review* (December): 21–27.

Raiffa, Howard. 1982 *The Art and Science of Negotiation*. Cambridge, Mass.: Harvard University Press.

Zartman, William. 1987. *Positive Sum*. New Brunswick, N.J.: Transaction Press.

Index